DRAWING FOR BEGINNERS

How to draw and shade for realism

by Jasmina Susak

Copyright © 2018 by Jasmina Susak
www.jasminasusak.com

Text and illustrations © Jasmina Susak
Page layout and cover design by Jasmina Susak

All rights reserved. No part of this publication may be reproduced, distributed, or transmitted in any form or by any means, including photocopying, recording, or other electronic or mechanical methods, without the prior written permission of the author. For permission requests, contact the author via email:
jasminasusak00@gmail.com

More tutorials at:
WWW.PENCILDRAWINGTUTOR.COM

This book is dedicated to my cats.

Being a painter means spending a lot of time between four walls, far away from people. My cats have been a perfect companion on my journey of being an artist and art teacher. I am so grateful for being allowed to travel with these little creatures through space and time on this big, round, spinning spaceship.

Table of Contents:

About the Author 5
Introduction 6
Tools 10
Drawing Tutorials:
How to draw a 3D ball 31
How to draw water droplets 38
How to draw a wine glass 49
How to draw a bald eagle 66
How to draw a wooden texture 82
How to draw a glass marble 88
How to draw a fish 98
How to draw a Teddy Bear 108
How to draw a flower 120
How to draw an anamorphic 3D "W" letter 135
How to draw portrait - part 1: Sketching 145
    How to draw an eye 165
    How to draw a nose 181
    How to draw lips 185
How to draw portrait - part 2:
    Shading the skin of the face 190
    Shading the skin of the neck 201
How to draw portrait – part 3:
    How to draw the hair 206
How to draw a cat 224
Epilogue 244
Inspiration gallery 245

About the Author

Jasmina Susak is a self-taught, graphite and colored pencil artist, art teacher and author of more than 17 how-to-draw books. She specializes in creating photorealistic drawings of animals, people, superheroes and everyday objects.

Jasmina graduated and worked as a dressmaker for many years. Now she is a freelance, self-employed artist. It is her full-time job, and she's been doing it professionally since 2011.

Jasmina has hundreds of thousands of followers and subscribers on social media, and her drawing videos have tens of millions of views all around the world.

Jasmina loves animals, science, astronomy, technology, web designing, reading, listening to music.

Visit her website for more tutorials, her drawing gallery, art prints and more.

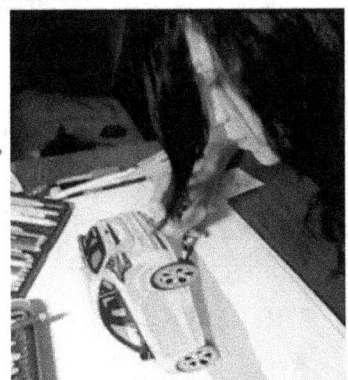

www.jasminasusak.com

INTRODUCTION

Many people think that drawing is unachievable for them. I would like to help you begin to create the realistic drawings that you have always wanted. I will show you that everyone is able to draw; only patience, strong will, and practice are needed. If you give up at the very beginning, you won't achieve anything!

Your first drawings won't be perfect, but don't let it discourage you from continuing. If you draw more, and compare your first to your tenth drawing, you will see how much you have improved and you will feel encouraged enough to keep working. You will surpass your previous drawings. So, drawing is not a skill that you learn overnight, but you have to gather experience through many months and years. After your first feeling of success, which can come only after persistent work, you will be thrilled and will want to draw more and more. With time and practice you will become better and better.

In this book, you will learn to draw shiny, black hair:

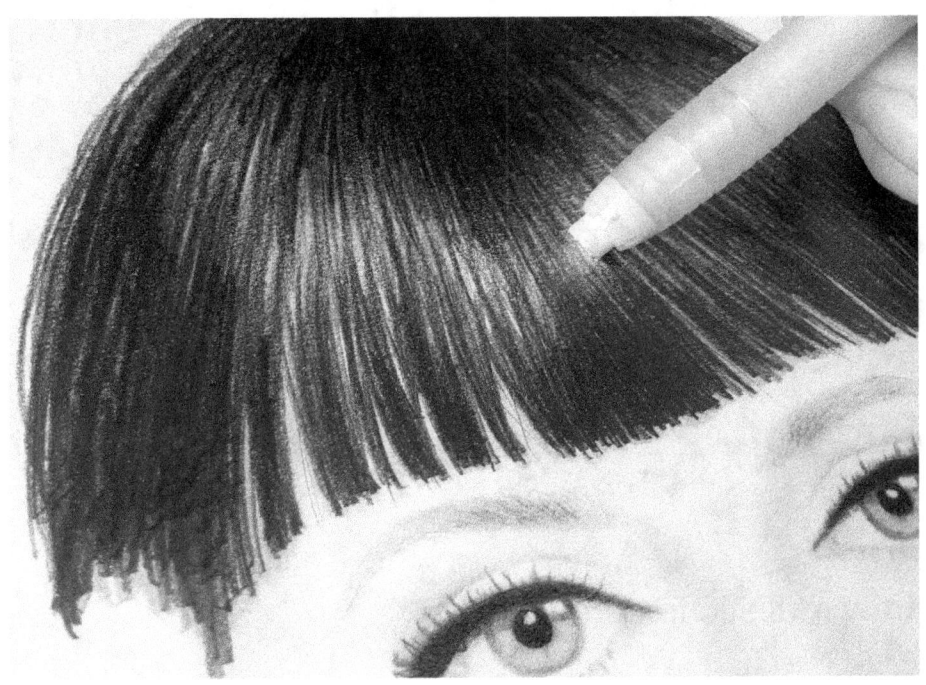

To create depth and create a third dimension:

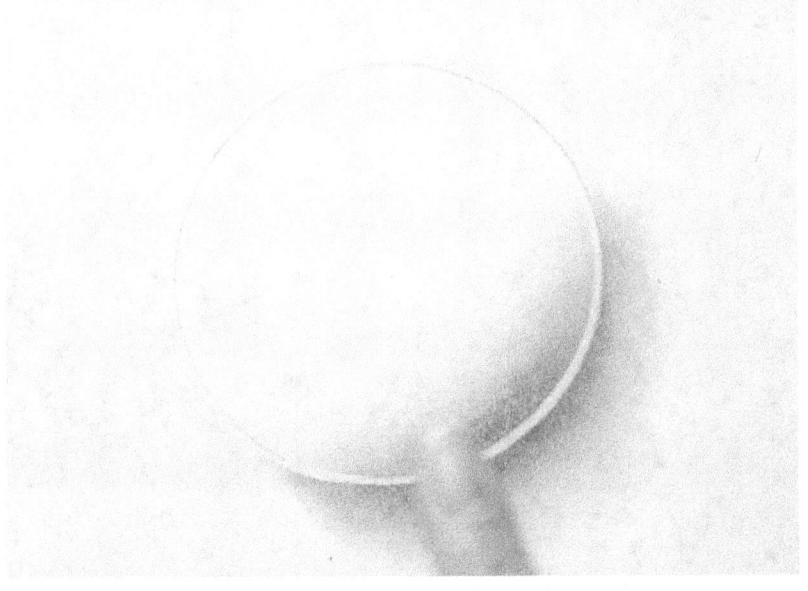

To make glossy objects:

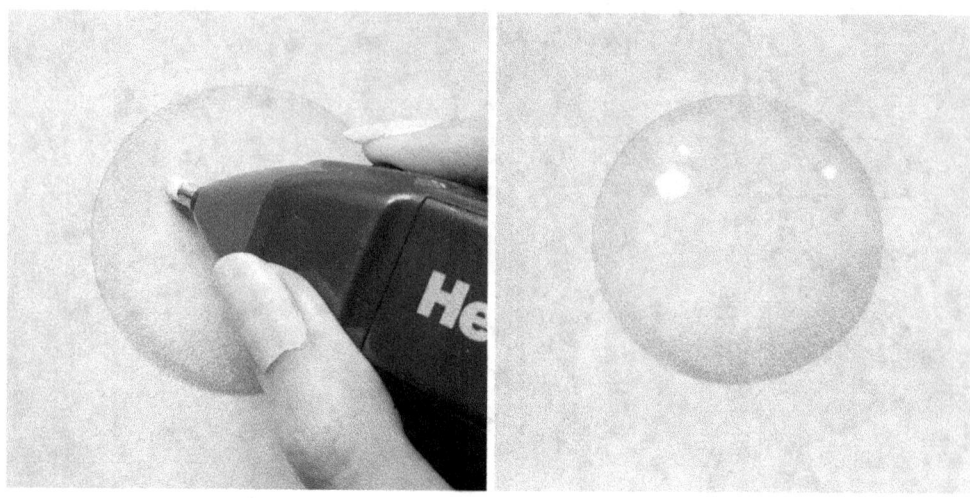

To draw realistic textures:

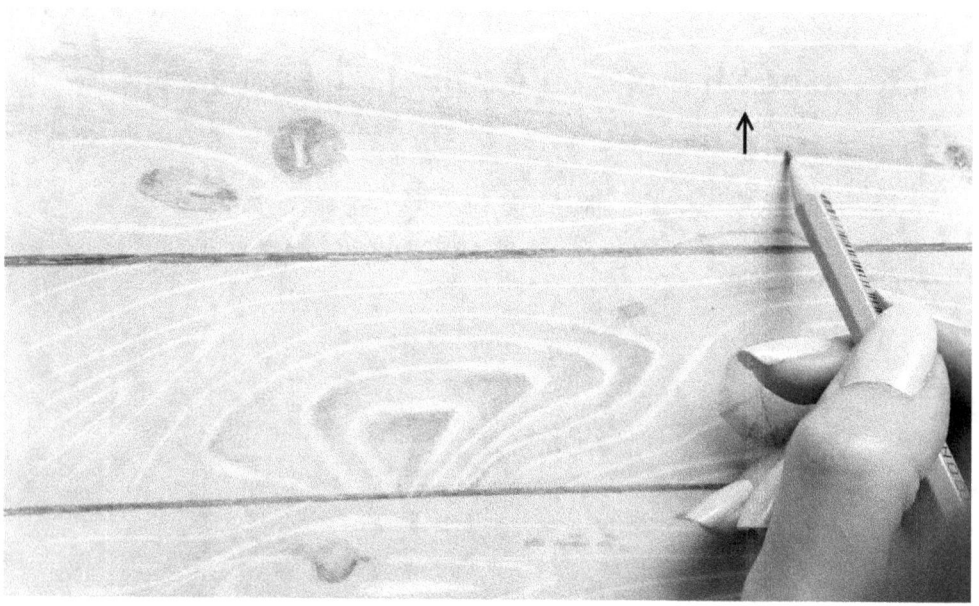

Drawing for Beginners

In the next image you can see:
Left: What you *won't* learn in this book.
Right: What you *will* learn in this book.

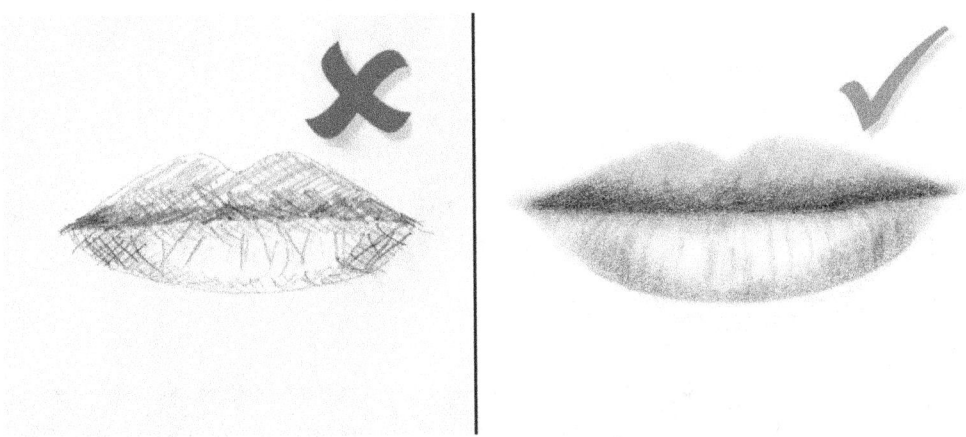

If you are ready for these, let's get started with what to use!

TOOLS

Pencils

Graphite pencils are the most common and popular drawing tool. The core of the pencils are made of a mixture of graphite and clay.

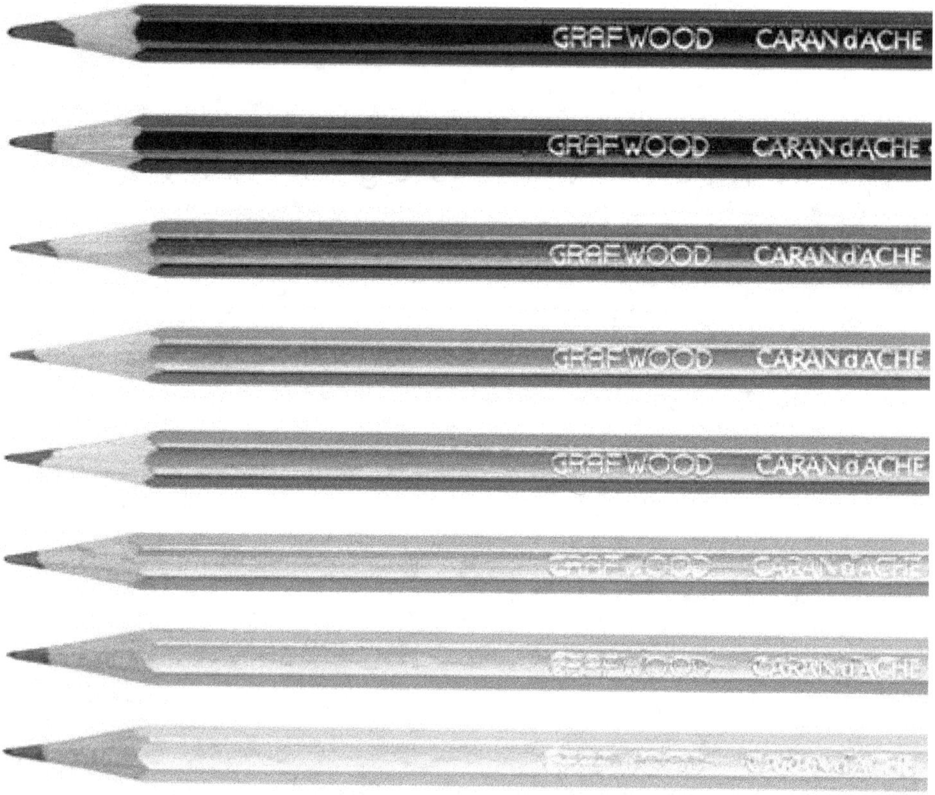

Brands of pencils

There are a lot of brands with graphite pencils, and in many aspects, the more expensive ones are usually better. The most popular brands are: Derwent Graphic, Caran d'Ache Grafwood, Koh-I-Noor Hardtmuth, Prismacolor Turquoise, Stabilo, Cretacolor Fine Art Graphite, Tombow Mono 100, Faber-Castel 9000, Staedtler Mars Lumograph, and General's Kimberly.

I personally prefer Koh-I-Noor Hardtmuth, and I will be using this brand for the drawings in this book. Even the graphite powder I have been making of Koh-I-Noor Hardtmuth progressos.

The hardness of the pencil

There are different grades of lead, depending on their hardness. It is important in terms of which pencil you use, and what you're trying to accomplish.
At the end of the graphite pencils you will find different numbers and letters, which indicate hardness. The pencil is based on a graphite manufactured with various additives added to the graphite, determining the hardness of it.

The short description of the meaning:
- H means "hard". They leave less graphite on the paper. The larger the number before the H-letter, the harder the pencil.
- B means "black". The B pencils are soft. The

larger the number before B-letter, the softer and darker the pencil is.
- F means "fine point". This F pencil (located between the two degrees of hardness), is still pretty hard, but leaves a bit darker trace than the H pencils.
- HB means "Hard & Black", so this is the nuance in the middle of the scale, good for mid-tones and shading. Can be easily darkened and lightened.

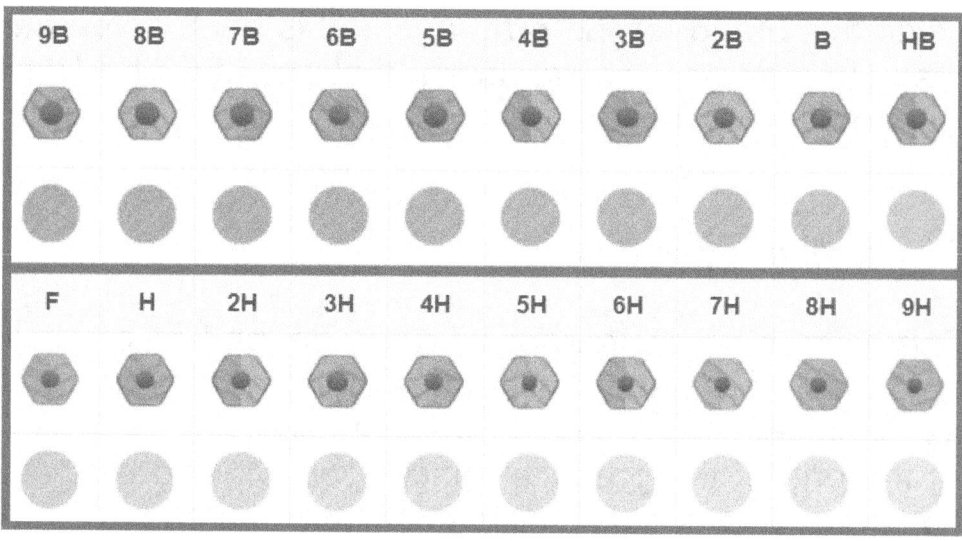

You can get good quality pencils, not just per piece, but also in different sets. Of course, this is just a guideline for the beginning. You will realize on your own how many pencils you need. Graphite is very generous. Not only are there different shades of different hardness pencils available. But the same hardness pencil can create different shades depending on the stronger or weaker pressure applied.

Which pencils will you need for drawing?
When I started to draw more than ten years ago, I had only two graphite pencils: 4B and HB, and I could draw this tiger and many other drawings, even faces, without lacking the rest of the nuances. The 4B pencil was dark enough for the black stripes, I couldn't make *this* black fur with HB pencil. I used HB to make the graphite powder for shading the fur and the background. I used an eraser to create the highlighted fur and whiskers over the previously shaded background. The fur that had to be white, I just left untouched. I also made the graphite powder out of 4B pencil and shaded with this darker powder behind the tiger to enhance the appearance of the tiger. You will have an opportunity to learn how to draw and shade similar animals in this book and I will explain how these steps have to be done.

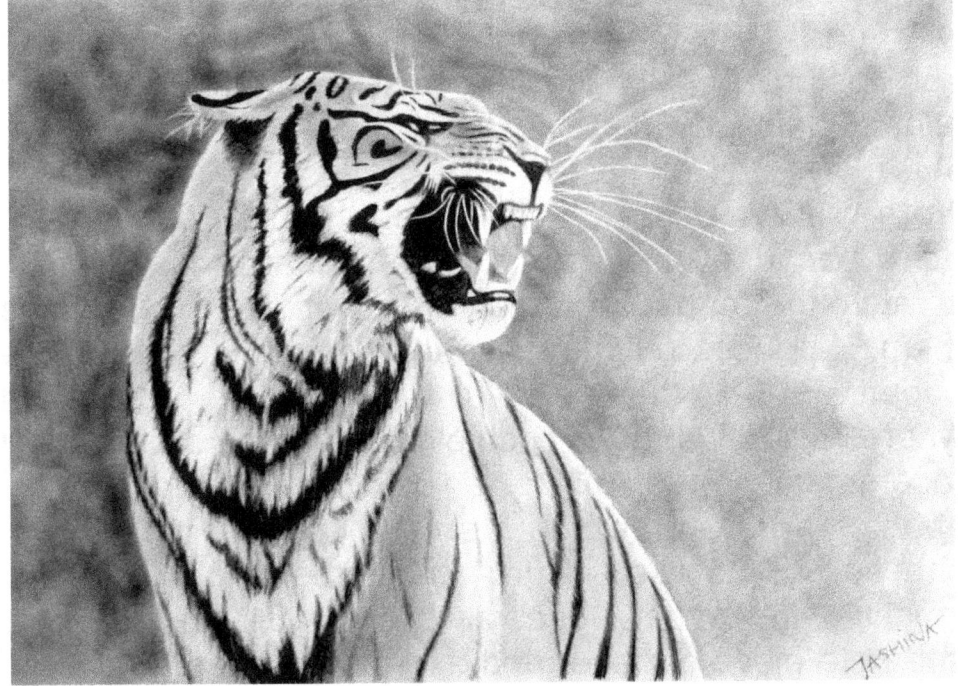

So, you don't have to have a lot of tools and a full scale of nuances regarding these pencils.

You will need HB for sketching, maybe B is even better because it does not scratch the paper as much as HB does, but you have to press lightly to avoid creating too dark lines. For the shadows and the darkest areas, you can purchase a very soft pencil for all black nuances: 4B or above. Any of them is similar as you can see in the hardness scale in the next image, so you don't need them all.

9H 8H 7H 6H 5H 4H 3H 2H H F HB B 2B 3B 4B 5B 6B 7B 8B 9B

Hardest → Medium → Softest

So, for the beginning, it is enough if you supply yourself with one HB, B, 4B and 5H. Also, I recommend purchasing a progresso, the best hardness is B, I will later explain why.

Note: When using 5H or harder pencil, don't press hard, because these pencils are so hard that they will scratch the paper, no matter how carefully you use them. H pencils leave traces, so to say "channels" in the paper, so use them carefully and never press hard where you want to achieve smooth surfaces. I recommend rather using a blending stump for the brighter areas, or if you want to use pencil anyway, choose 4H, 3H or softer and press lightly, barely touching the paper. Also, always try the pencils on a separate piece of paper and experiment with them a bit, to see how they behave. You will also note how 4B or the darker options are so soft, that they are similar to Prismacolor Premier colored pencils, which are very creamy. On one hand, you can relax with these, because these soft pencils won't scratch the paper and they draw smoothly, which is more enjoyable. On the other hand, use them carefully, because the blackness of these pencils is much more difficult to erase.

Mechanical pencils

If you don't like a lot of sharpening or creating a mess, and you want to save time, you can use a mechanical pencil. Other good reasons why you might choose a mechanical pencil over a wood-cased pencil is that, with a mechanical pencil, you have the continuity with the width of drawn lines the whole time, and you don't have to sharpen it to get the sharp tip after a little use.

I recommend this tool for sketching mostly and a lot of details can be drawn with this tool. You can use the same tool for years, unless you break it, and you can find refillable leads in several different widths and in all the existing graphite nuances, mentioned before.

Graphite powder

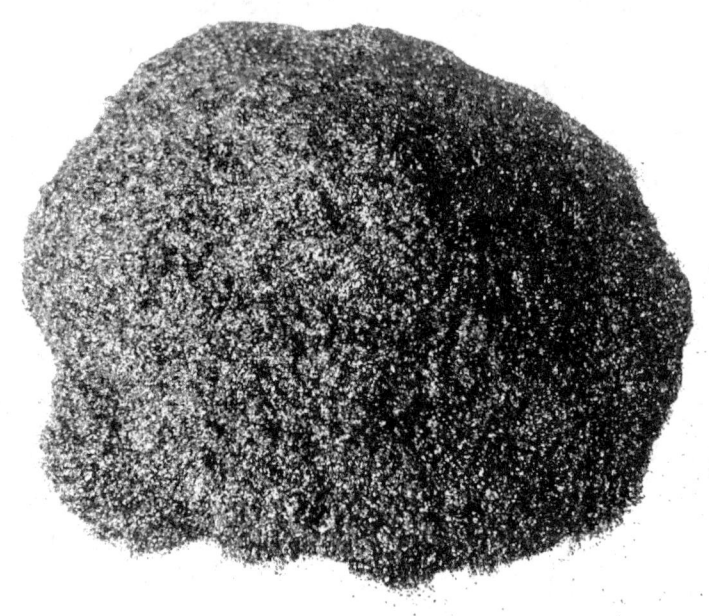

In this book, we will use a lot of graphite powder for shading to achieve a smooth and fine texture, for human skin, backgrounds and so on, instead of drawing line by line where the lines remain visible and the drawing is less realistic.

Graphite powder is the same graphite from which the graphite pencils are made. You can buy graphite powder, or you can make it at home, yourself. I've always made the graphite powder myself. To do this, you will need to carve the lead of the graphite pencil in order to get the powder from it. You can make it with a sharpener or a knife.

I realize that the finest graphite powder I can make is from the progresso graphite pencil. When I use a simple, wood-cased graphite pencil for making it, I always had the pieces of wood getting into my powder, no matter how carefully I carved it. It scratched the paper when I was shading and the final result wasn't smooth, but full of lines and scratches. That's why I've chosen progresso, which is a woodless graphite pencil, consisting only of the graphite core. I never use this tool for drawing the lines, but only for making powder.

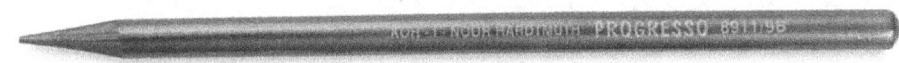

Put a progresso in a manual sharpener and turn it slowly, not pressing it hard into the sharpener. This way, you will get a fine graphite powder. Also, this way, you can create brighter graphite powder from H progresso, and dark graphite powder from 4B or darker progresso.

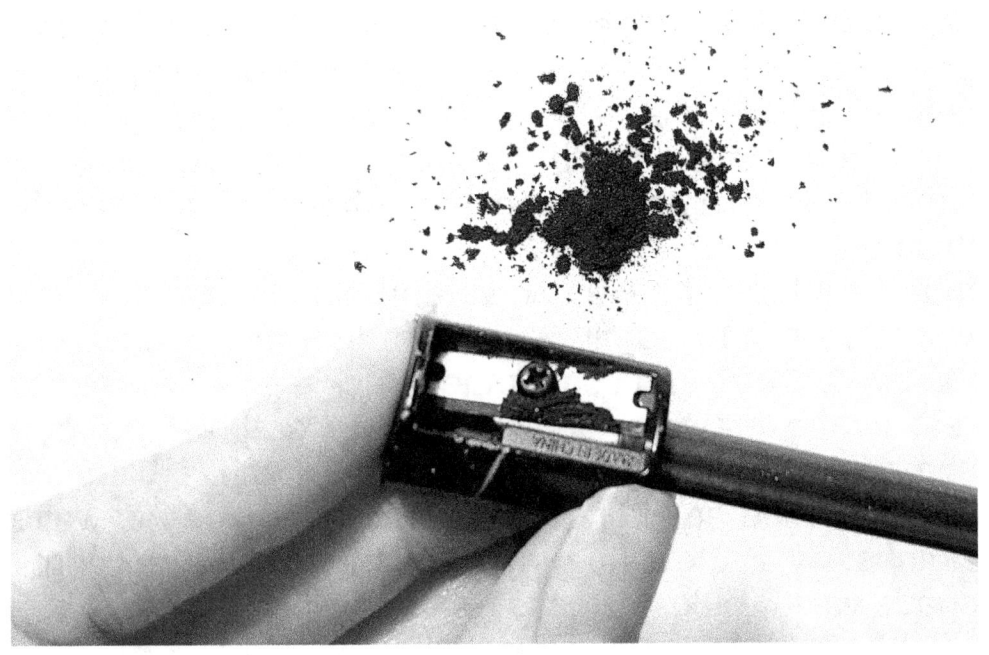

If you push it deep into the sharpener, you will carve bigger pieces out of the graphite. They will draw the lines while shading, when you're trying to create a smooth surface without any lines. So, it is essential to make the finest powder. Finally, to make it safe, you can sieve the powder through a cotton bandage, multiple times even, to exclude any bigger grains left and to ensure only the finest powder is ready for use.

We can use the graphite powder in a few ways. One of the techniques is the brush technique, which I recommend for the advanced artist. For beginners, it is best if you use a tissue, cotton pad or cloth. The brush requires a more experienced hand. Besides the tissue or cotton pads, which are good for shading the larger surfaces and backgrounds, I recommend the already mentioned blending stump for shading tiny details, and also a cotton swab, something that everyone has at home. You can create shades if you draw line by line, crosshatching, parallel strokes (and similar) using only pencil and not graphite powder, but your drawing will be less realistic. This is why I always recommend the shading techniques with graphite powder. This is what we will place emphasis on throughout the tutorials in this book.

In the next image, you can see an old drawing of mine, where there are barely any areas that are drawn, only the eyes, teeth, and some other black areas. I made the rest of the drawing, 99% of it, with graphite powder, spreading it with tissue, cotton swab, and a blending stump. I used an H graphite powder to shade the white clothes. If I drew the strokes to create the bright shadows, it would look less realistic, including the skin.

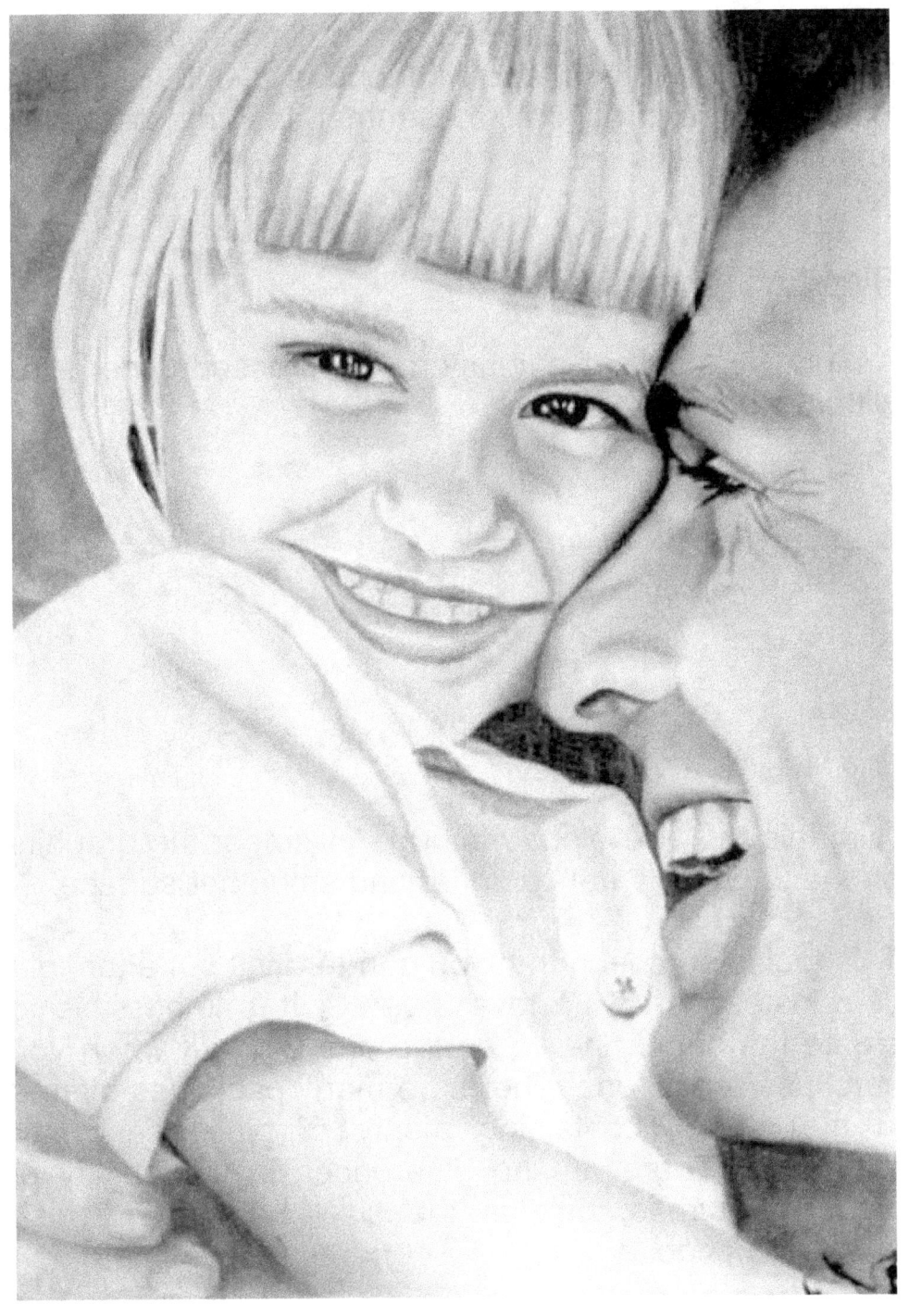

There should be very few hard lines on portraits. Portraits have to be made with tone gradients, not lines. But we will go through all these "theories" in detail in the tutorials in this book.

Blending stump

A blending stump is a tightly rolled, pressed paper stick with two pointed ends.

With this tool, we blend, smudge or smear the graphite on the paper to create a softer and smoother surface.

This tool is so cheap that you can throw it out after light use, instead of trying to sharpen it. It is impossible to create the same fine tip as the one you get when you purchase a new one. There are many packages offered in the stores, containing plenty of pieces and still affordable. There are no differences in the quality of blending stumps, only in the size, no matter which brand you choose.

Similar tools are tortillions, which have only one end

pointed, so I think the blending stump is a bit more useful, but you can acquire both and see which ones you'd rather work with.

Erasers

When drawing with graphite pencils, erasers are very important. Not only to correct mistakes, but to help in creating the highlights over the drawn and shadowed areas. I recommend you supply yourself with many kinds of erasers since they are not expensive and will make your work easier and more enjoyable.
The most popular is the <u>kneaded eraser</u>. I personally rarely use this kind of eraser because I find it too sticky. I have more experience with other kinds of erasers that I will list in this chapter. Kneaded erasers are very soft and can be kneaded with your fingers to achieve a desired shape. After a certain period of use, they become too dirty because they accumulate the graphite, and when it is impossible to find a clean part, you have to buy a new one. It costs a few dollars, so you don't have to begrime your drawing with an old kneaded eraser.

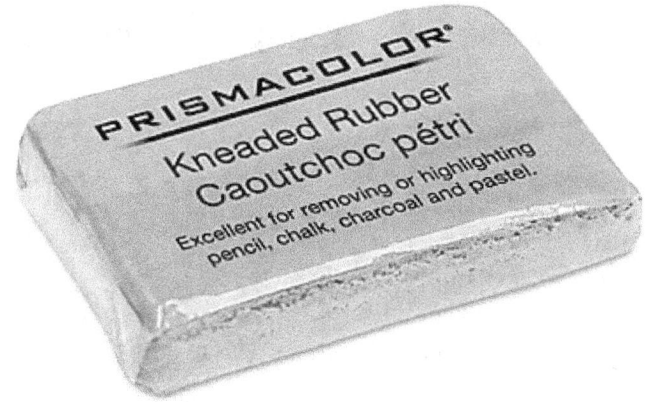

The mechanical pencil eraser is a similar to the mechanical pencil, but with a push button, and instead of the graphite leads you use gum leads, which are much thicker. You can even find a mechanical pencil and gum inside both triangular shapes, which helps with even more precise erasing and allows you to create hair and similar, tiny highlights.

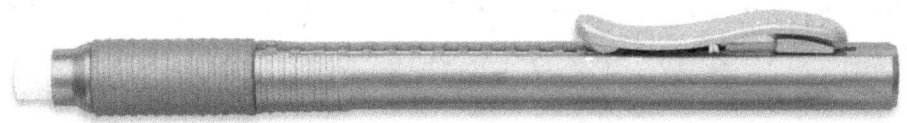

When the top of the gum on a mechanical eraser becomes dirty, I simply cut off the top with a knife to get a clear, sharp edge again.

The soft eraser pencil is a very practical eraser that looks the same as a wood-cased graphite or colored pencil, but the lead inside is made out of gum. You just sharpen it with the pencil sharpener, and it is ready to work with as you get the new, clear top on the eraser. This is also good for fine details and small areas. I have this tool by Faber-Castell which has half white and half red gum inside, so you can use both ends as you please.

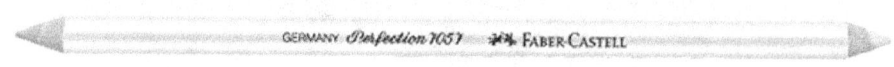

For erasing the larger areas, the plastic eraser is a

good tool. This eraser can also be cut with a knife and shaped to get the sharp edges and tips for fine details. This was the eraser that I used at the very beginning, and I used this kind alone for many years without having any difficulties achieving what I wanted.

I would also recommend a battery-operated eraser which I always recommend for colored pencils. I use an electric erase by Helix, which is amazing.

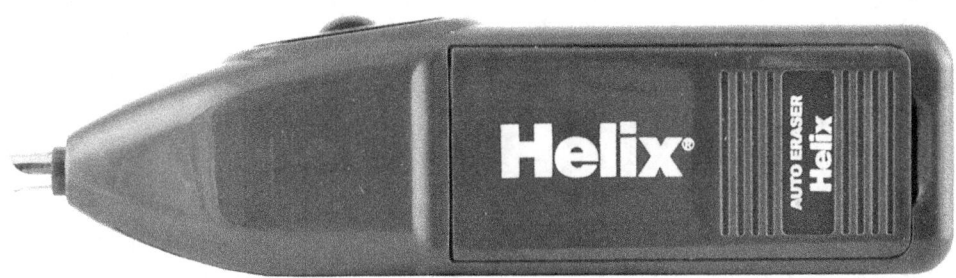

Paper

The papers are not all the same, and what kind of paper we use is important. Different types of drawing sheets are produced for different types of artwork.
If you use cheap, print paper your paper will ruffle and tear under the pressure of the tools you use. The erasers will tear up the cheap paper, particularly if you erase more times over the same area. The final result will appear underwhelming and poor, therefore wasting all that effort you put into it.

The weight of the paper

The weight of the paper is one of the most important things we have to pay attention to. The thickness of the paper is determined by the gram weight of 1 square meter. Traditional printing paper weighs 80 g / m2, but as mentioned, it is better to choose a harder paper for drawing. We should choose a paper weighing between 180-220 g / m2.

Besides the weight of the paper, we also have to pay attention to what kind of medium we will work on. There are different kinds of paper offered for different mediums:

Watercolor paper: These are the thickest sheets because they need to absorb the water and remain straight. Their weight generally ranges from 200 to 300 g / m2. Smooth, hot pressed watercolor papers can also be ideal for drawing.

Paper for graphite or charcoal drawings: it does not require the same durability as the watercolor paper, but it must be more durable than the common printer paper. They generally have a weight of 180 to 220 g / m2.

For colored pencils: Colored pencils work well with many kinds of paper surfaces, such as paper for graphite, pastel or watercolor.

Whether I recommend the paper in my books on colored pencils or on graphite, I always recommend *thick* and *smooth* paper. You don't have to buy a particular brand. Any kind of paper in your local store is good as long as it is thick and smooth. Thick paper can endure many layers of blending, erasing, and pressure. If you are looking for good and high-quality brands of paper, I recommend Strathmore Bristol, Fabriano Bristol, and Stonehenge.

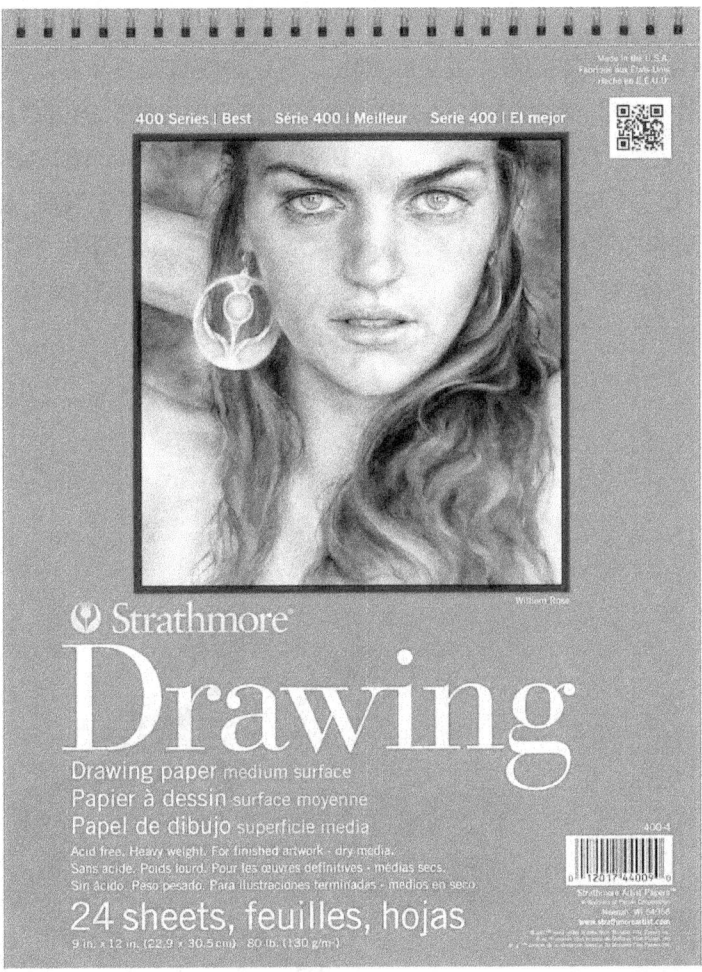

Paper size

Here is a list of the most commonly used sizes:
A1 -- 594 x 841 mm -- 23.4 x 33.1 in

A2 -- 420 x 594 mm -- 16.5 x 23.4 in
A3 -- 297 x 420 mm -- 11.7 x 16.5 in
A4 -- 210 x 297 mm -- 8.3 x 11.7 in
A5 -- 148 x 210 mm -- 5.8 x 8.3 in

For the drawings in this book I recommend an A4 paper format. If you want to create a really detailed drawing later on, you might want to try to draw on larger paper, but for the beginning, A4 is the perfect size for you.
I use Fabriano Bristol paper for every single drawing in this book and also for my colored pencil drawings, so I can highly recommend this paper.

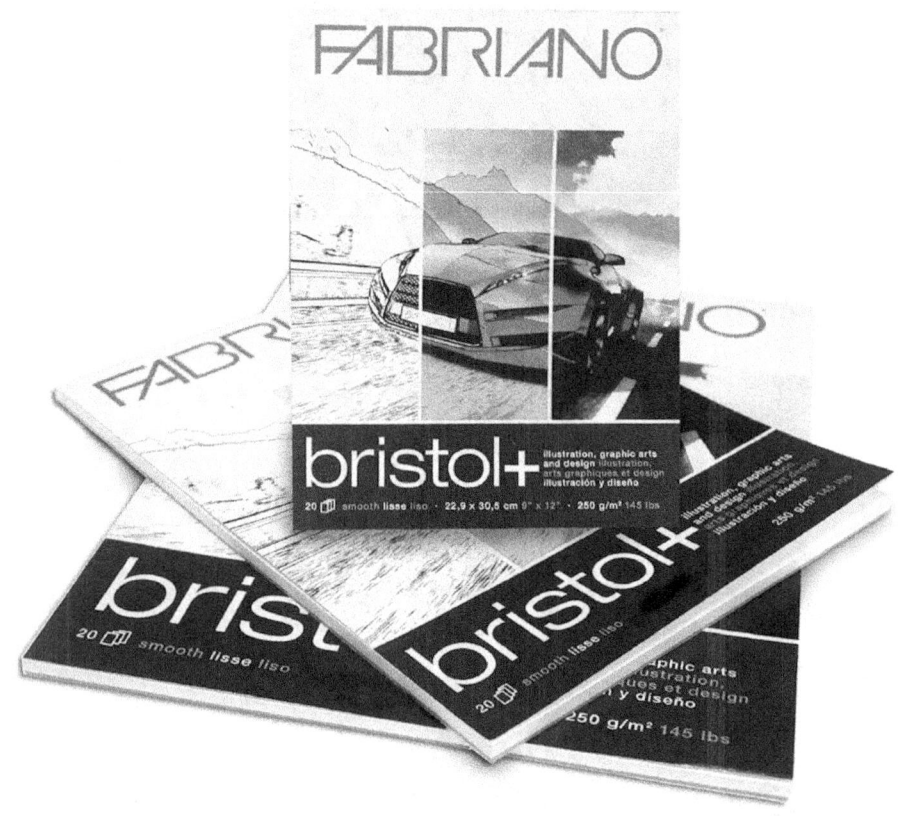

Additional tools that you might find helpful:

Pencil lengthener

As our pencil gets shorter after use and sharpening, the balance changes and it is not that comfortable to hold anymore. Also, if you have purchased expensive graphite pencil brands, you will want to use them to the end, and with minimal waste. For this, you will have to get a pencil lengthener, which can also be used for colored pencils, and for many shapes of pencils: hexagonal, round, triangle and so on.

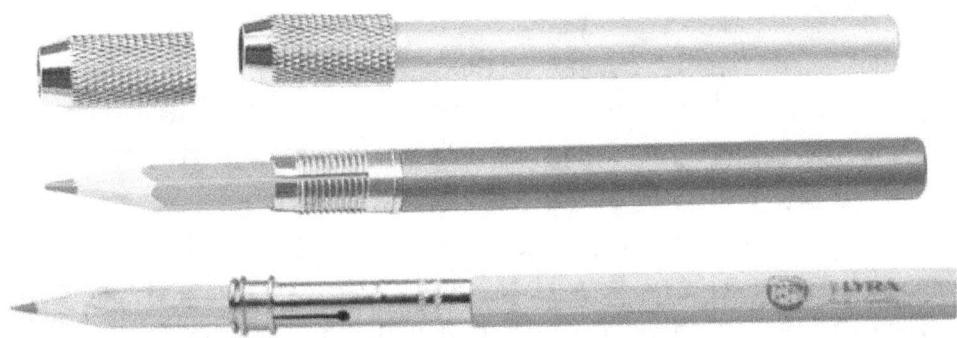

Even after using a pencil lengthener, there will still be a tiny part, about 0.5 in (1 cm) long, which will fall off out of the lengthener, so to use even that tiny part, you can glue it to the unsharpened end of a new pencil with superglue and use it to its fullest.

In the next image you can see an example of how I have done it with colored pencils. My white colored pencil was falling out from the lengthener, because it was already too small, and I glued it to the silver colored pencil, which I rarely use. Now, I could use the white pencil wholly. If you have pencils that have erasers on one end, simply use pliers to take them off together with the ferrule that holds the gum on the end of the pencil and glue the ends.

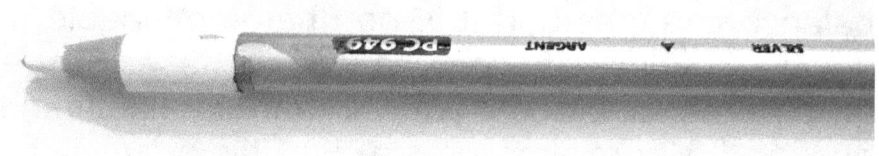

White ink gel pen

Besides all these tools, I recommend using a white ink gel pen for the tiny highlighted areas, which can be easily applied over the drawn and shaded areas. Of course, you can leave untouched the part of the paper that you want to stay white, and it is often recommended, but when you want to draw a cat's whiskers for example, it is difficult to draw around them during the whole drawing process. It is much easier to draw them at the end of the drawing over the graphite. Also, it is very useful when drawing the eyes, lips and similar shiny things. You will see this tool in action throughout the tutorials in this book and you can decide whether you want to buy it for yourself. This tool is cheap and long-lasting.

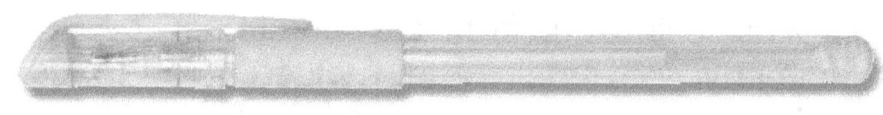

You can easily create the brightest highlights over the graphite, brighter than erasing the graphite with an eraser. For this purpose, you can also use white fine markers, such as the one by Uni Posca 0,7 mm, or even 5 mm for the larger areas.

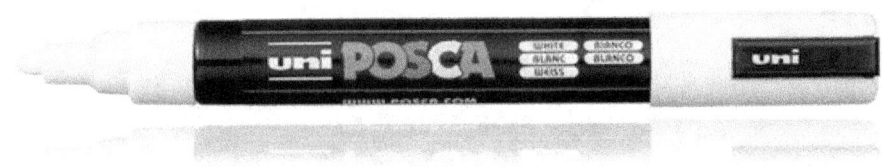

You can use white gouache, white paint, white acrylic paint, white pastel or anything else that can be easily spread over the graphite and look absolutely white.

Fixative

Spraying fixative on a finished drawing will add protection against unwanted smearing and will diminish glare. The drawing absorbs the fixative and still allows you to draw over it again. So, when you are working on a piece, you should start in the upper left corner (if you are right-handed), and as you finish the area, spray it with fixative and draw the area to the right or under it. It will protect the finished area from the dust and dirt while you work on the rest of the drawing. I always use the fixative outside or I open the windows as its smell is very strong and is not healthy to inhale.

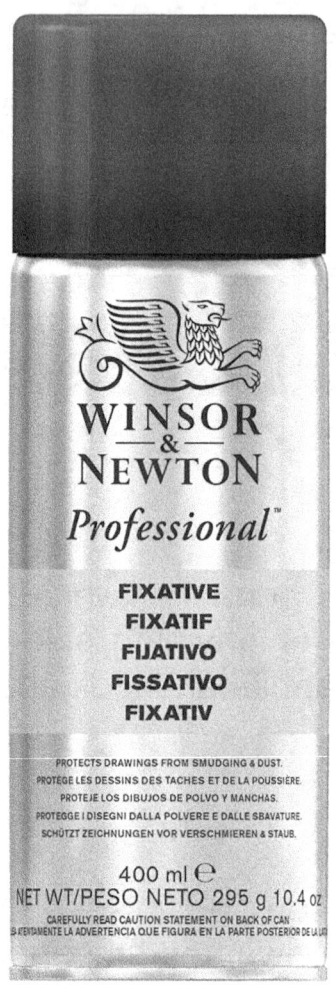

Another reason for fixing the drawings is that the reflectivity of the dark graphite lessens. Graphite has a strong reflective attribute. For this reason, you can consider choosing a matte fixative over the glossy one.

Drawing Tutorials:
HOW TO DRAW A 3D BALL

Let's start by practicing the shading on a simple ball. The first step is to create a perfect circle, which is the best to do with a divider tool. Create the circle somewhere in the middle of your paper sheet.

The next thing is to give this ball a round shape by shading the self-shadow. Draw a circle of the same size on another piece of paper and cut it so that you can place over the surrounding area as shown in the next picture. Here, we have to determine the light source, which usually comes from above.

Place the cut paper a bit further from the edge to avoid shading the area of the reflected light. Take a look at the picture in the next step to see how I have left this area untouched.

Pick up a little graphite powder with your finger or cotton tab and make a gradual transition by pressing harder next to the lower edge of the ball and releasing the pressure as you shade towards the center of the ball until you reach the brightest shade.

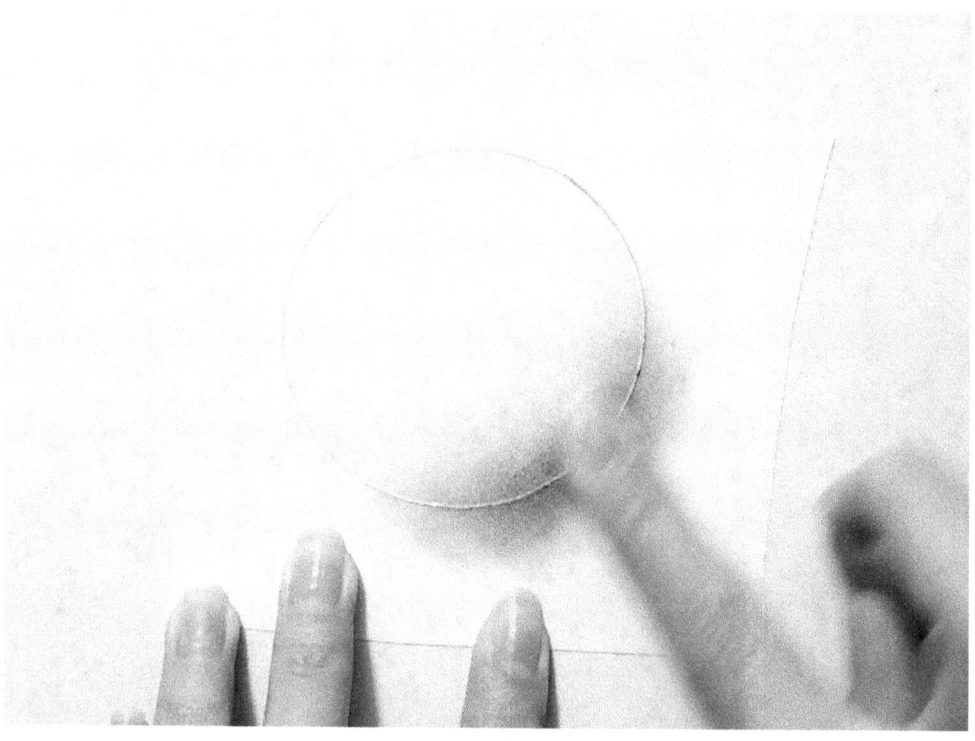

When you remove the cut paper you will get the gradient shading and the surrounding area will stay clean. Now you can see the untouched area of the reflected light that I mentioned in the previous step. However, this area shouldn't stay white, but for now, we just have to prevent it from getting as dark as the darkest part of the self-shadow.

Now you can shade the area for the reflected light lightly using a blending stump. Just try to make it a bit darker than the white area of the background and avoid too much shading.

Here you can see how I have shaded the cast shadow a bit further from the ball, and how we got the bouncing or floating ball. This cast shadow should be the darkest in the middle and try to make it gradually dissolve into the whiteness of the paper by releasing the pressure as you shade outwards.

If the light source is strong, the cast shadow will have sharper edges. Here you can see how much we can achieve with shading. I erased the brightest surrounding areas around the cast shadow to create a shadow with sharp edges, and it already looks as if it were affected by direct sunlight.

Try to play with this cast shadow, for example, by placing it on the right or left side, under the ball, but pay attention to the self-shadow. If the self-shadow is on the lower-right area, the cast shadow should be placed under the ball in the middle or on the right side.

The higher the ball is bouncing above the surface, the smaller and brighter the cast shadow will be.

Now we can make it as if the ball were laying on some surface. Just erase the previously added cast shadow or make a new ball as you did in the first two steps.

Here, we have to create the same flawless gradation as we did inside the ball with the self-shadow, but this time place the cut piece of paper over the ball including the area for the reflected light. Press very hard next to the edge of the ball and less and less as you shade outwards on the ball. This is good if you have the cut piece of paper placed over your ball because this way you will be able to press really hard over it in order to create the darkest shade next to the edge of the ball.

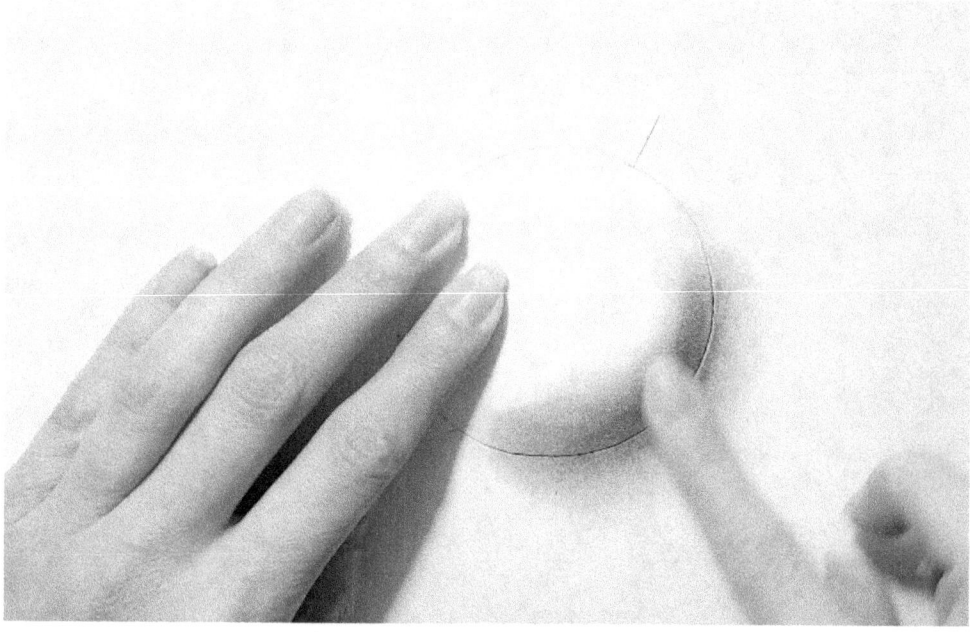

When you remove the cut paper, shade a bit over the reflected light. This area should stay as bright as possible, yet not absolutely white, so give it a bit of the shade.

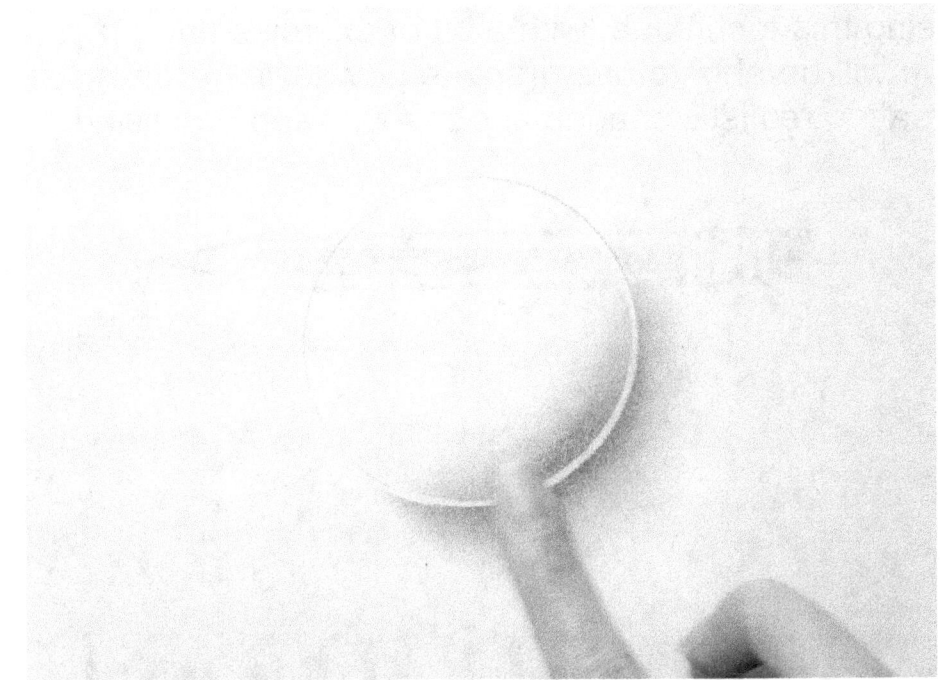

In this next image you can see how it finally looks. If you are not satisfied with your result, make a new ball and you will see where you went wrong and how to improve.

Using this technique, with a bit of exercise and practice, you will be able to use graphite powder for drawing and creating realistic shades and tones. Keep practicing!

HOW TO DRAW WATER DROPLETS

Start by creating random circles on your paper, from small to large, as many as you want; you can even only start with one for the beginning if you want. In the next picture you can see the circles that I have drawn and scanned. Use an HB for this and don't press too hard. Don't use darker tones than an HB because the dark, strong contour lines appear strangely around the transparent material.

The next step is the most difficult and the most crucial. You can draw this step with a pencil, but I recommend using graphite powder because shading with graphite powder will make the drops look smoother.

Here, we have to use the gradation technique, to create a graduated tone or gradient transition between the nuances of grey. It is a drawing technique which can be used to create larger, even areas, and to make a sense of space and form. It is a very useful skill to develop for both graphite and color pencil drawings.

As mentioned in the "Tools" chapter, create the graphite from your HB or softer pencil or progresso. The lighter grades will not give enough depth to the darkest tones, but I don't recommend the darker tones for these drops. We will only have to darken the edges in one of the following steps.

But for now, let's shade the droplets so that they can appear round.

Start by shading the edges which have to be darker and slowly build up the tone working towards the center of the drop. I use a cotton pad for applying the graphite powder. I always cut a piece of paper, and I place it over the outer area of the object I want to shade, so that surrounding area doesn't get any of the powder and I can press harder over the edge.

You can see what I mean in the next image. It is pretty complicated to cut many papers, but the effort is worth it, and you will have less to erase around the droplets. Not to mention that the gradual transition will look more flawless. I will use this trick throughout many of the tutorials in this book, so I recommend you try the same.

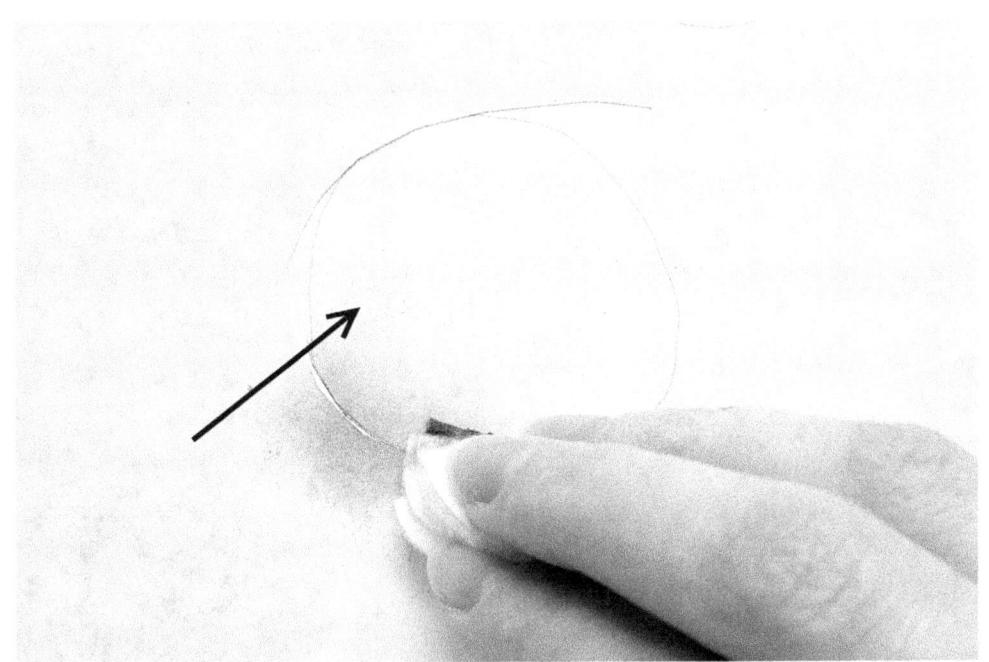

As you work towards the center of the droplets, gradually ease the pressure until you can no longer see the powder on the paper. You then patiently repeat this process all around the droplets.

Do the same with the rest of the droplets, if you have drawn more than one.

You can use your blending stump or bright pencil 2B or softer to adjust any irregular areas. Try to keep the tonal changes as smooth as possible until you achieve the variety and intensity of tone you desire. Also, strengthen the edges with a blending stump, digging it into the darker powder, made out of either 2B or B pencils, or use these pencils, but don't make the edges too dark, yet tend toward darker than the inner area next to the edge. Blend these tones to make a gradation between them. This step requires a lot of time and patience.

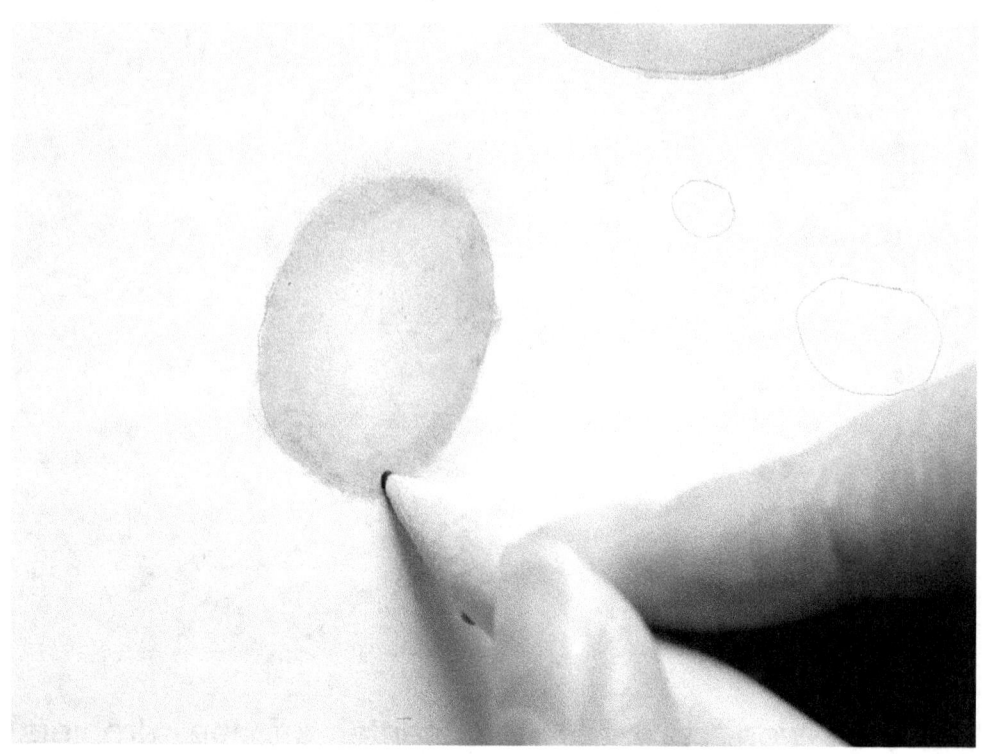

The second way to shade these areas is drawing instead of applying graphite powder. The point is to use the nuances of one next to another as they are in the scale of graphite nuances. Always have the chart from the next image next to you to see which nuance to use as a continuation to the one that you used.

9H 8H 7H 6H 5H 4H 3H 2H H F HB B 2B 3B 4B 5B 6B 7B 8B 9B

Hardest → Medium → Softest

Start to draw the tiny line all around the edge with an HB, and press harder when you draw over the edges, releasing the pressure as you draw the inner areas. Then continue to draw with the brighter nuance next to

HB, which is F. You can also skip the F pencil (or if you don't have this one), and use an H. This is why you should press lightly when you finish the shading with one tone, so the brighter tone of the next pencil will have the same value, and the edge between the pencils will be invisible. This way, you will achieve a flawless gradation.
Lastly, blend the entire gradation with your blending stump, cotton swab, tissue, or anything else that you would like to blend with.

I have created more droplets, you can see in the next image how they look after adding the shading. After shading with graphite powder, we have to erase the surrounding areas of the droplets because no matter how carefully we shade, and we put the cut paper over the surrounding areas, it will always get some powder. So, use the sharp edge of the eraser to eliminate this dirt.

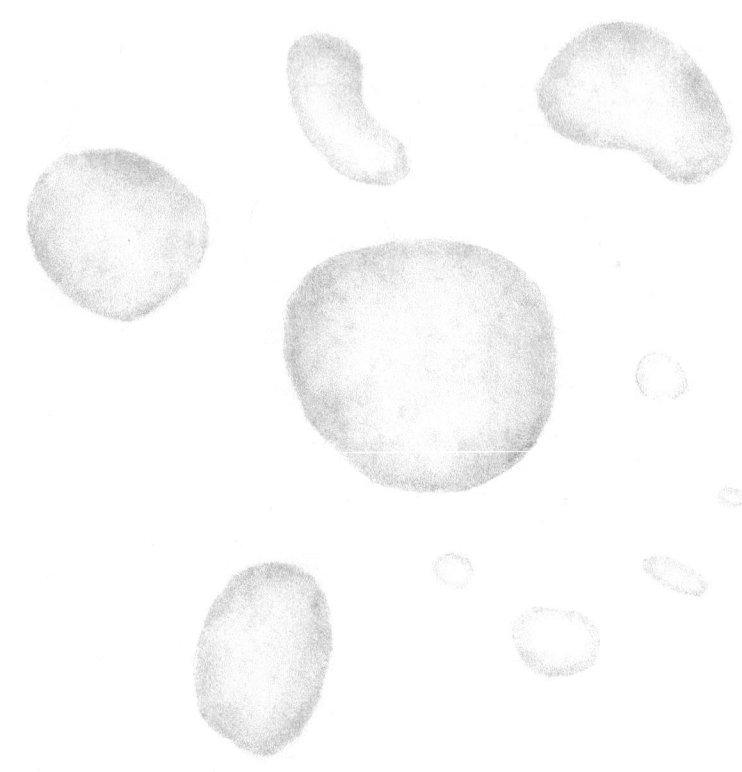

If we want to make these droplets come off the paper and look more realistic, we have to create the cast shadows. At first, determine the light source. My light source is found in the upper-left corner of the paper, so my cast shadow will be placed under the droplets, towards the lower-right corner of the paper. You can make these cast shadows by placing the cut paper over the droplets (like in the case of the 3D ball) and shade it with powder and tissue, releasing the pressure as you shade outwards the cast shadow, or you can draw it, using a bit darker pencil, such as B or 2B next to the droplet. I have chosen to draw the cast shadow. Sharpen your pencil often to get the nice, clean edge between the droplet and the cast shadow.

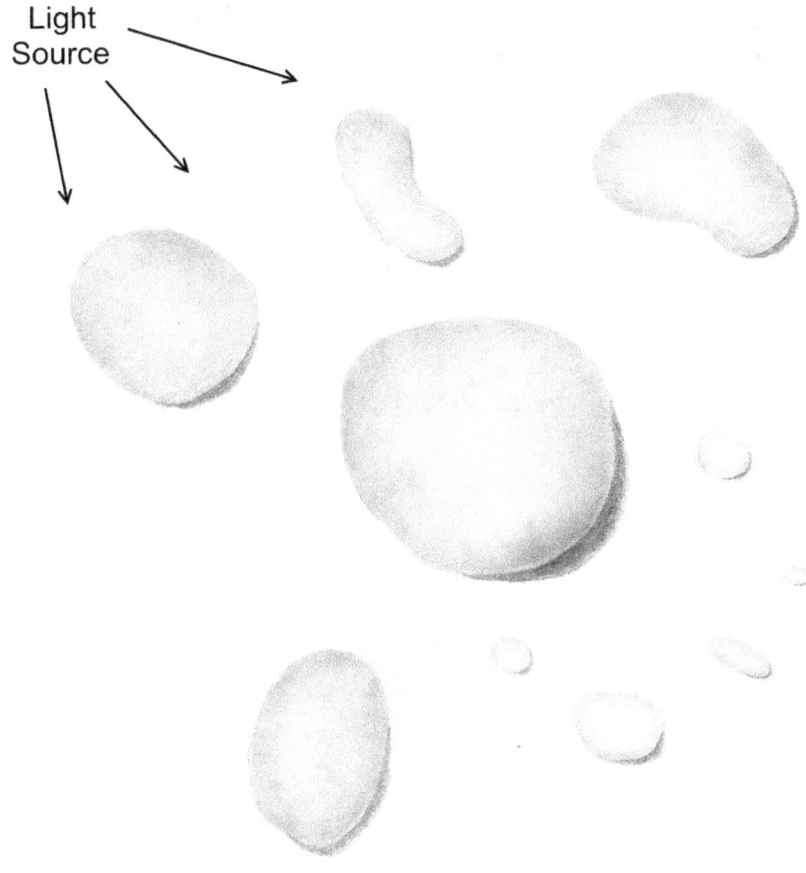

Continue with a brighter nuance, HB and softer. Blend

the edge of the shadow with blending stump and make it gradually disappear into the background. Don't forget a few rules: the bigger the droplet, the larger and darker shadow it casts, and that the shadow is the thickest in the middle. Analyze the next image before you start shading. It is good to draw more droplets, instead of just one, so that you can practice. If the cast shadow of one droplet hasn't succeeded, you can try again on the another droplet. As mentioned, the gradation technique is very important to acquire, because you will have to use it in almost every single drawing.

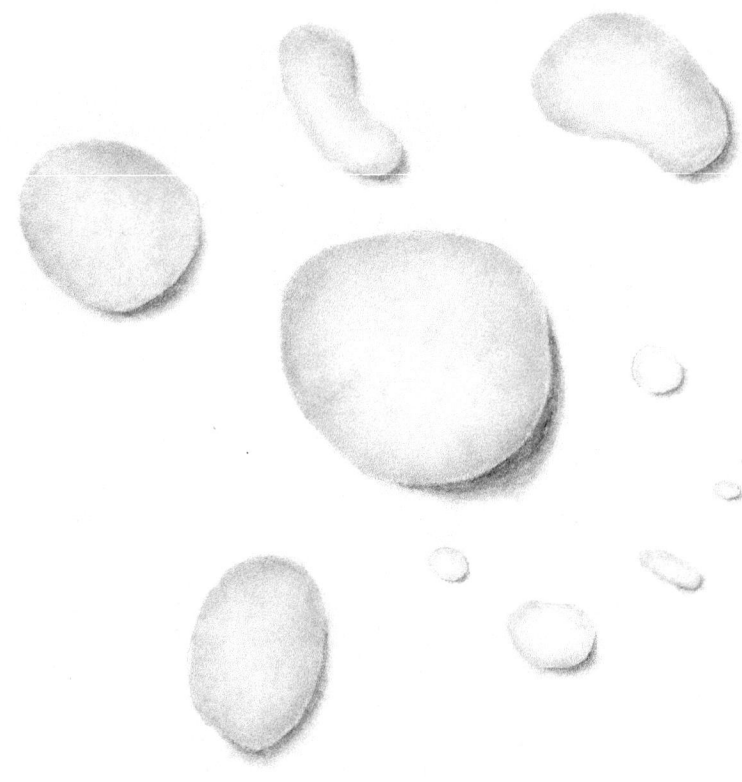

So far, my droplets look nothing like water. They could be pebbles or similar objects. What we need here, is to make these droplets look wet and shiny by adding the highlights.

If you have determined your light source in the upper-left corner – as I have – your droplets will illuminate on the upper-left areas. Here, you have to erase the highlights. These highlights can be round, ecliptic, even square, make them as you please. Again, if you have drawn more droplets, try to apply different shapes of the highlights (above mentioned and more) so that you can see which one appears the best for you. To make them even shinier, you can make the rays of light coming out of the center of the highlights by using well-sharpened edge of the gum, or with the peak of the kneaded eraser. Place the clean top of the eraser in the middle of the highlight, and with rapid movement, draw it outwards, the highlight releasing the pressure at the end.

You can create these highlights with the tools that I have mentioned in "Tools" chapter, white ink gel pen, or if you want to apply the bigger dots easily, you can use a Uni Posca white marker, which will make it look even brighter. Remember that once shaded, paper will never be absolutely white anymore. You can also make more highlights over a single drop, just like I have done with my biggest droplet.

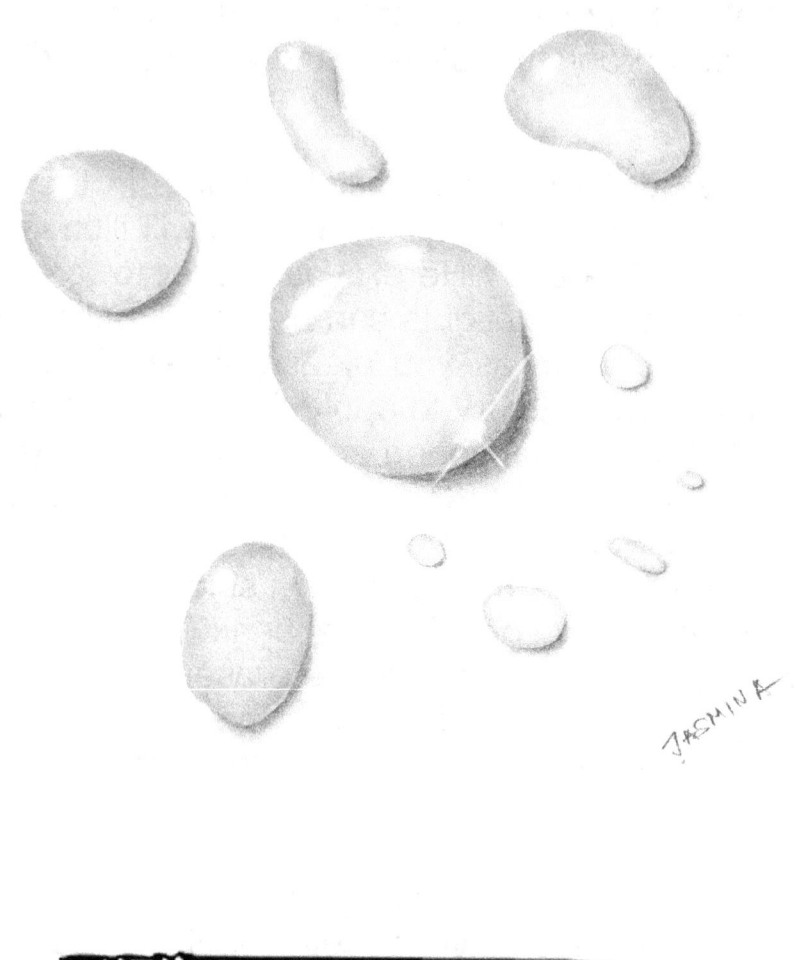

HOW TO DRAW A WINE GLASS

At first, draw a vertical oval. You should draw a shape that is similar to an egg. To make it symmetrical, take a look at the oval shape in the mirror. If it looks symmetrical in the mirror as well, then you have a perfectly symmetrical oval.

Then, draw a vertical line starting from the center of the oval, going through the bottom of the oval, extending below it, as shown in the next image. This line will be the center of the stem. If you are not sure where the center of the oval is, measure the width of the oval and divide it in half, for example, if the oval is 2 inches (5 centimeters) wide, you should place the line after 1 inch (2,5 centimeters) measuring from the left or right side of the oval. If that is easier for you, draw the vertical line first, and then draw the round shapes of the oval the same on the both sides of the line.

In the next image you can see how the vertical line that I have placed in the middle divides the oval into two equal parts. This is the base of our realistic, symmetrical glass.

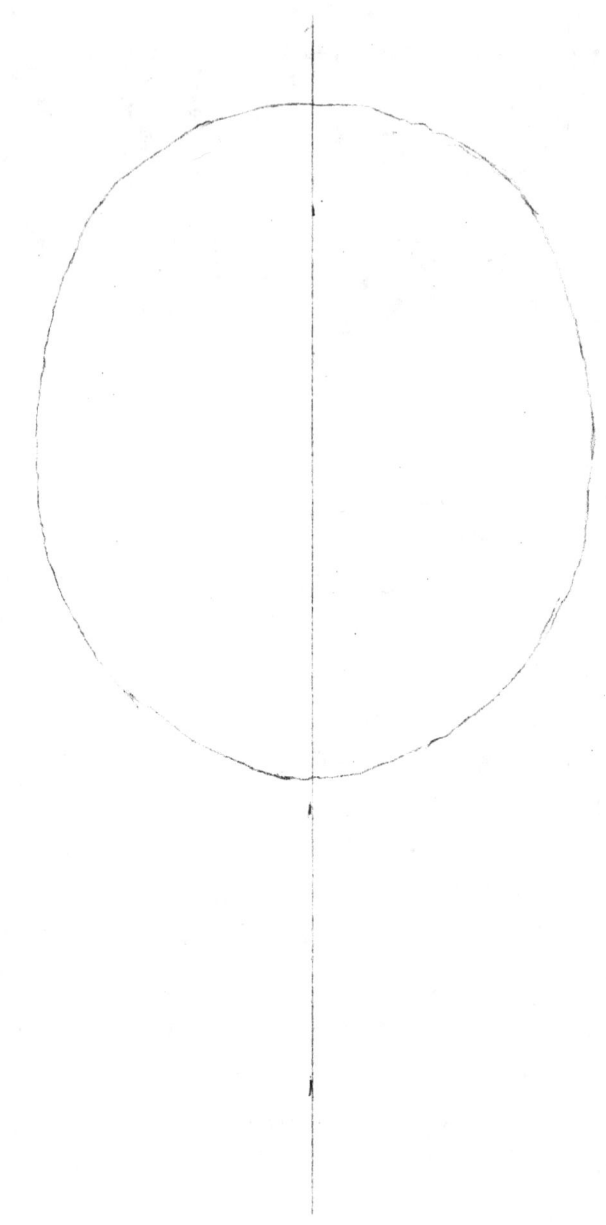

Let's focus on the upper area on the bowl for now, so that we won't smudge the stem and foot while drawing the bowl. In the upper part of the oval, draw an ellipse which will represent the rims. This ellipse doesn't have to be in the same place as mine. You can put it wherever you want, the point is to make it also symmetrical, and to check it in the mirror. Erase the outline of the oval above the rims. Here, you can also determine the amount of wine you want to draw by adding a horizontal line somewhere in the middle of the bowl – like mine - or wherever you want.

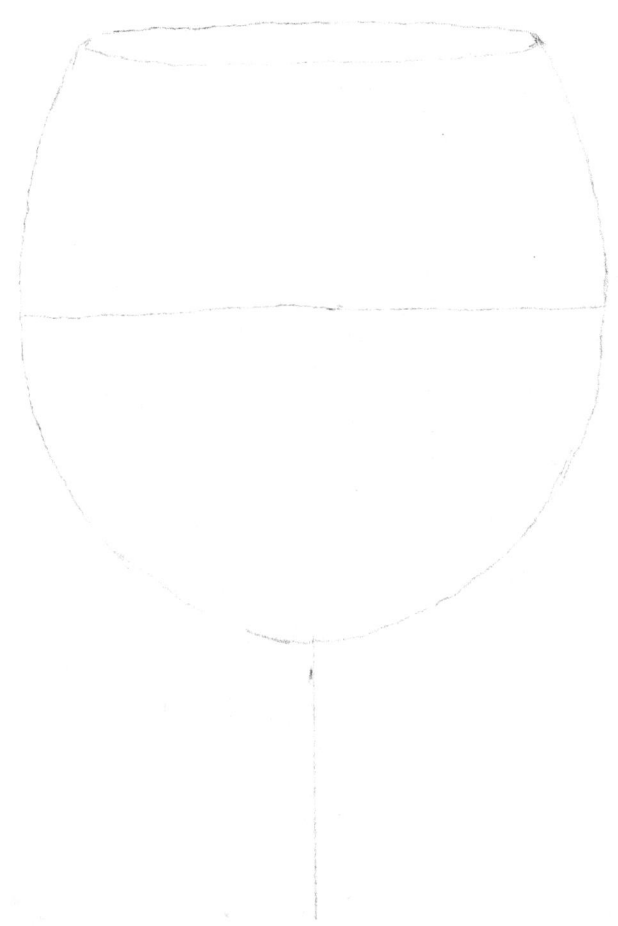

Now you can start shading. As mentioned many times,

it is best if you cut the piece of the paper in the shape of the background around the glass and place it over the surrounding area. Pick a bit of the graphite powder with tissue or cotton pad and spread it gently over both the left and right sides of the bowl, and also over the rims. Press harder when shading the edges and release the pressure to get the shading to gradually dissolve towards the center of the bowl.

Now, using a B pencil, strengthen the upper edges on the left and right side of the bowl, next under the rims in the area that contains no wine.

Erase all around the rim with the sharp tip of an eraser. This way, you will get the highlights of the rim. Strengthen the edges around this highlight using an HB pencil and blend it with blending stump.

Erase the highlights where you want over the area on the left and right sides of the upper area of the bowl. The reflection of the light should be square or rectangular on the glass, only the rounded objects, such as a ball, eyeball etc. usually have circular highlights. I used a battery-operated eraser to completely eliminate the graphite. It was easier to make the highlight completely white because I erased over the shading. If we erase the drawn parts, it would have left some lines and the paper wouldn't be purely white again.

Since we have finished the upper area of the bowl, which contains no wine, we can start to draw the area with wine. You can choose to draw red wine - as I have

- or white wine, but you will have to use much brighter nuances for the white wine. Anyway, the relation between the nuances should differ the same way when you draw white wine.

Firstly, draw in the middle of the glass area, which is not affected by the light from any side. Use a 6B or darker, I used an 8B for this. Press hard and go over multiple times to fill the tooth of the paper and to eliminate the visible white dots of the paper texture. Take a look at the next image to see the shape I created, and try to make it similar. Doesn't have to look the same as mine.

If you want to draw a glass containing white wine, use a a 4H for this area.

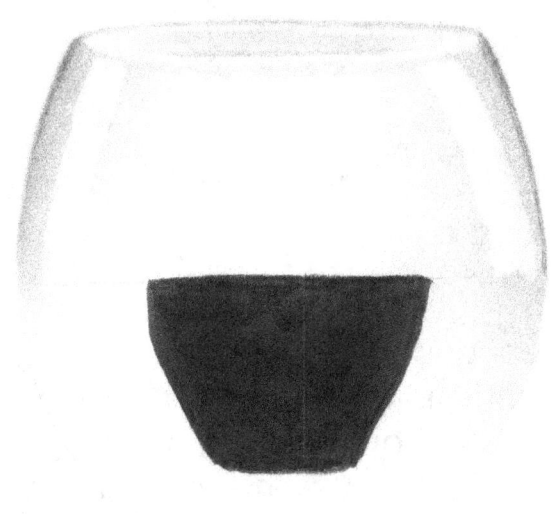

Using a B pencil, draw the outer edges of the lower part of the bowl as shown in the next picture.

You can make the line thicker or thinner in some places. It shouldn't have the same thickness all around because it would appear unnatural.

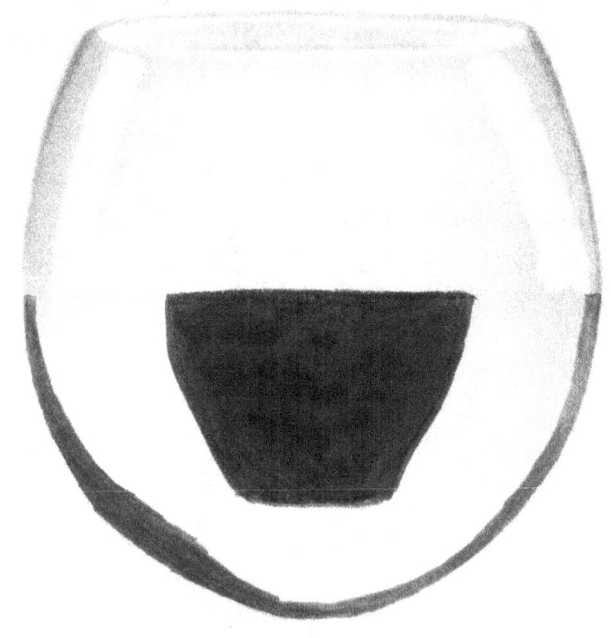

Fill in the area under the darkest part in the middle using an HB and make the gradient transition between this area and the bottom, using a blending stump or a B pencil, pressing lightly over the area drawn with an HB, and pressing harder as you shade into the bottom area. Analyze the next image before you start shading.

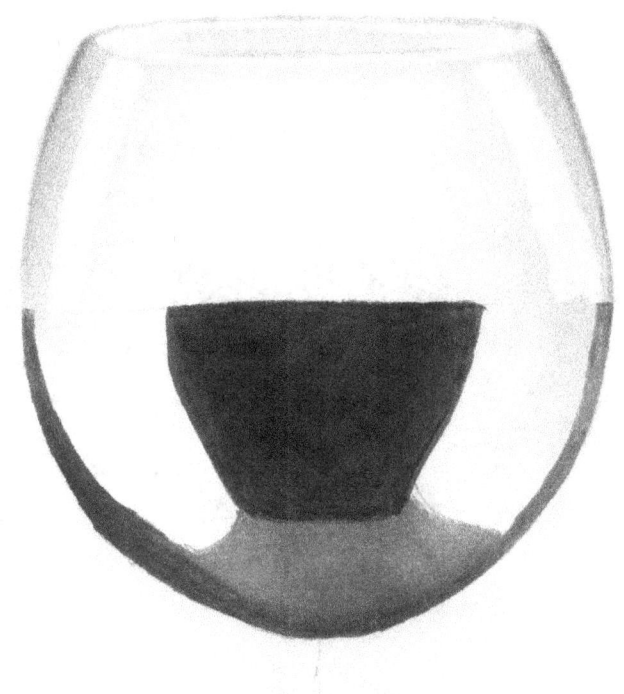

You can fill the area on the right side using a 2H and a blending stump to make it smooth.

Here also, it is important to create a gradient transition between the tones. The tones will always depend on the surrounding tones. For example, if the glass with wine is placed on the white table, the lower area of the bowl will have brighter tones because of the table's reflection. If it is placed on a black table, it will hardly have any brighter tone; it would be almost completely black.

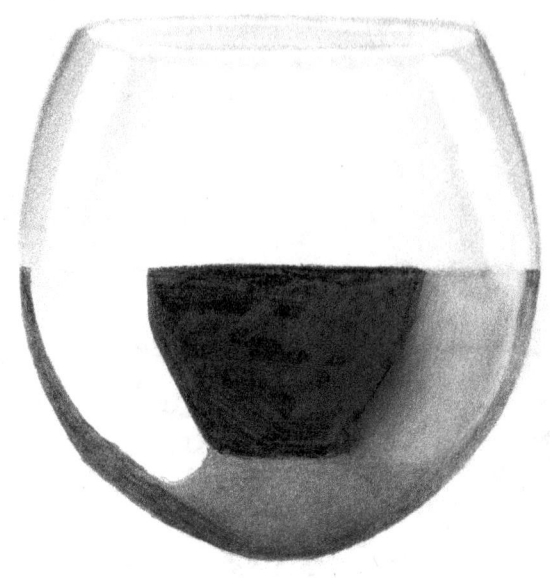

On the left side, you can shade brighter or darker than you did on the right side.

You can also add some different highlights to make it more natural because the reflections, highlights, and shadows are rarely the same on the both sides of the glass or bottle.

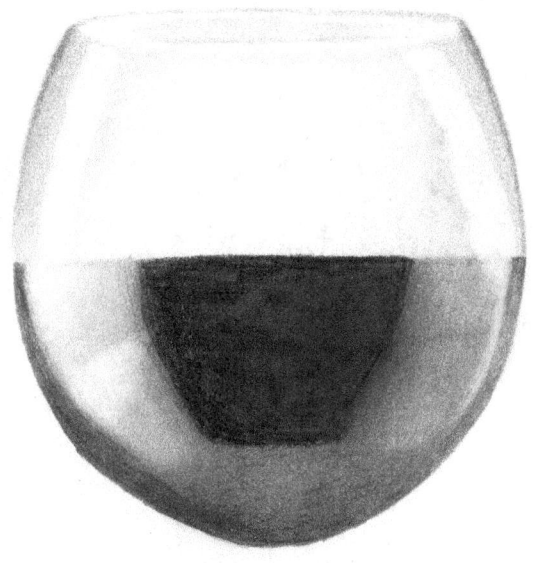

If you are satisfied with the bowl, you can move to the stem.

The stem shouldn't have any dark tones in the middle, nor should it have drawn lines. The best option is, again, to create the paper to place over the surrounding areas, and to shade the edge of the stem as shown in the next image. This way you will press harder over the edge and achieve the gradient transition which is very important when drawing a rounded object like this one.

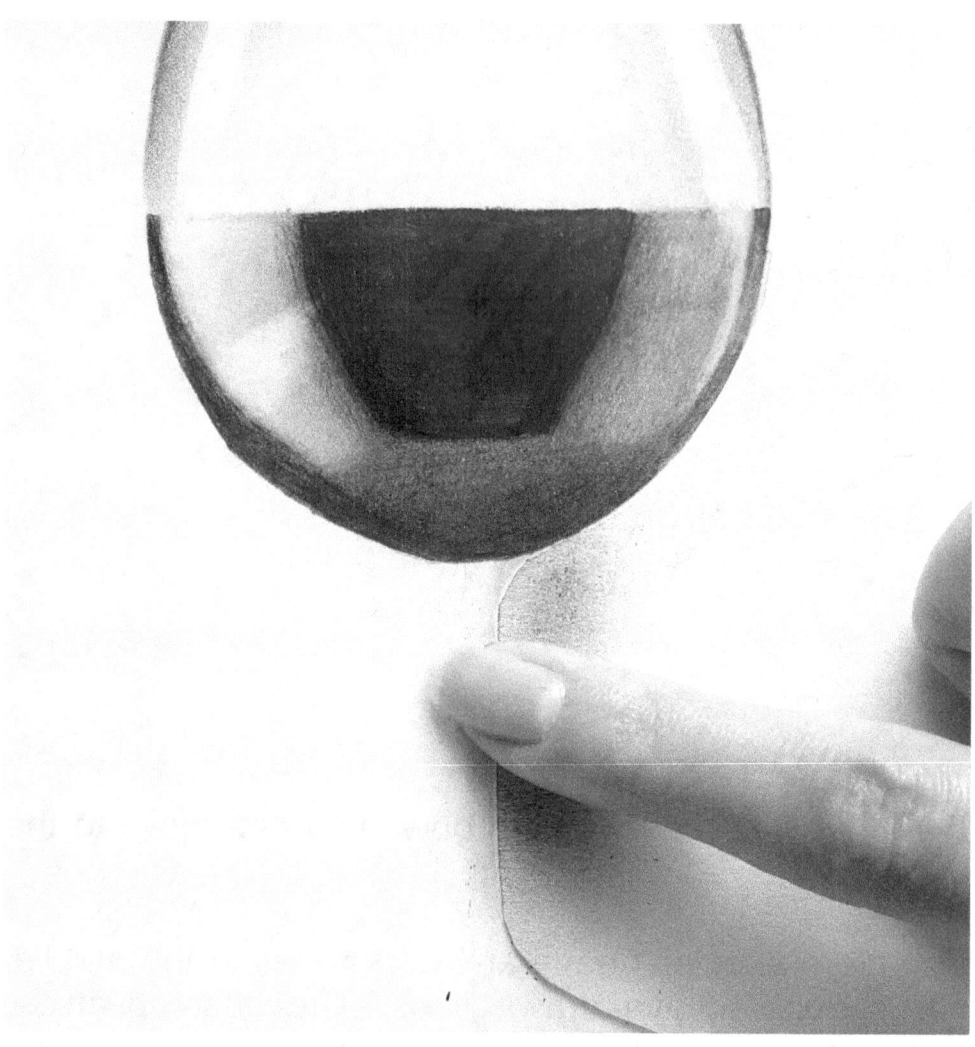

When you remove the protecting paper, the stem will look like this in the next image which appears to be just like the rounded glass of the stem.

Any drawn line would be unnecessary and would make it look completely different and less realistic.

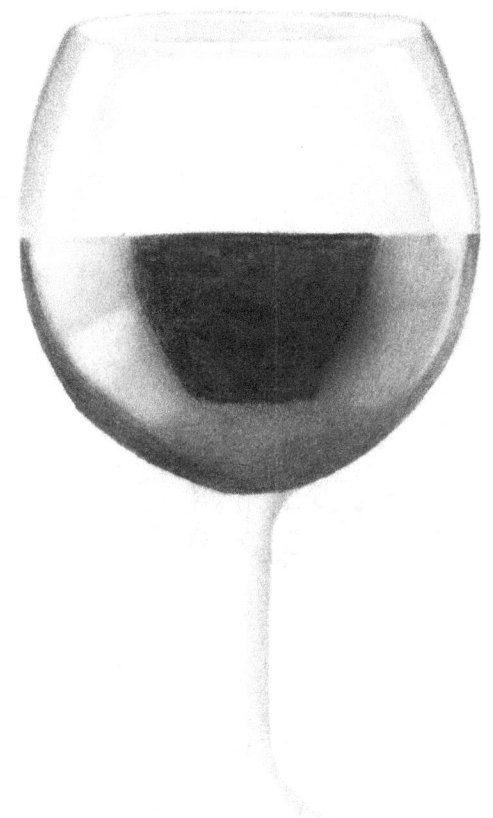

There's nothing left but to do the same on the left side of the stem. Shade the edge the same way, having placed the cut paper over the surrounding area. Here we have done this with the longest area of the stem in the middle. You can erase your vertical line if that's too visible and if you don't need it anymore for orientation. You can leave only the lower area of the line so that you can have it when drawing the foot.

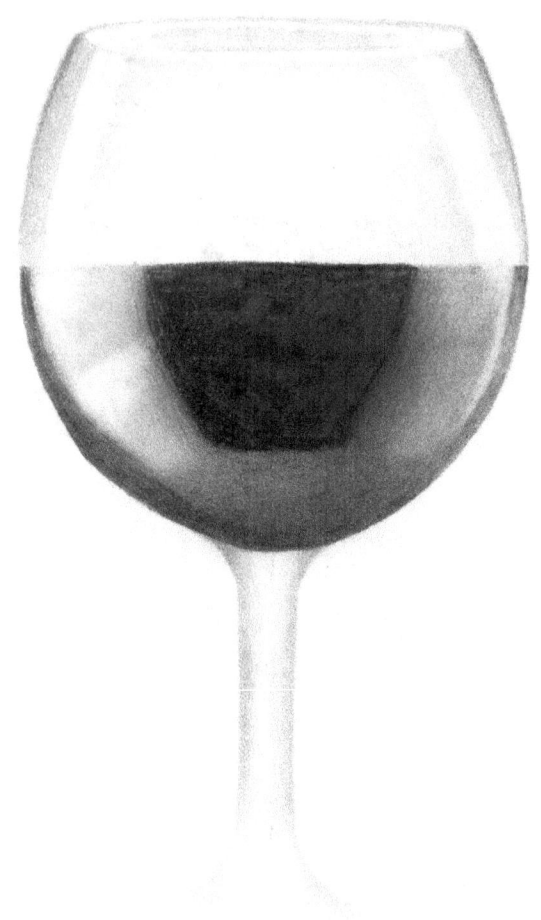

Now we can create the shadow under the bowl, in the upper area of the stem. Here you can use a B or darker pencil (I used a 4B) because the black wine should reflect through the upper area of the stem which is a bit wider and rounder than the longest part of the stem. Using a blending stump, blend the tiny area above this dark shadow that you just created. Press harder when shading next to the bowl to eliminate the strong edge between nuances. You can pick up some graphite powder with the tip of the blending stump and apply it right under the bowl.

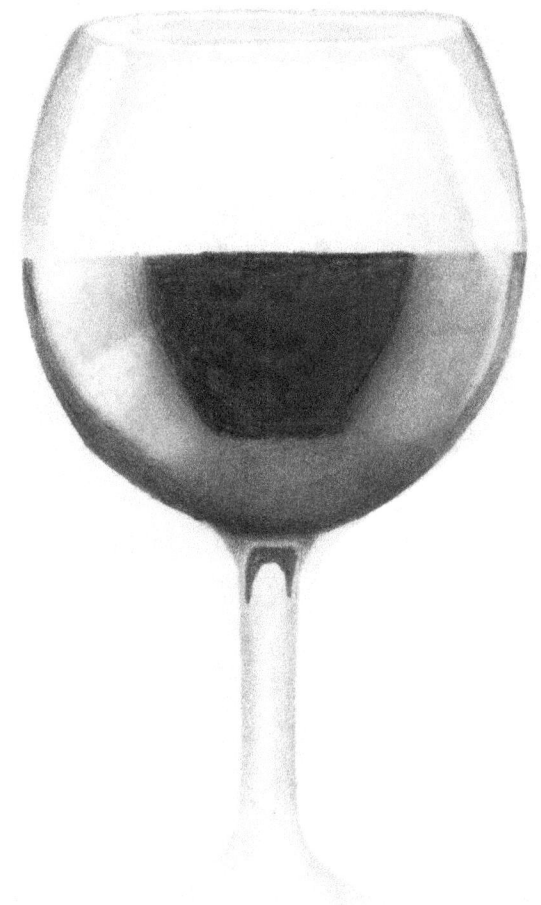

At the end of the horizontal line (hopefully you still have it visible), draw a horizontally flattened oval for the foot of the glass under the stem. Do not use dark nuances or pencils. The best choice is the blending stump. Create a symmetrical, oval shape going all around with the blending stump. Shade randomly within the oval to get some more shadows in the middle of the foot. Take a look at the next image to see how I have shaded.

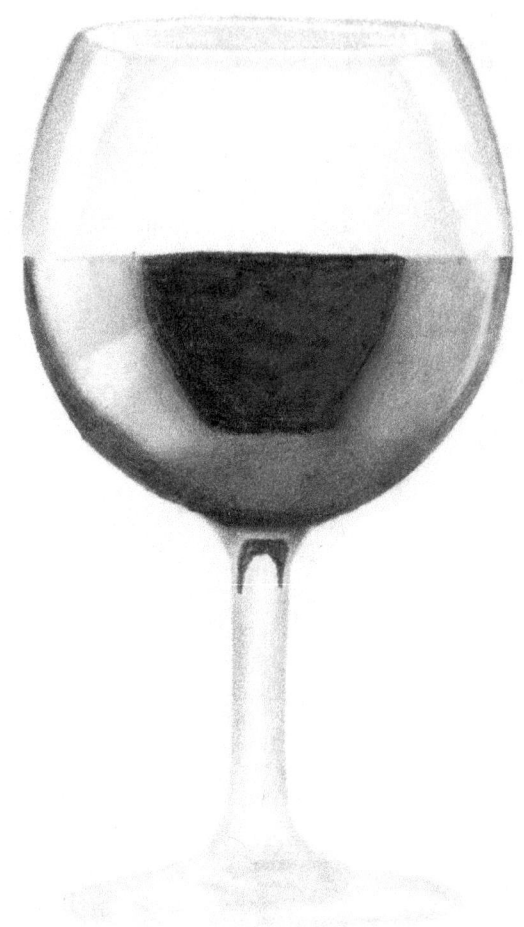

As a last step, add some stronger shadows to the foot, because the bowl with black wine should have a bit of reflection on it. You can add it randomly where you want, using a B or softer, and blend it with a blending stump. Always, check it in the mirror for symmetry.

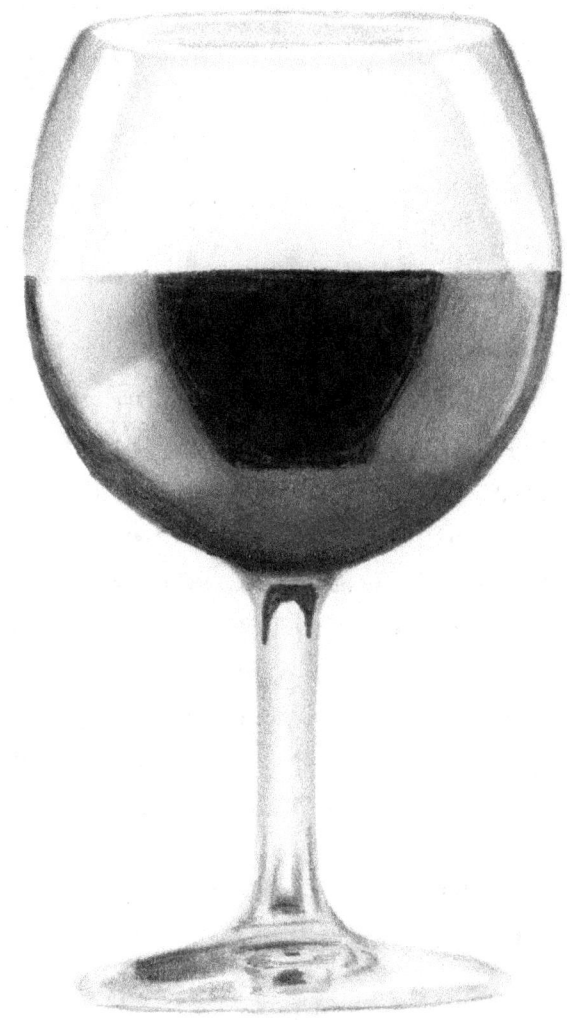

HOW TO DRAW A BALD EAGLE

Many people ask me how I draw white animals on white paper. It seems logical that you can draw black or grey animals on white paper, but what do you do when the animal is snow white? Well, I always answer: then I draw the background, and the animal stays white. I also often draw animals with brighter fur on grey paper, and I suggest you try the same after having practiced a bit with tutorials from this book, but in this case, you should use a white graphite, white charcoal, or white colored pencils, which is much more difficult.

In this tutorial, I want you to draw a bald eagle with me. In this case, the feather of the head is absolutely white, so we will want to outline the eagle before we start to shade and draw anything else.
Let's start by determining the shape of the eagle's head. I want to focus on his head and the upper area of his torso, so we won't draw his full body this time. Using an HB pencil, outline the shape of the head, similar to mine shown in the next image. It doesn't have to be the same, just approximately something like this. I have determined the edge between the white feather of his head and the black feather of his torso as well. The

white area of the head is just a bit longer than its width.

In the next step shade the background with graphite powder and a cotton pad, but you can also draw it with a B or softer pencil if you want. The texture of the background doesn't have to be smooth. I just find it easier and faster to shade the background than to draw it. You can try both to see which method you like more, and which way is more successful for you. You can see in the next image how my background looks and how the shape of the eagle appears when the background is added.

I have placed the cut piece of paper over the eagle's head to avoid smudging it with graphite. This way I got a clean edge between the eagle and the background. I recommend a B or darker pencil or graphite powder for the background.

It's time to create the facial feathers. Since a bald eagle's beak is the most captivating part of his head, let's start by determining its position. In the next image you can see how I have divided his head into two vertical areas with "D" line, so that I can place the beak in the left half. Also, I have divided his head into three equal horizontal parts with two "A" lines, so that I can place the beak in the mid 1/3. Here you have to determine the upper area of so-called cere.

I have shaded the upper edge of the beak as a first step. Here, also, I have cut a piece of paper and placed over the left area of its head, and shaded the tiny edge of the beak. Make the shading of this edge gradient to get a round shape of the beak. As always, you can create a gradient transition by releasing the pressure as you go outwards towards the darker part of the shadow.

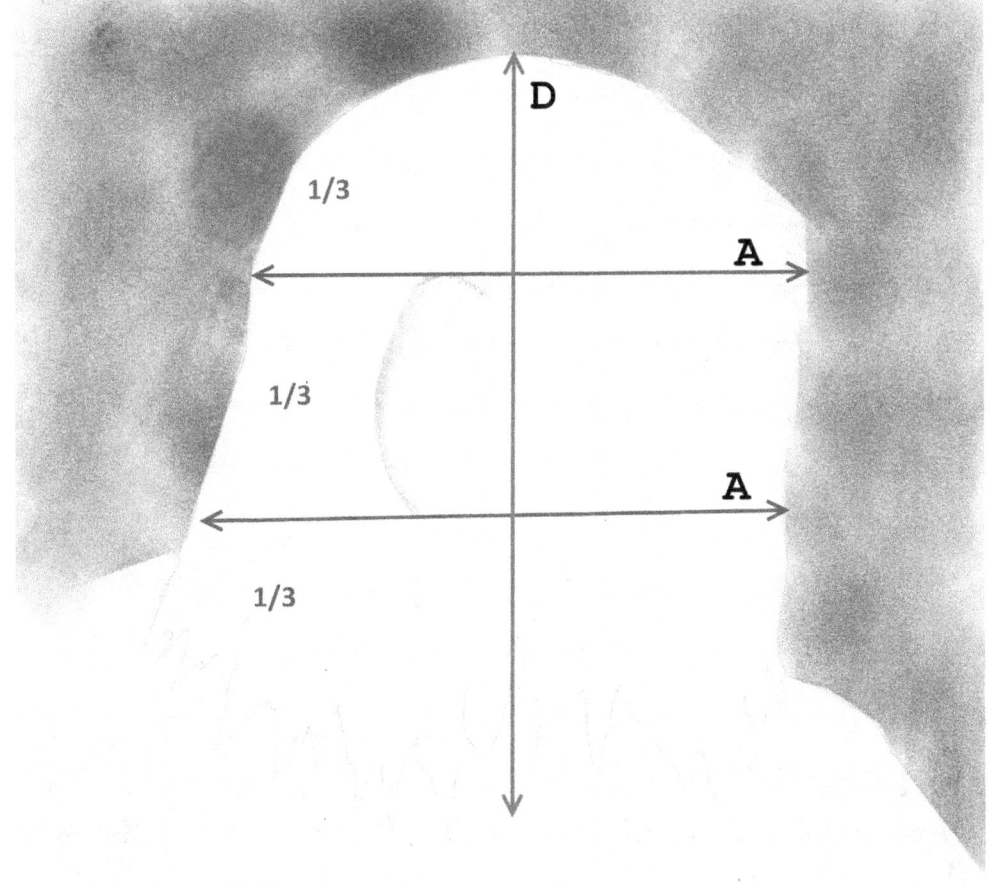

You can draw the nostril and the "lips" on the visible side. You can see in the next image where I have placed these features. Also, outline the lower area of the beak. Here it is important to determine the position of the main features of the beak so that there is just the shading left.

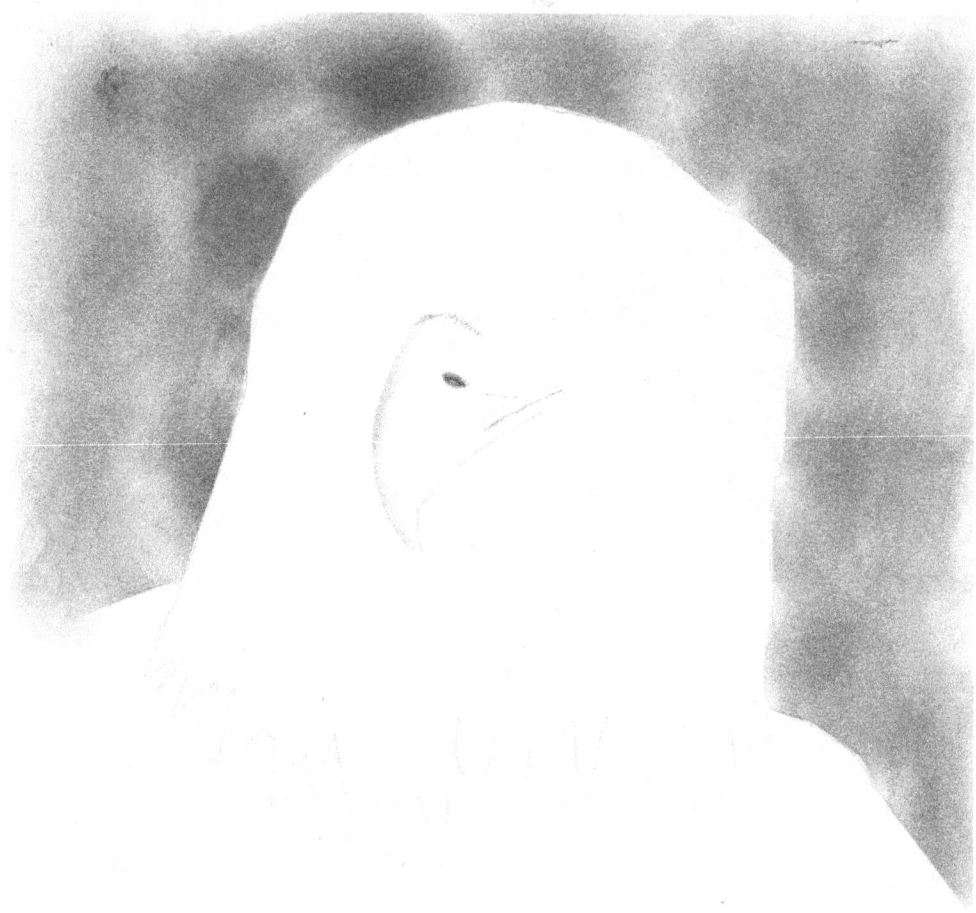

Place the cut piece of paper under the beak and shade the same way as you shaded the upper beak. This lower beak should be much darker because it gets less light. Press hard over the lower edge of the beak and press gently in the middle of the beak.

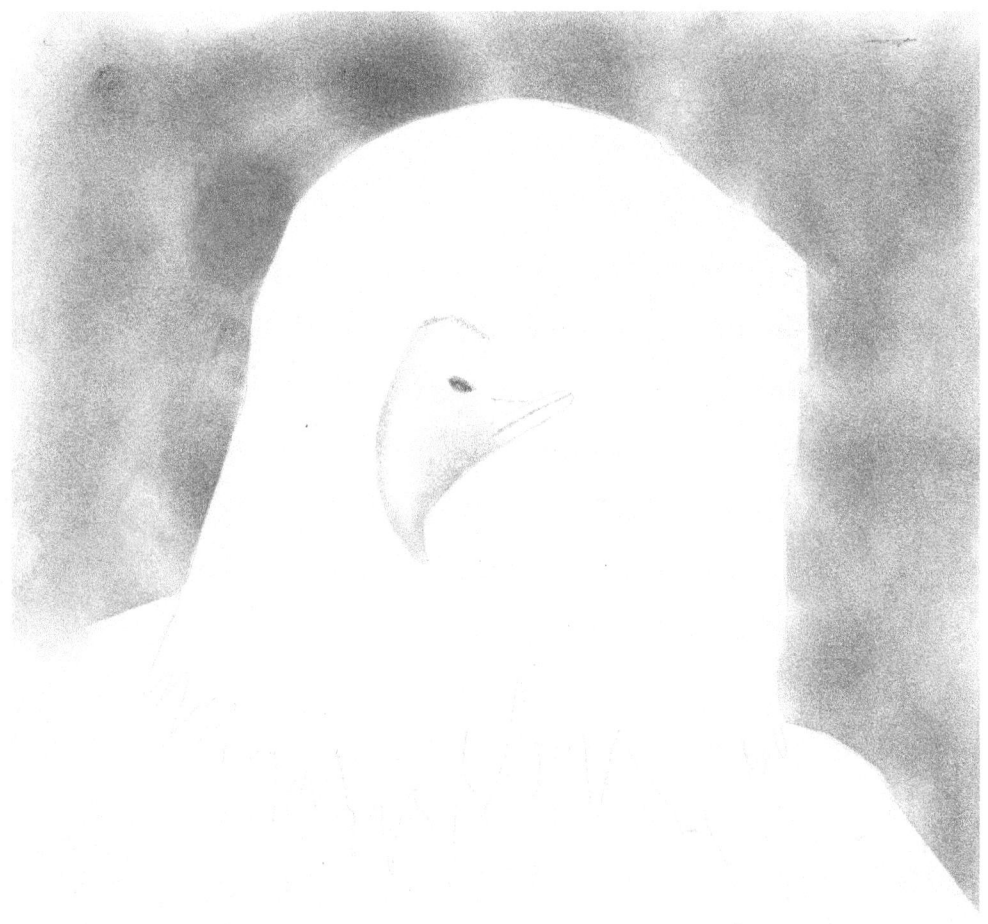

Now you can start drawing the eyes. Before placing the main features of the eyes, such as pupils and black eyelids, create two arches above the eyes, which represent the shadowed area of the white letter. These features are very specific for bald eagles and it is very important to put them in the right places in order to make this kind of bird recognizable. I have created these two arches with a blending stump.

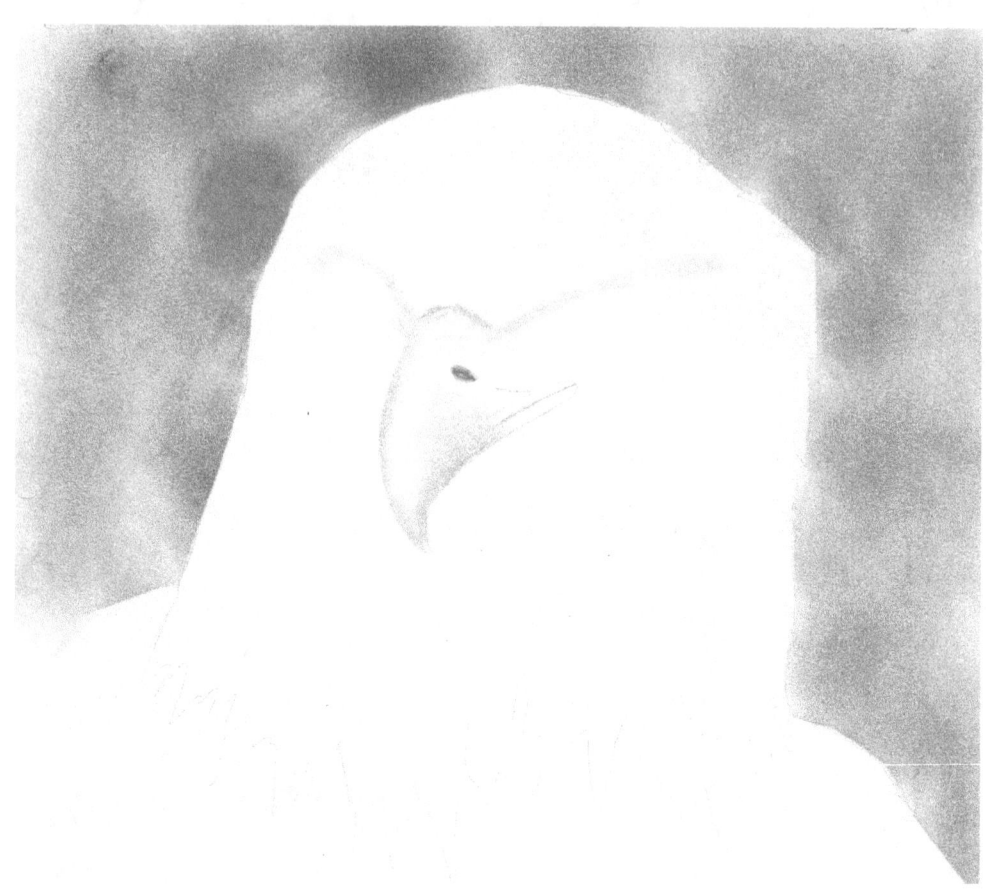

Remember the D and A lines that we marked in one of the previous steps. Use these lines again as a help for placing the pupils. Draw the pupils over the upper A line, and draw the black eyelid around the pupils as you please. The pupil on the left side shouldn't be circulated, but a vertical ellipse. Use a 4B or darker pencil for the pupils and the eyelid. Do not draw the upper eyelid because it is always absolutely covered with the white feathers from the forehead. You can outline these features with an HB or softer pressing gently, so that they can be easily erased if you want to change something. A 4B or darker can't be totally erased when pressed hard into the paper. If you are satisfied with the positions of the pupils and eyelids, just go over it with a 4B or darker.

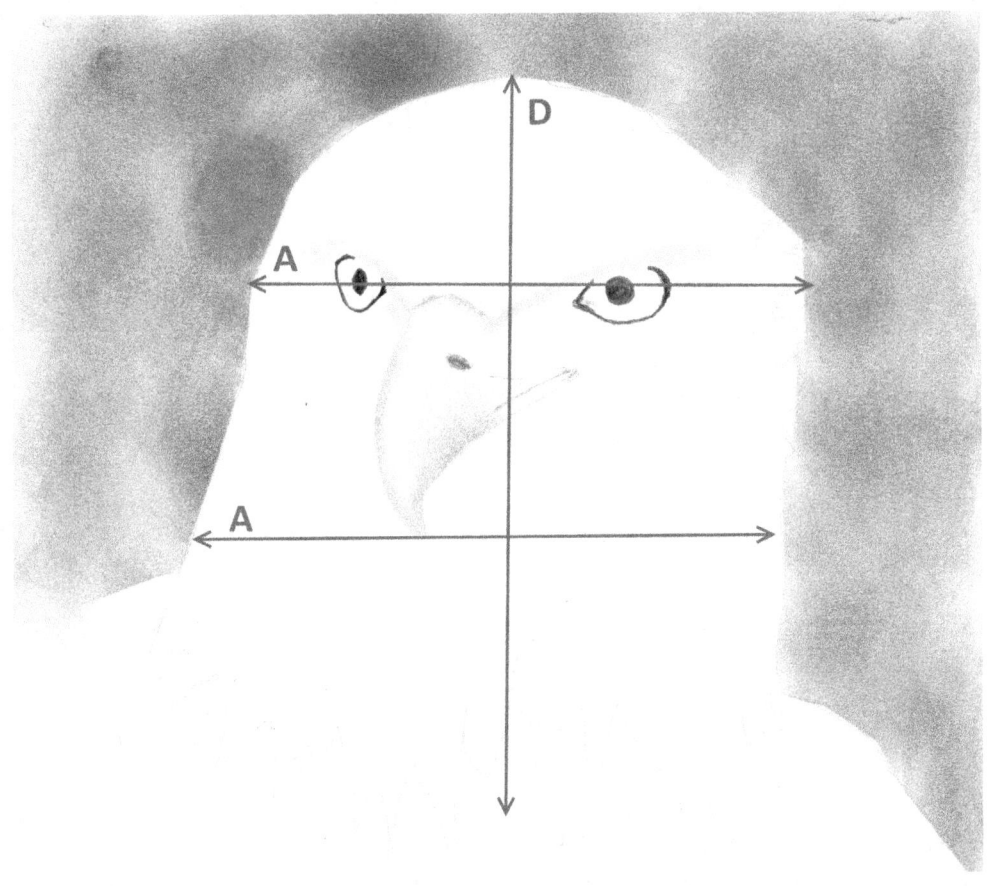

You can start to shade the shadowed areas that the white feather of the forehead above the eyes casts. Use an HB for these shadowed parts and fill them in completely as shown in the next image. Try to draw tiny lines in the same direction when you shade. This will make it look like tiny feathers.

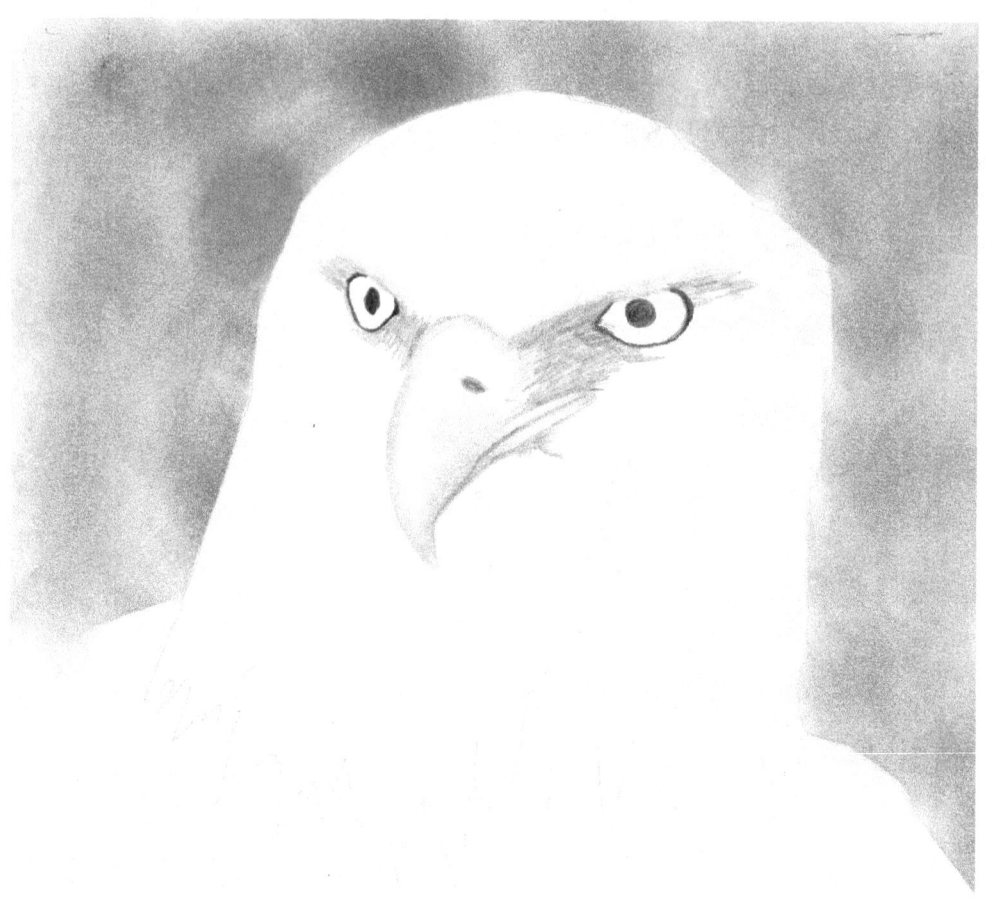

Use a B pencil to make the stronger cast shadow directly under the feather of the forehead, which is found between the inner corners of the eyes and the beak. This will add even more depth to these areas and make the eagle more life-like. Don't be afraid of using dark pencils, you can always erase them as much as possible or start a new drawing. But the depth and realism that you can create with darker pencils is worth trying and experimenting with.

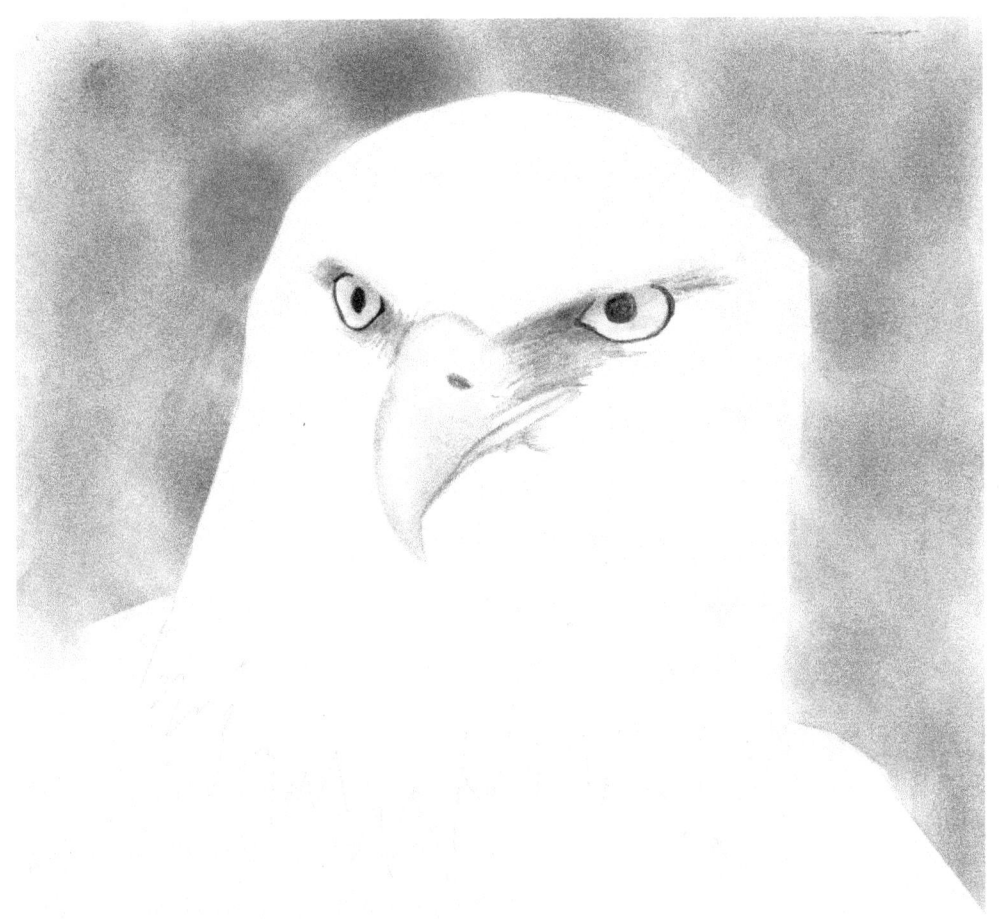

Now you can finish the upper area of the head.

Using a blending stump, lightly shade the feather all over the forehead. This way you will create the illuminated white feather, which has to be absolutely white with a few bright shades that should be created above the eyes mostly. Also, make the edge between the eagle and the background blurry by spreading the graphite from the background into the white feather. Do not press hard. Press gently.
Take a look at the next image to see how I have shaded

these areas.

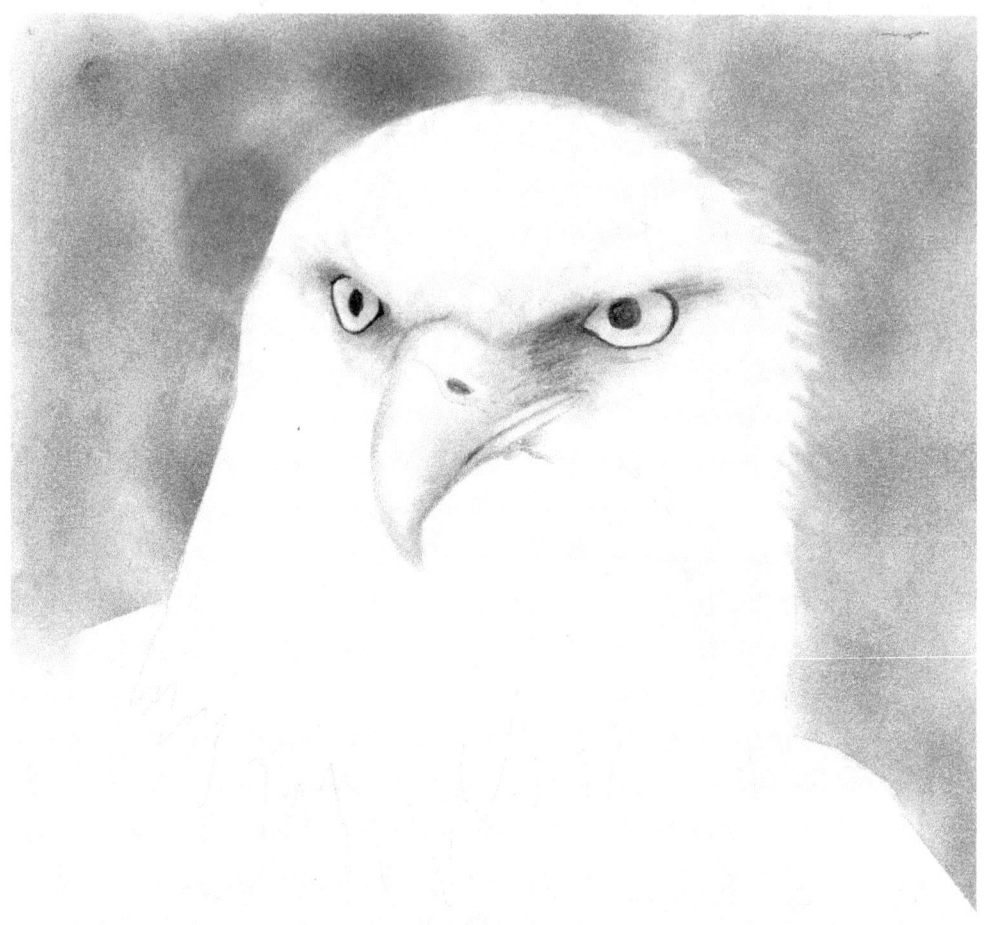

If you are satisfied with the upper area of the head, you can move to the area under the beak.

The first step is to create the cast shadow that the beak casts. Use a 2H to mark this area under the beak. You can see in the next image where I have determined the position of the cast shadow. The cast shadow always depends on the direction of the source of the light. In this case we can imagine that there is no direct sunlight, otherwise we would have to create the clear edge between the shadowed and illuminated white feather. Since we didn't do that when we created the cast shadows around the eyes, we shouldn't make it under the beak.

As in the case of the bouncing ball in the first tutorial, you can erase the brighter, outer areas of the shadow to get the cast shadow which is cast by the direct sunlight. By experimenting like this, you can learn a lot.

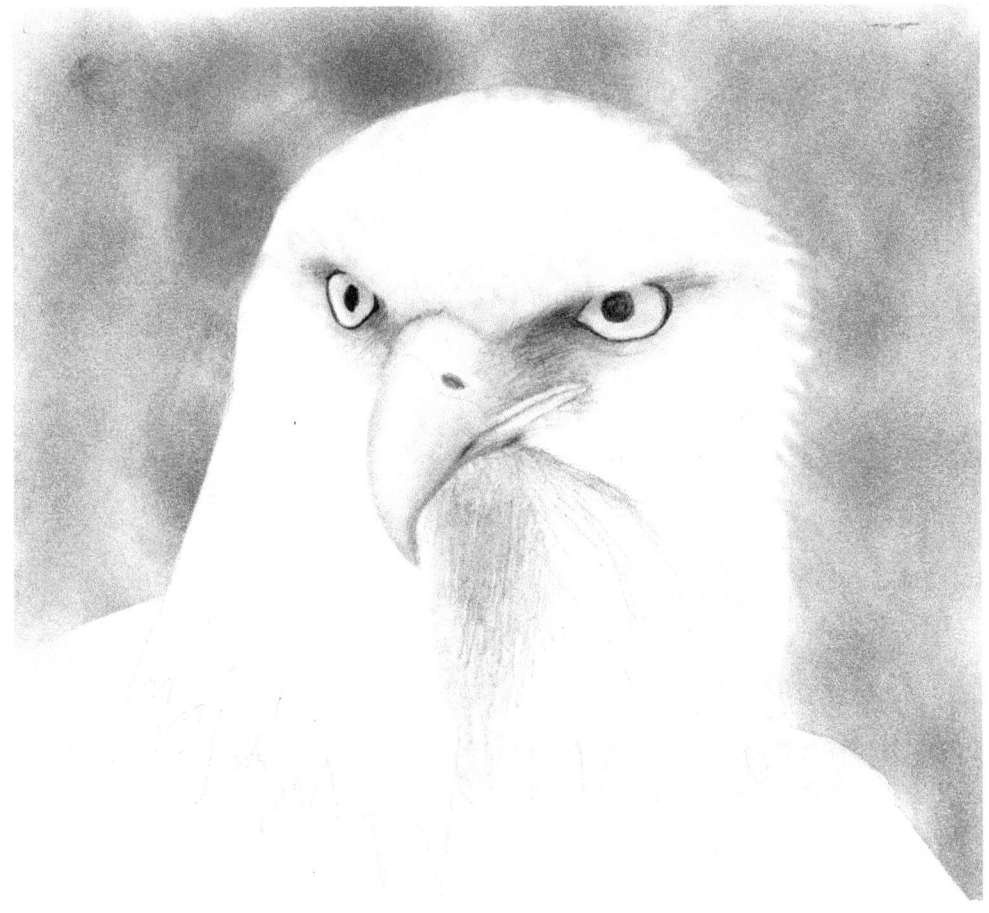

After this, shade the larger area around and over the cast shadow created in the previous step, using a cotton pad or tissue. The point is to make this area darker than the upper half of the head, yet bright enough so it can look like shadowed white feathers.

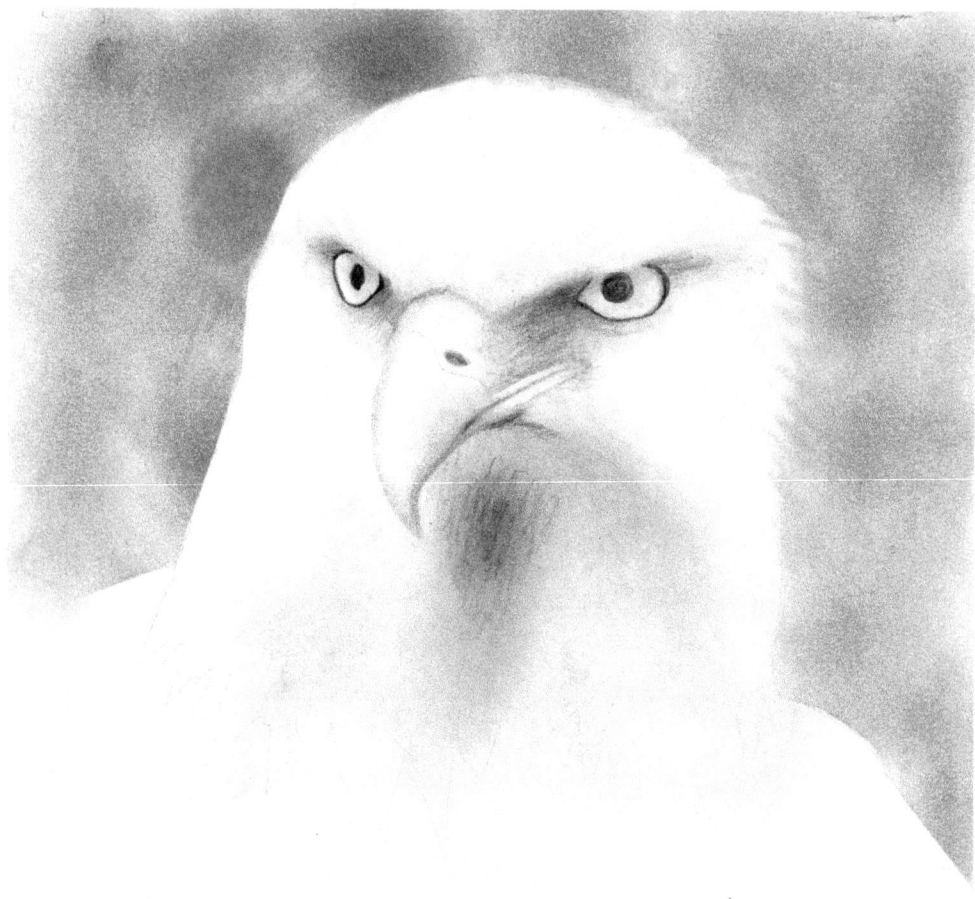

Now you can create the highlights over the shadowed area with an eraser.

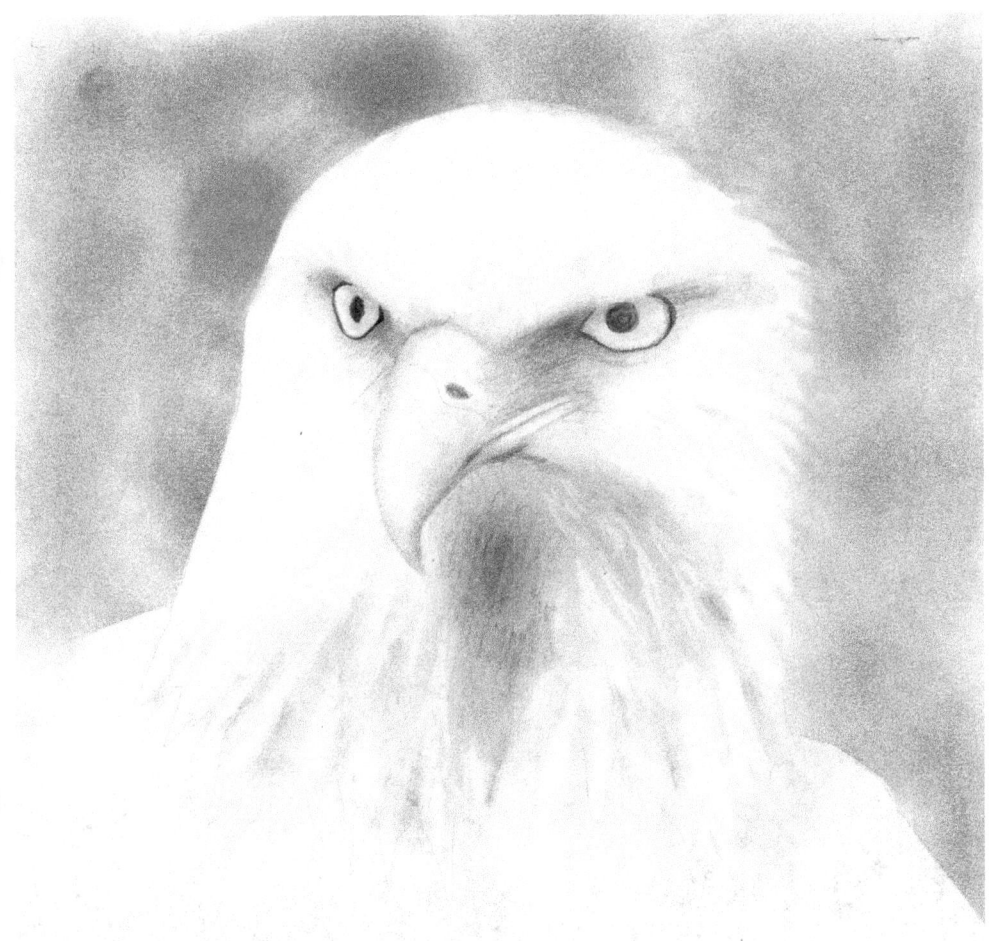

There's only the black feather left.

Using a 6B or darker, fill the whole area under the outline of the white feather. You can see in the next image how I have drawn this area and drawn around the white feather that reaches over the black feather. This step is pretty easy, even if you draw a bit over the outline of the white feather, it will still look good.

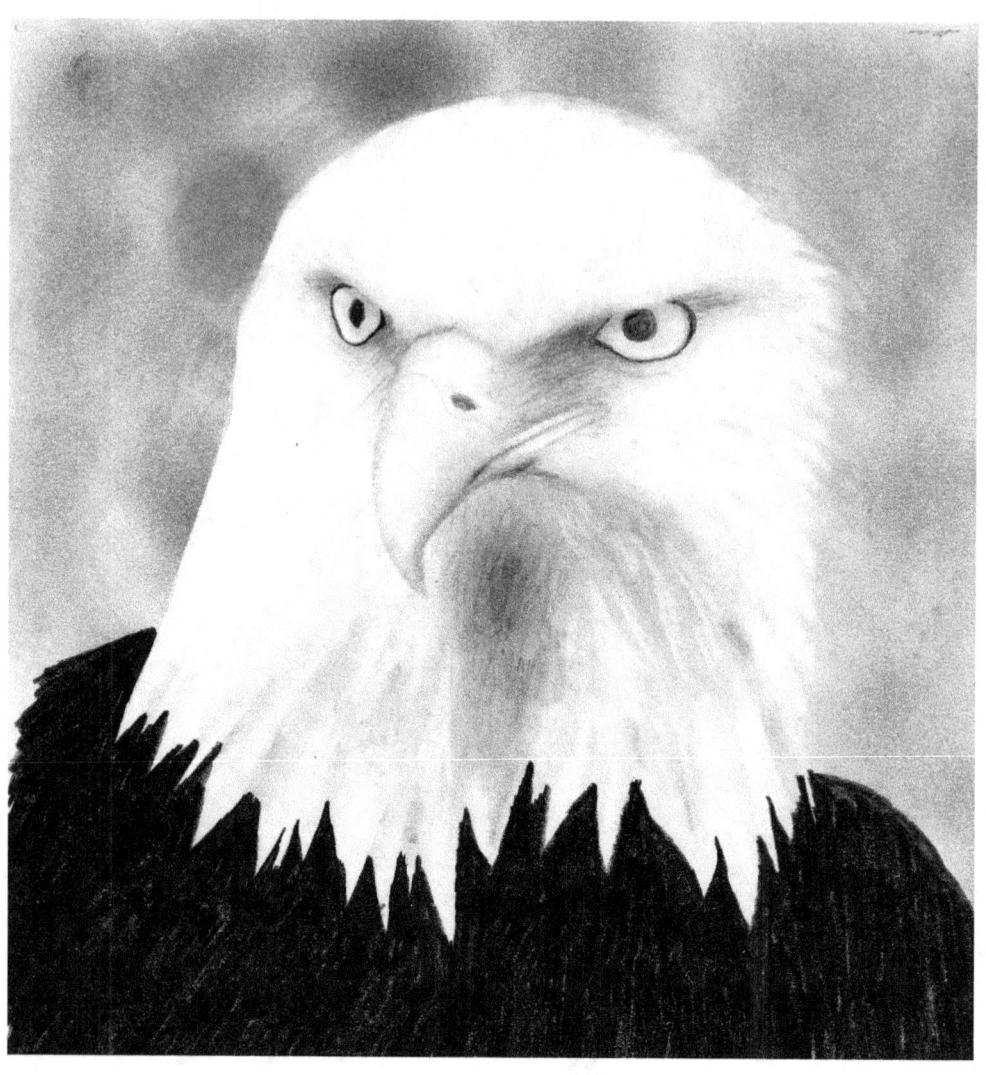

Lastly, blend the edge between the black and white using a blending stump. This will soften the white feathers. Place the tip of the blending stump over the black drawn area and draw into the white area, between the white feathers. This way you will pick up a bit of the graphite and make the edges of the white feather blurry.

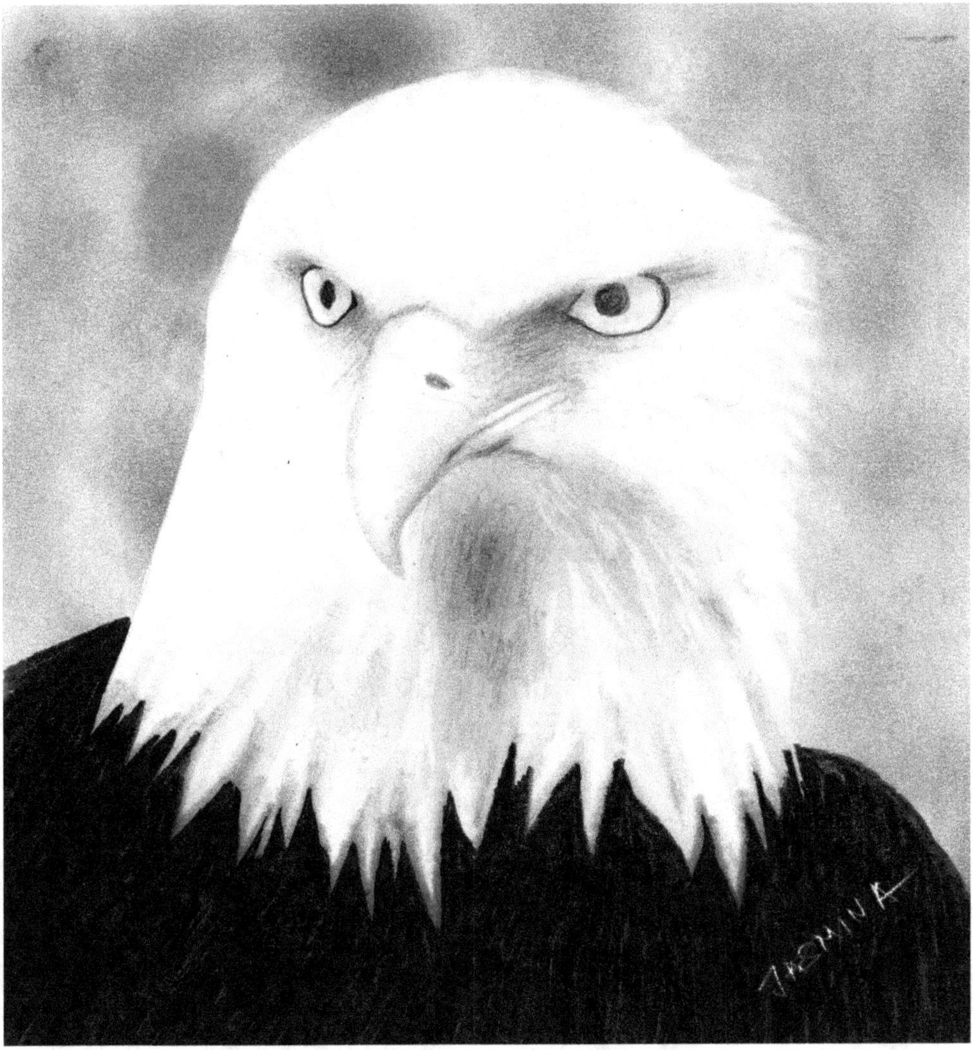

HOW TO DRAW A WOODEN TEXTURE

Let's draw a simple wood texture. As a first step, shade the whole paper with graphite powder and tissue. Here you don't have to create an absolutely smooth paper, there can even be some "dirt" or accidental lines on the paper. The important thing is to make horizontal movements when you shade, if you want to make horizontal boards; and vertically if you want to make vertical boards. I have chosen a small A5 paper for this one, so this kind of shading took a couple of seconds. I used powder from an HB pencil because I didn't want it to be too dark.

Determine the position of the boards by drawing the gaps between them. Use a ruler if necessary and an HB or F pencil for these gaps. They shouldn't be drawn with a 2B or darker, because these gaps are usually not so deep to be that dark. You can make one thinner than the other – like me – to enhance the realism.

It's time to add some patterns that can be found anywhere over the wood texture.

You can check up for some pictures on the Internet or look around you if you have wood flooring or wood furniture, if you are not sure how the patterns may appear and how should you make them. In the next image, you can see where I have added a few patterns using an HB pencil. These patterns – as anything else on this texture – shouldn't be drawn with a 2B or darker.

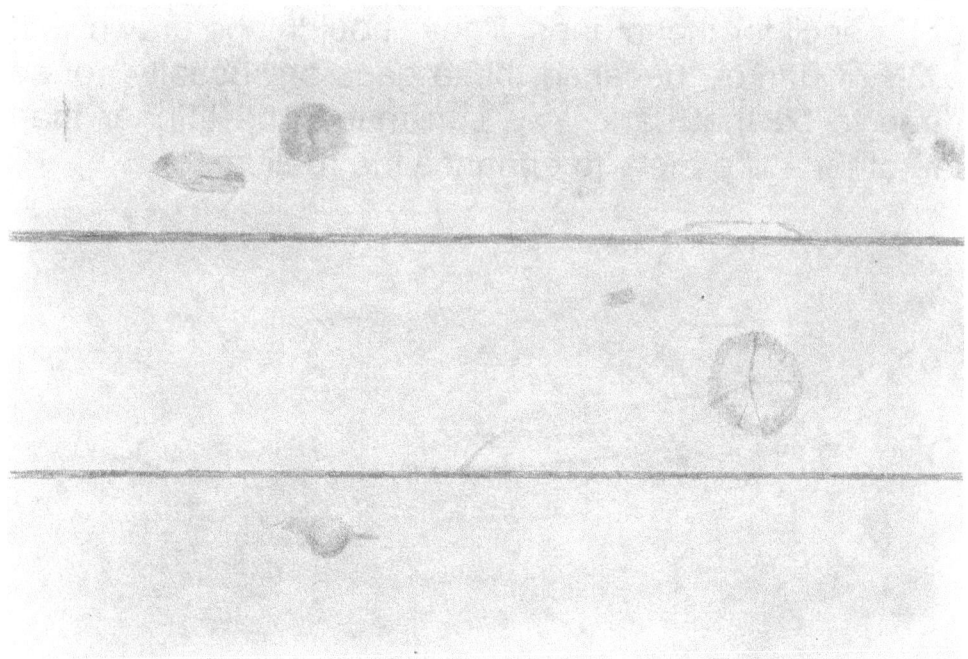

Now we can create the highlights by erasing the graphite powder. For this, I used a mechanical eraser, but any other kind of eraser can be good, even a shaped kneaded eraser. Also look for the patterns somewhere, and examine the next image before you start erasing. Your patterns don't have to be the same as mine, just try to make them appear naturally. That's why it is good to check up on some pictures to see how the patterns may look, and also how they shouldn't look.

I started on the left side of the paper, and continually moved the eraser over the graphite to the edge on the right side. Also, when erasing any other part inside the patterns, just keep pushing the eraser without lifting it up, to achieve the unbroken lines which will make the wood appear realistic.

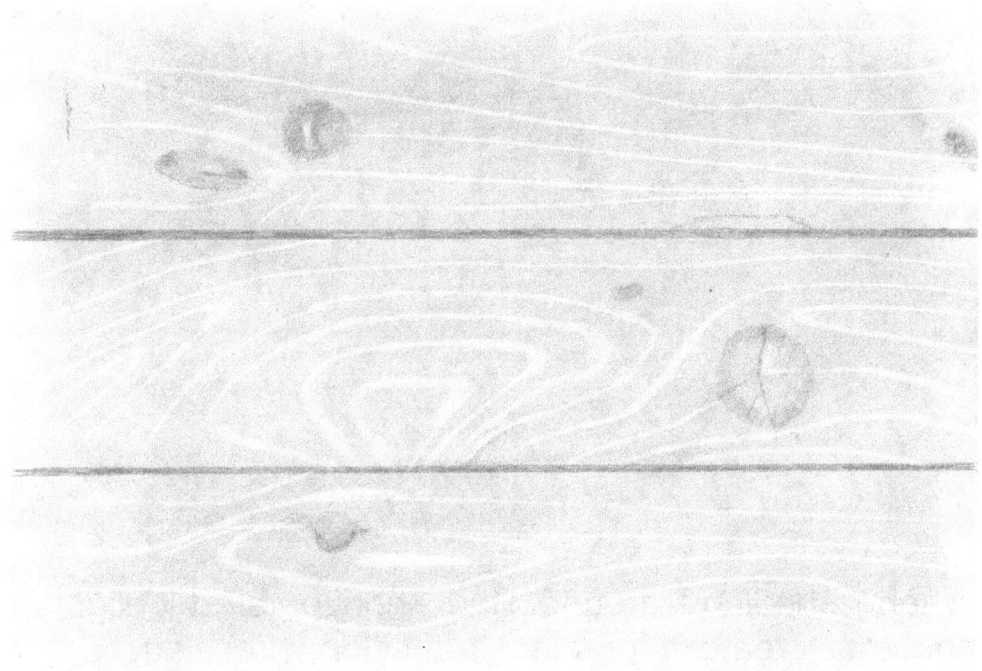

You can start to shade around these highlights. The best is to make the gradient transition starting from the certain side of the highlights and releasing the pressure as you shade towards the adjacent highlights.

In the next image you can see how I have created the shades around the vertical bright lines, working line by line, starting next to the highlight, pressing harder and releasing the pressure somewhere in the middle between the two highlighted lines.

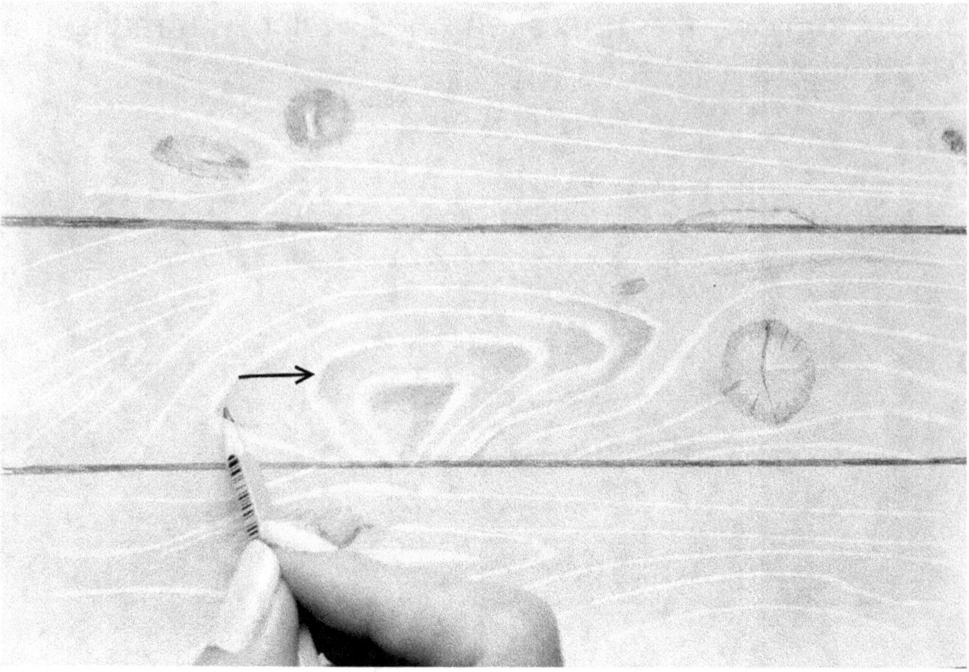

When shading around the horizontal highlighted patterns, create a gradient transition, pressing harder above or below the line.

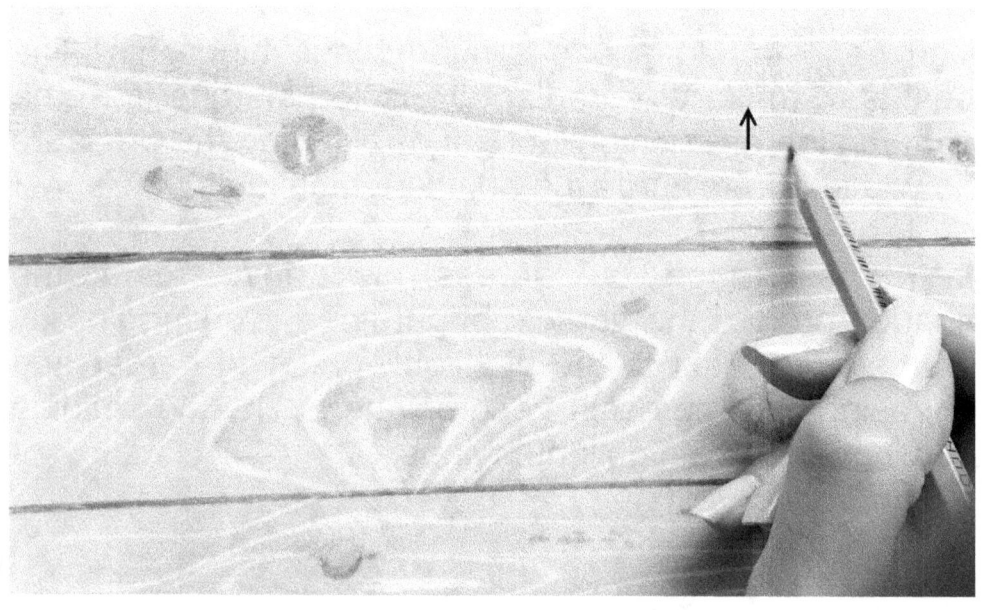

I started above the line, but you can even start under the line, doesn't really matter; the point is to make the gradient in the same direction of all the areas between the highlighted lines. So, if you started by pressing harder above the line, do the same everywhere. Just release the pressure somewhere in the middle between the bright lines.

Blend these drawn shadings with a blending stump a bit, if you want. If the texture looks raw, and not blended, it is not a problem because the texture of the wood can look different, having both sharp and blurry patterns. Add some random, short lines and dots all around the paper, using both a pencil and eraser to make it look even more realistic.

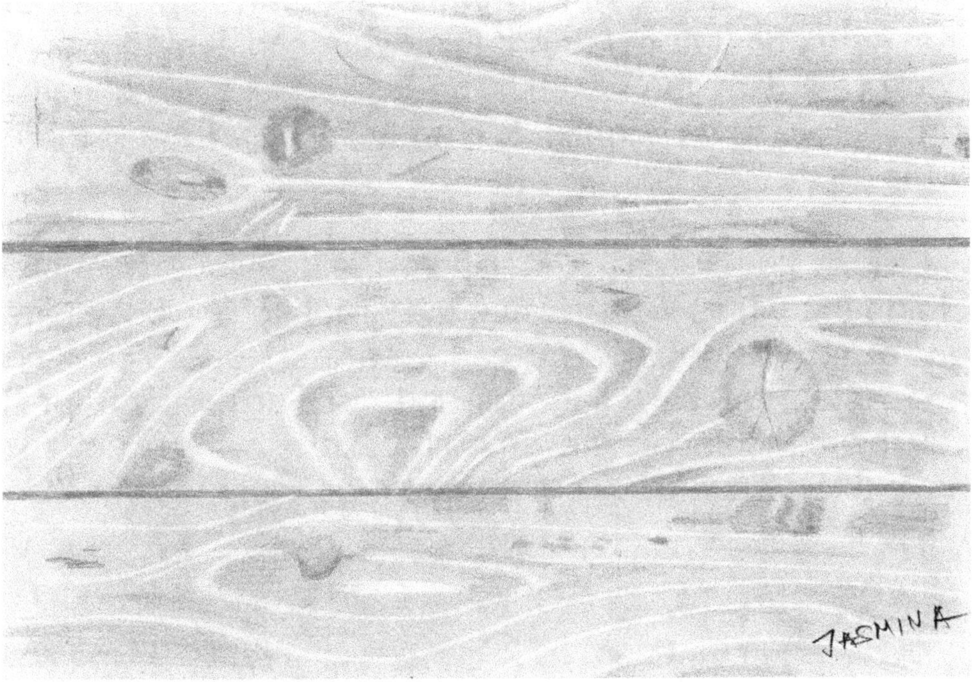

HOW TO DRAW A GLASS MARBLE

Let's make a transparent marble.

For this drawing, I would recommend grey paper and white graphite, but they require more experience and skills. For the beginners, it will be good if they shade the whole paper in the same manner as in the first step of the previous tutorial, and this way achieve the grey background of the paper. The grey background helps enhancing the highlights and make them more prominent.

So, as a first step – just like in the previous tutorial - shade the whole paper using the graphite powder made out of an HB pencil. You can create shade by making horizontal, vertical, diagonal and circular motions, until you have achieved the smooth texture, which doesn't have to be absolutely smooth, just as much as you can make it.

Using a divider tool, create a circle in the middle of the paper.

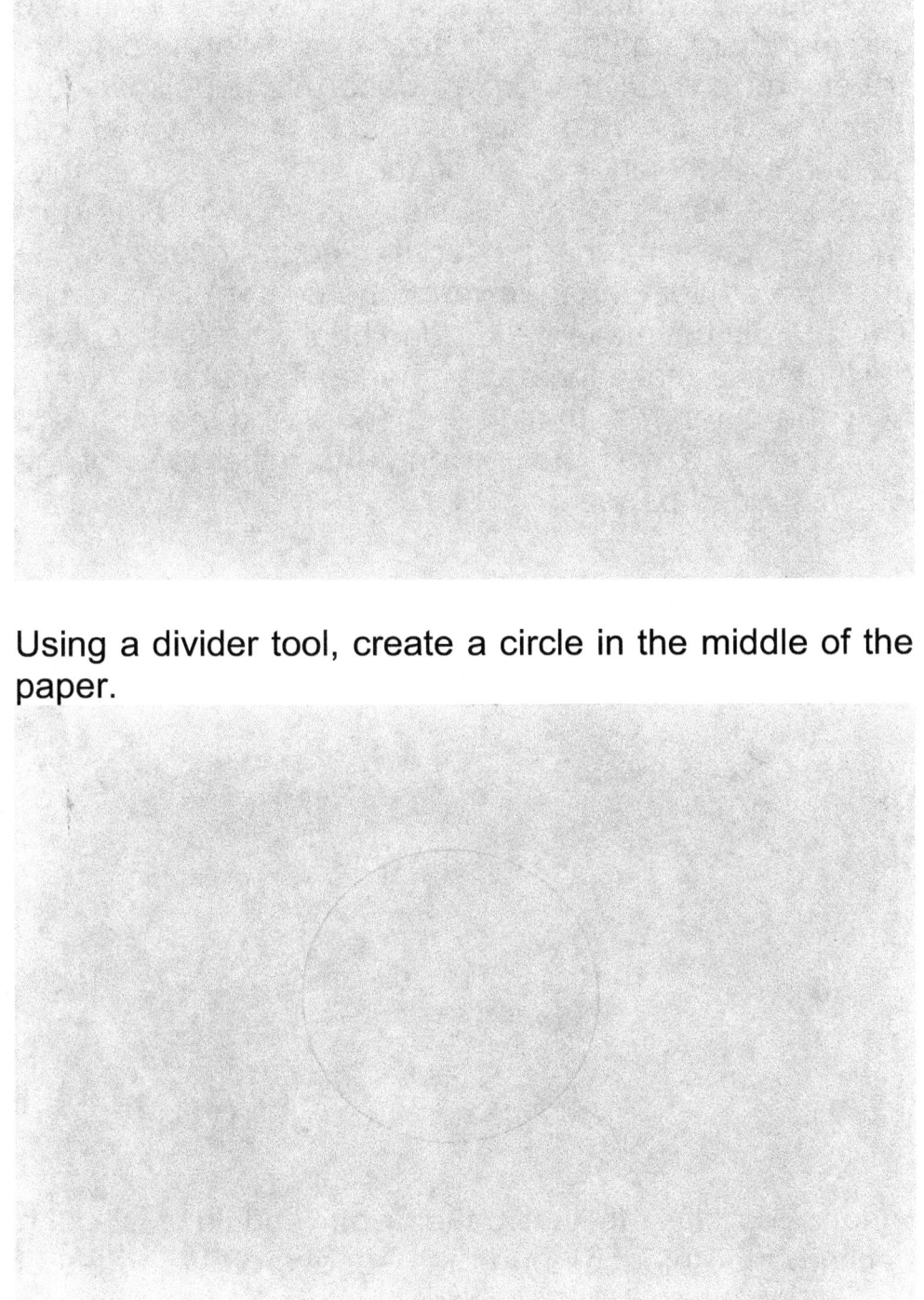

Keeping the same distance on the divider tool, make one more circle of the same size on a separate piece of paper and cut out the circle. Place this paper over the drawn circle on your shaded paper so that you can have only the inner area of the circle approachable. Shade the edges of the marble – as shown in the next image – pressing hard over the edge, releasing the pressure as you shade inwards the center of the circle. This marble can have darker and brighter edges, so you don't have to make the same shade all around.

Only the outer 1/3 should be shaded, and the inner 2/3 can stay as it was, having only the initial tone of the whole shaded paper.

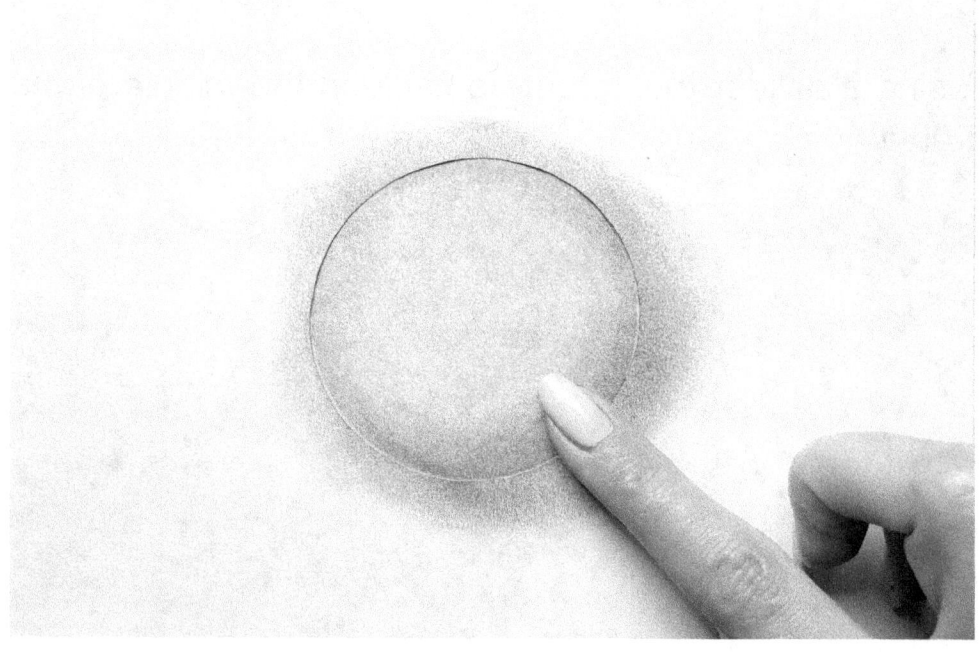

When you lift off the paper you should have the background untouched and the shades of the edges of the marble should have gradient value, as you can see in the next image.

We have to imagine where our source light is coming from. I have decided to make my glass marble as if the source light would hit it from the left upper area of the paper.
Now we can make it look like a glass with adding strong highlights. If you have a battery-operated electric eraser, just place it over the point that you want, and switch on the button. It will eliminate the graphite and you will get an absolutely white dot. You can erase it with any kind of eraser and, if it doesn't become white enough, color it with white marker or white ink gel pen.

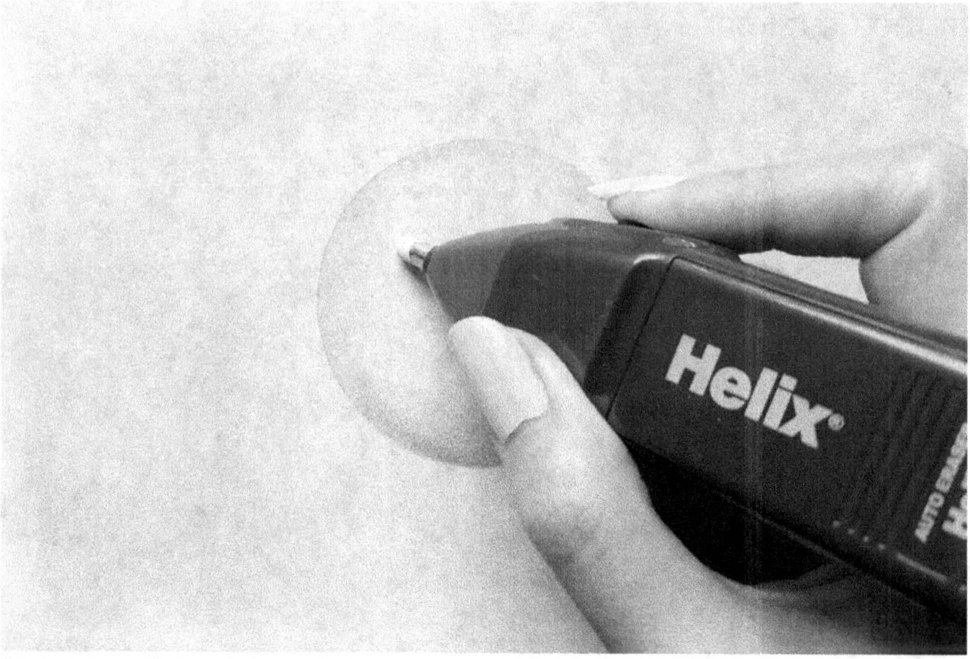

Beside this big dot, you can add some more dots randomly where you want, they should be in the upper area of the marble.

Create the strongest shadow which is cast by the edge of the marble and transmits no light. Use a 4B for this. Take a look at the next picture to see where I have outlined the cast shadow. Since the light source is coming from the left-upper hand corner, the cast shadow will be in the right-lower area, starting directly under the marble. Press hard when drawing the shadow under the ball.

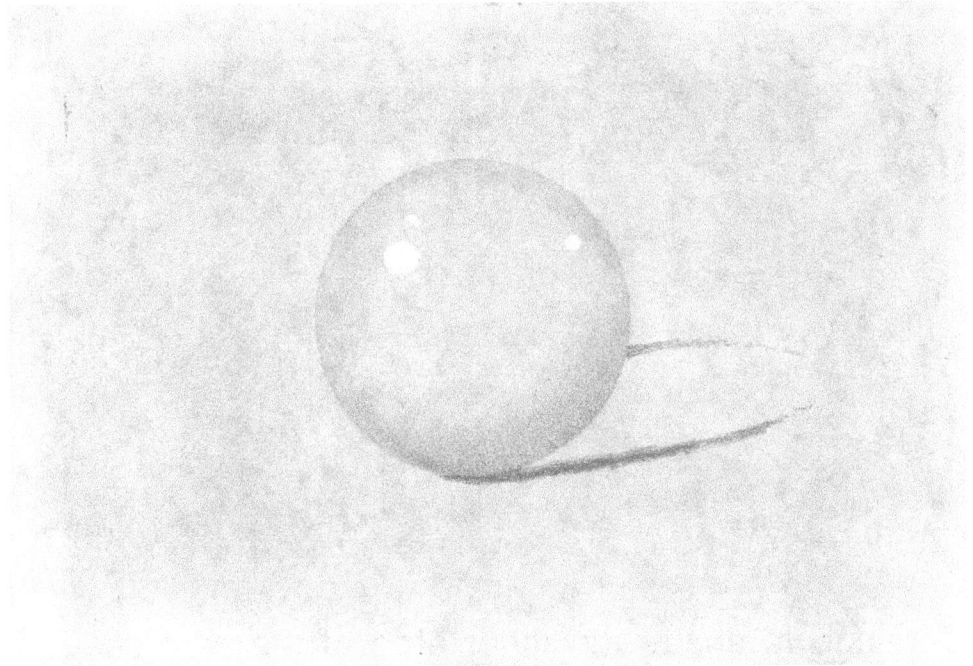

Continue with a B in the inner area of the shadow, towards the center of it, and try to make the gradient transition between the tones as flawlessly as possible. Go a bit over the previously drawn areas to make the edge between them invisible. This will help a lot for making the gradient tone. It is important to make it brighter as you shade towards the center of the cast shadow because the ball transmits more light in its inner area. The closer to the center of the ball, the more light it transmits. So, keeping this in mind, we have to create the shadow with a gradient effect.

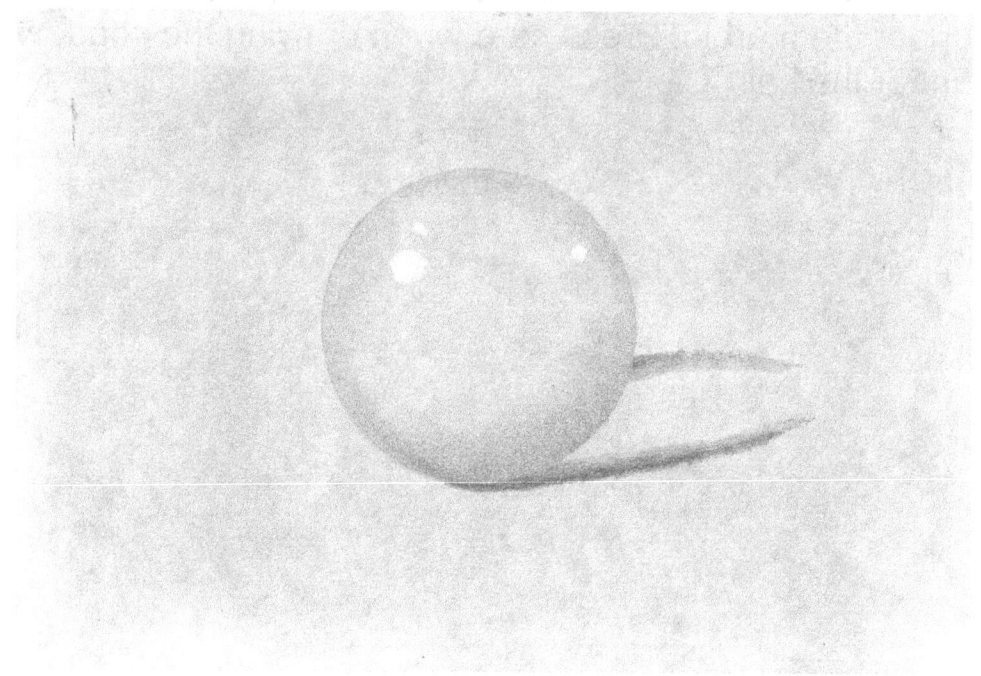

Continue to shade the inner area of the cast shadow using an HB, somewhere in the middle, away from the edge to the center of the shadow.

Use blending stump to blend all of these tones of the cast shadow, and try to make it as blurry as possible, except for the outer edge of the ball; it should stay pretty clear and sharp.

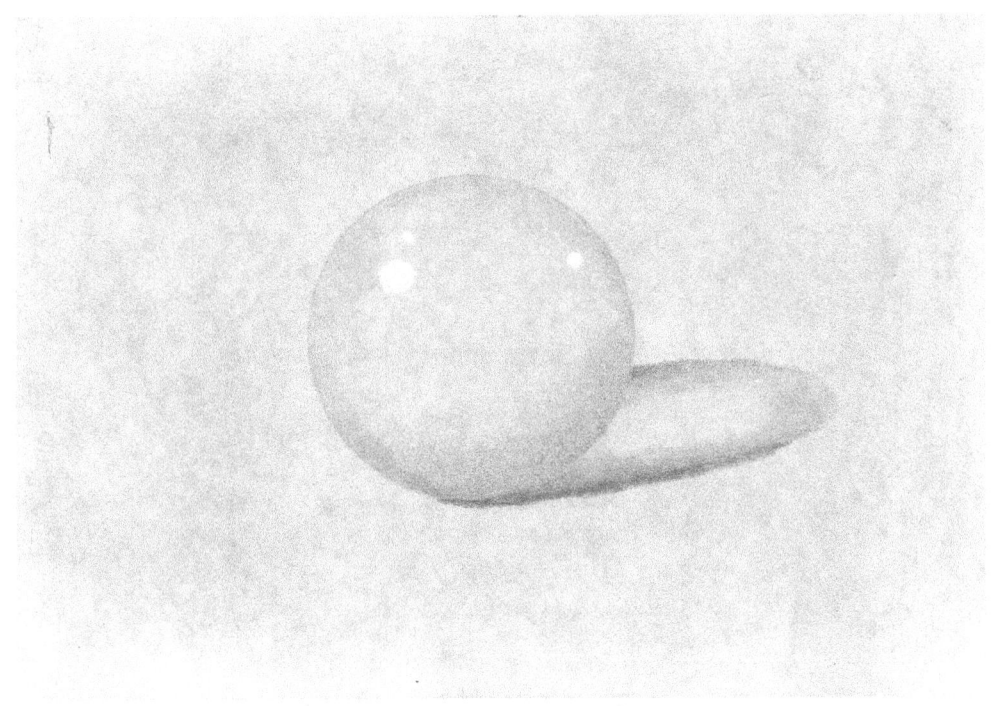

Now, using an electric eraser, erase the area in the middle of the cast shadow – as shown in the next picture - starting next to the edge of the marble and going to the edge of the previously shaded part, which we did with an HB.

Here also, if you have any other eraser which cannot eliminate the graphite completely, or as much as the electric one can, color the area with a white marker, white gouache, white pastel, white charcoal, or even white graphite, anything white that can be easily applied over the graphite will do.

Now it looks as if the clustered light was hitting the table through the glass marble.

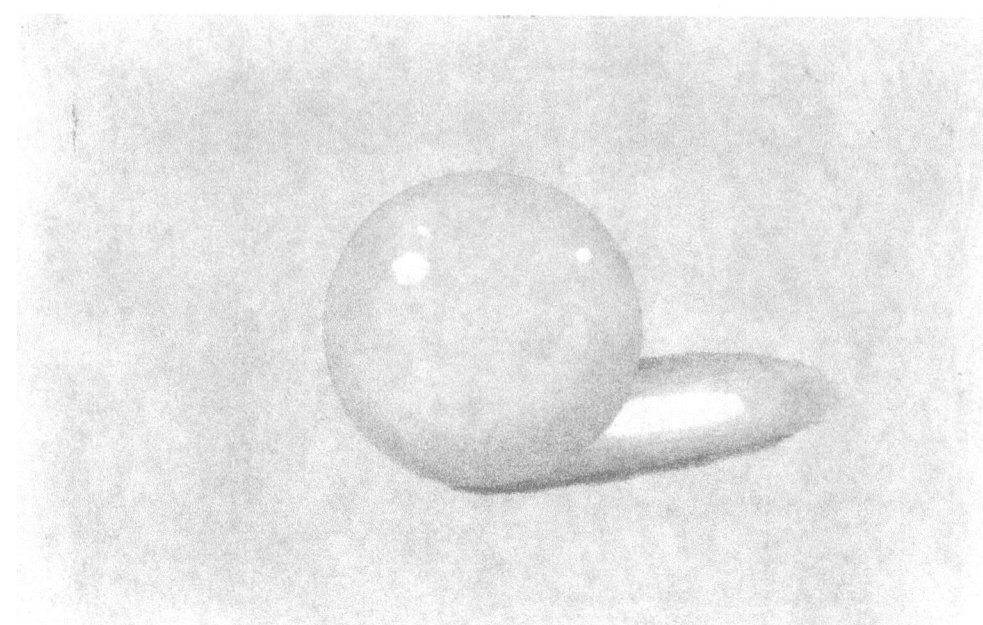

Blend the edge between this white area and the surrounding graphite with a blending stump.

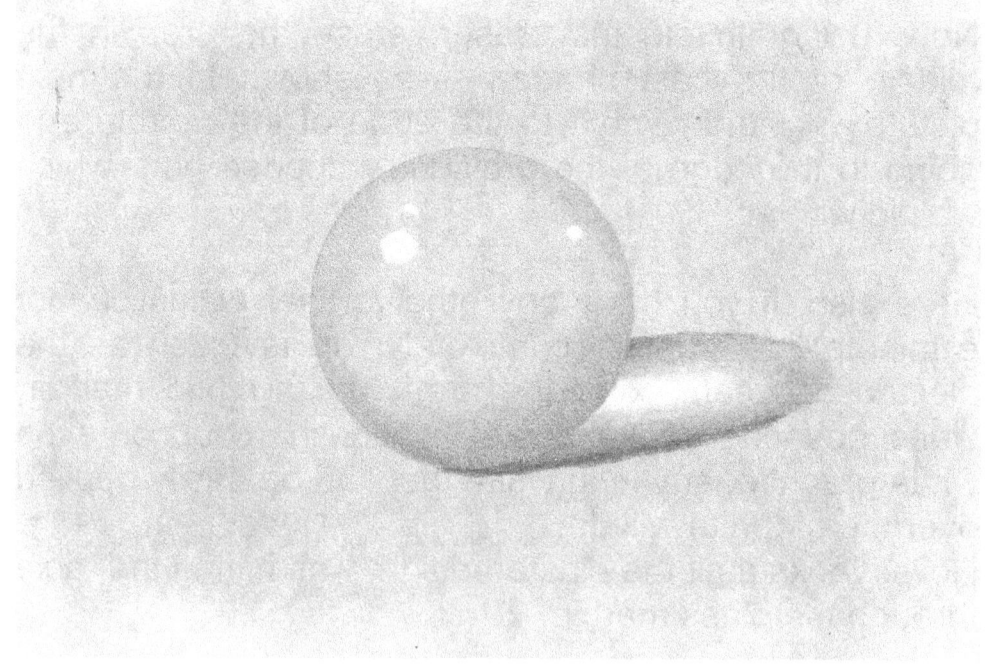

You can go over the inner part of the highlight a bit. Maybe you would make it a bit smaller, but the edge between these two values will become blurry and look more natural.

Erase the highlights on the lower edge of the marble, next to the cast shadow and some other areas of the edge, randomly, or you can erase all around the marble.

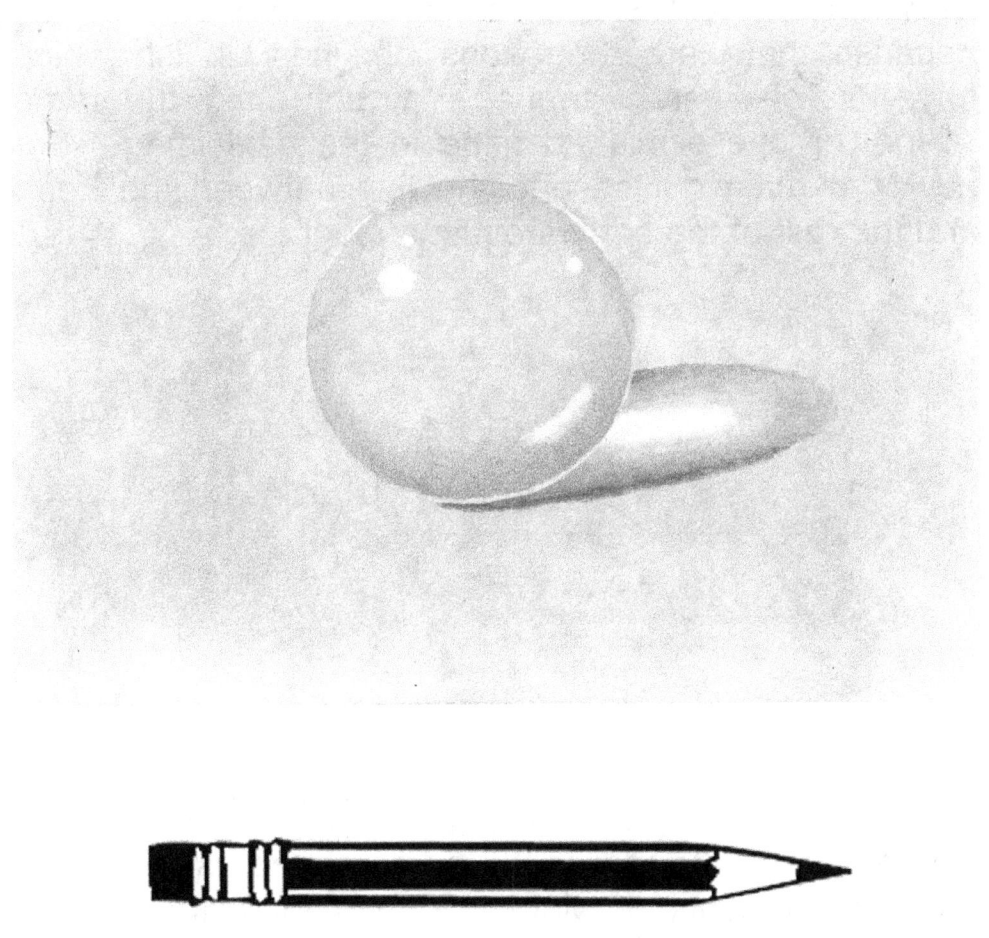

HOW TO DRAW A FISH

Draw the typical shape of a fish. You cannot fail because there are thousands of kinds of fish which have lots of different shapes. You can make the same shape, or one similar to mine in the next image. For now, the main outline and the line between the head and the rest of the body are just enough.

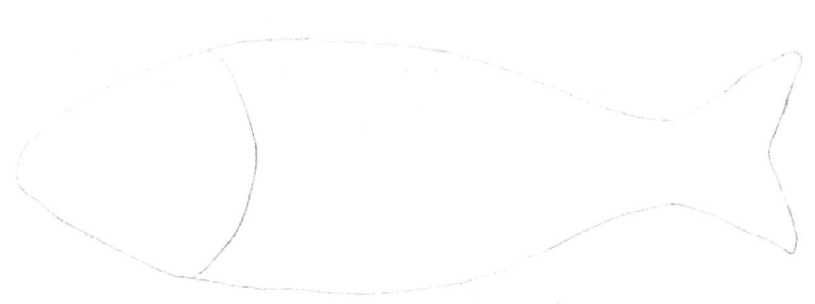

Cut the piece of paper in the same shape as the upper area of the fish and place it over the background to cover it completely. Use a cotton tab or a tissue and apply graphite powder all along the edge pressing hard.

The edge should be very dark. Use gentle circular motions as you run out of the graphite from your tissue and shade downwards. Take a look at the next image to see the gradient transition that I have created this way.

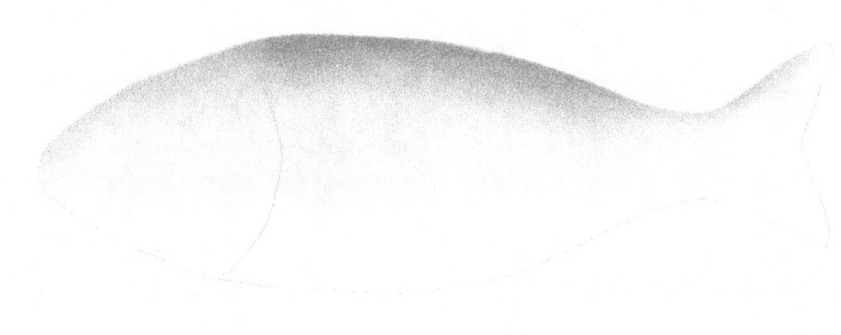

Do the same with the lower area of the fish, but this time apply much less graphite because – as we know – the belly of the fish is almost white and their back is usually very dark. It is even better if you use powder made out of a 2H or brighter graphite because you cannot make it too dark.

This white belly is found in the shadow. That is why it also has to be shaded. This way you will make the round shape of the fish and make the basic shading done.

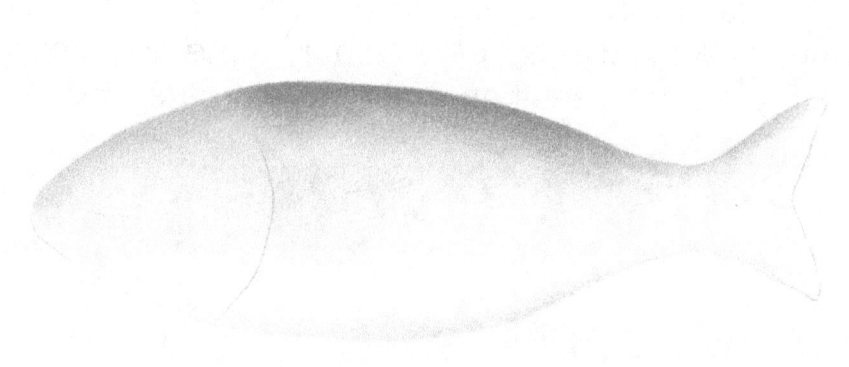

Now you have to decide how big to make the scales.
In the next image, you can see the 4 parts of preparing and starting the creation of the scales. Here, also, you will have to cut a piece of one scale out of paper, something like mine shown in image 1. I have cut one bigger and one smaller. The bigger is for the scales in the area next to the head because – as you may know – the further from the head, the smaller the scales are. So, the smaller cut mold will be used for the scales closer to the tail. But let's start by making the scales next after the line for the gills. You can see in image 2 that I have placed the cut paper so that the area for the first scale is left for shading. Press hard over the cut paper because you want to create the scale with a darker edge and create a gradient transition. In image 3 you can see that I have placed the side of the cut scale next to the edge of the previously shaded scale and shaded one by one as many as could fit in the width of the fish. In image 4 you can see how I started to create the second row, and I have placed the ends of the cut

shape of the scale on the top of the previously shaded scales in from the first row.

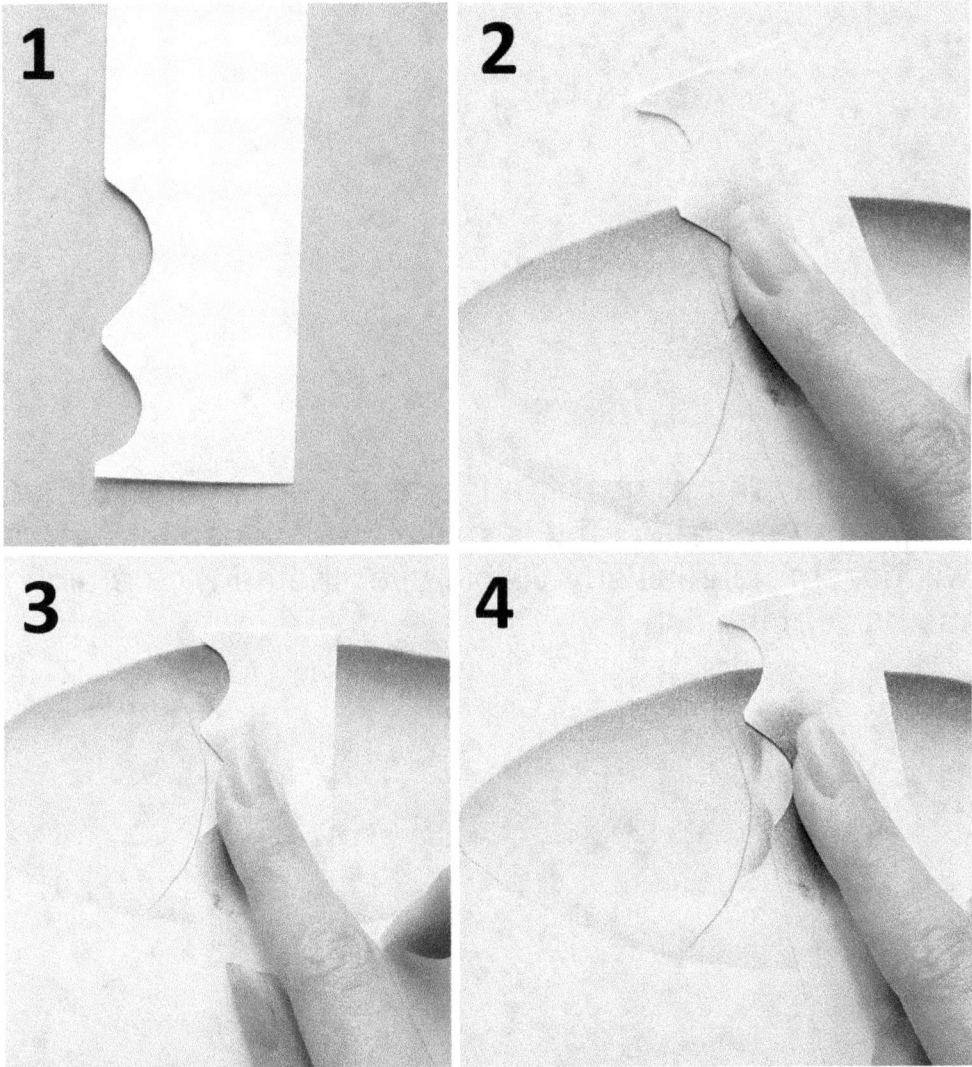

Going this way, row by row, scale by scale, shade the rest of the scales and somewhere in the middle start using the smaller cut. This is how the whole area with the scale turned out on my fish. Hopefully you could create something similar, so let's add some highlights over the scales.

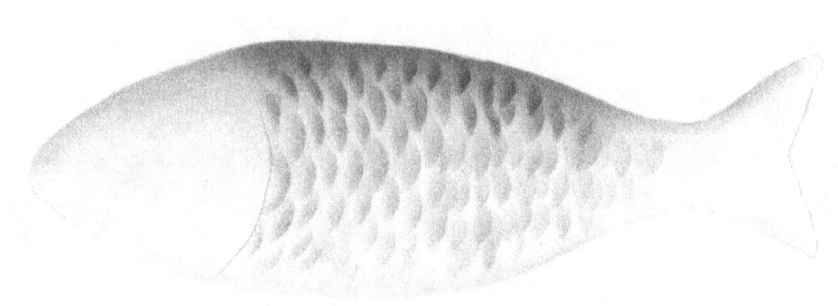

Using the sharp tip of an eraser, erase the edges between the scales a bit to make the scales shiny. This will become particularly visible over the dark tone along the back of the fish.

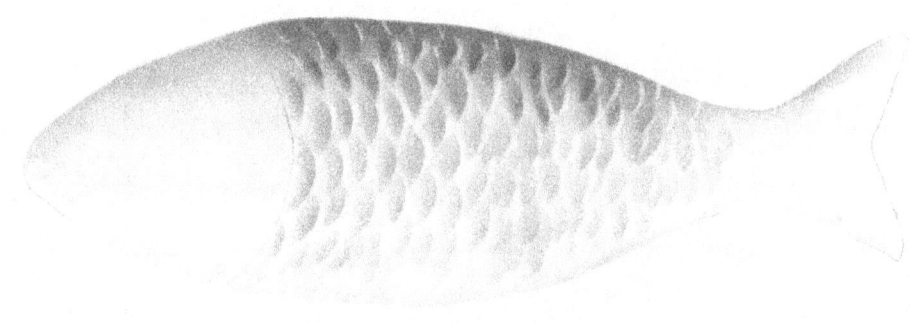

Now we can draw and shade the features on the head. To create the eyes, draw a small circle somewhere in the middle, closer to the left side, and fill it with a 4B or darker. Leave out the tiny dot for the reflection of the light to make the eye shine. Outline this with one more big circle as you can see in the next image and shade a bit around it, particularly under it with blending stump to make the eye pop up. To create the mouth, just draw a line, slightly bent downwards, and shade a bit further from it with a blending stump all around the line in order to make the lips.

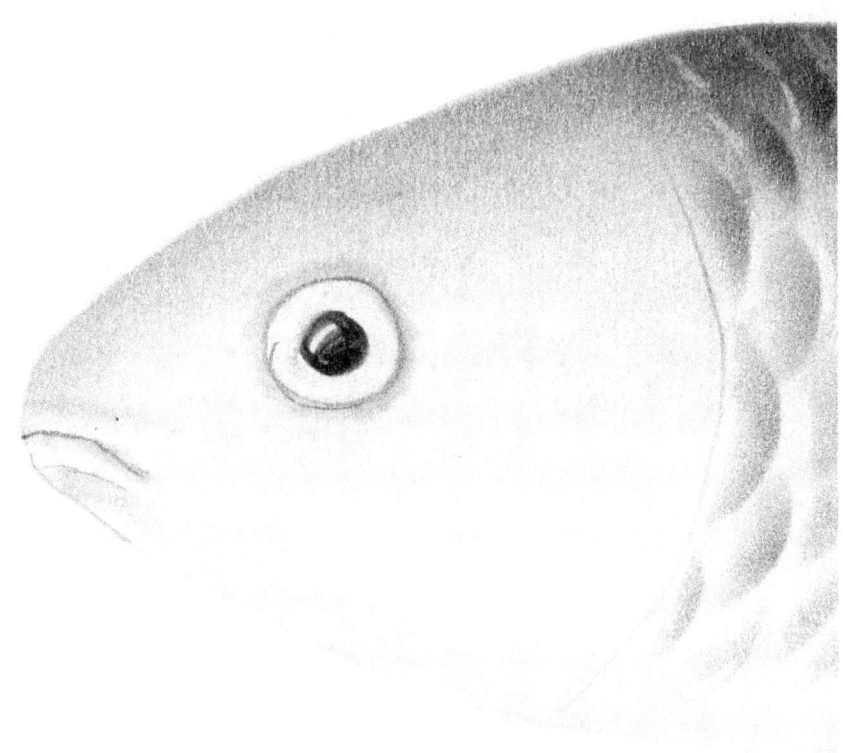

Create a few big scales with a blending stump. You can

see in the next image their placement, but you can make them in other places, differently, or omit them if you want.

Also, you can add even more details if you find these insufficient.

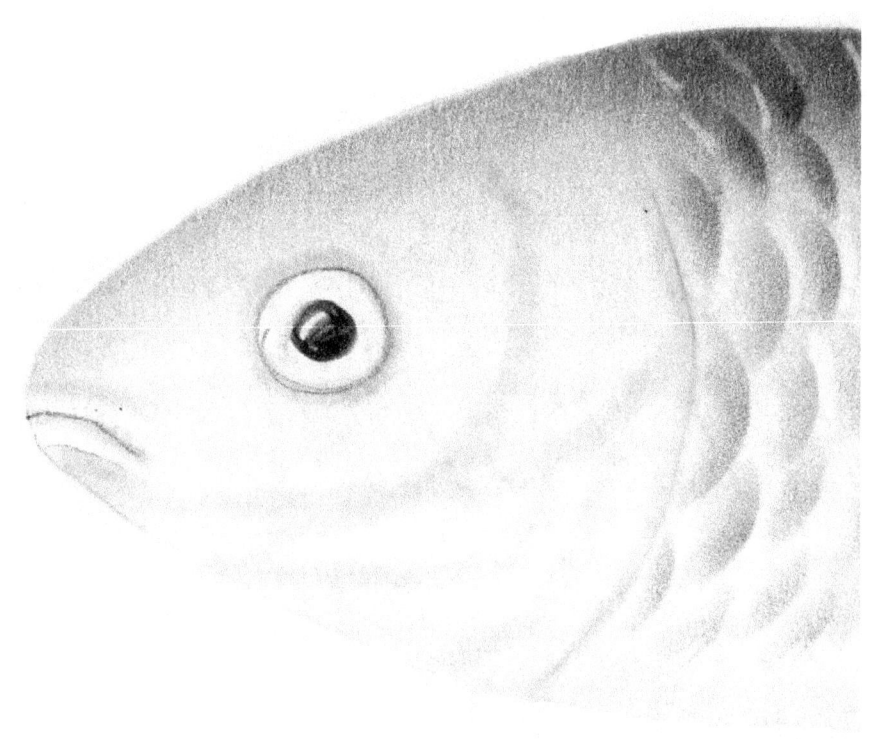

If you are satisfied with the body of your fish and don't want to add anything else, you can draw the fins. The fins also can be found in many different areas of the fish, but let's draw the most basic ones.

Draw one long fin along the back of the fish as shown in the next image.

Then draw two smaller fins under the belly of the fish. Their shape can be different as they turned out in my drawing.

Lastly, draw the pectoral fin over the shaded scales of the fish, in the lower area right next to the head and gills. Note these outlines in the next image and create them on your drawing.

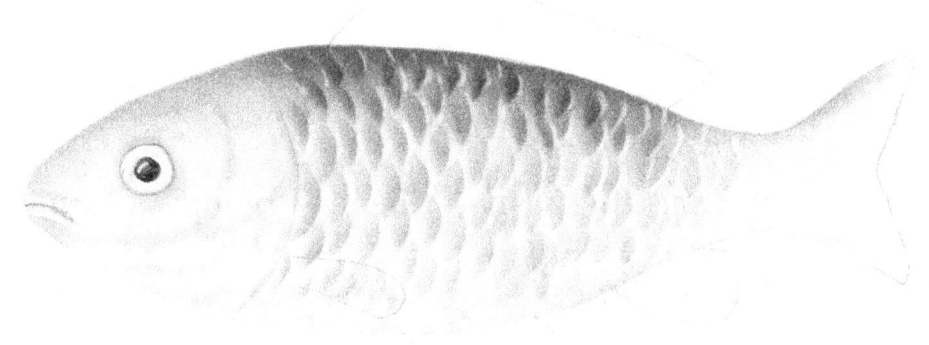

To shade the fins, use an HB pencil and make stripes over every fin except for the pectoral fin, leaving out the width of the stripe between the stripes, as you can see in the next image. It is important to draw these stripes in the direction of their growth, as they grow from the body of the fish, and to draw them to the top of the fins.

Now you can shade the tail too in the same manner. See the next images for the placements and ideas.

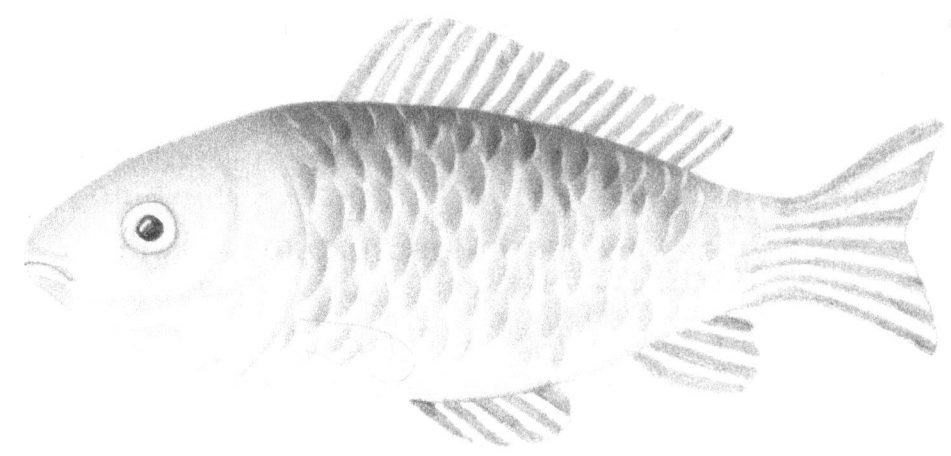

After having done the stripes, using a blending stump, blend the areas of the whole fins. Going over the previously drawn stripes and also over the left out ones.

Press hard until the edge between the stripes and white areas is blurry and invisible. You can shade the brighter areas more if you want or erase some areas for the highlights.

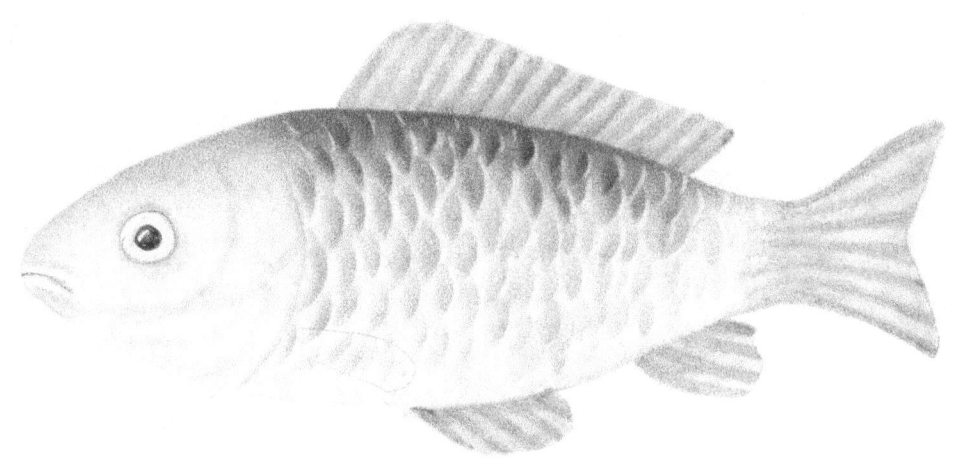

Lastly, the pectoral fin should be shaded evenly, not too dark, but to make it much darker than the tone of the belly. Use an HB for this and blend it with blending stump.

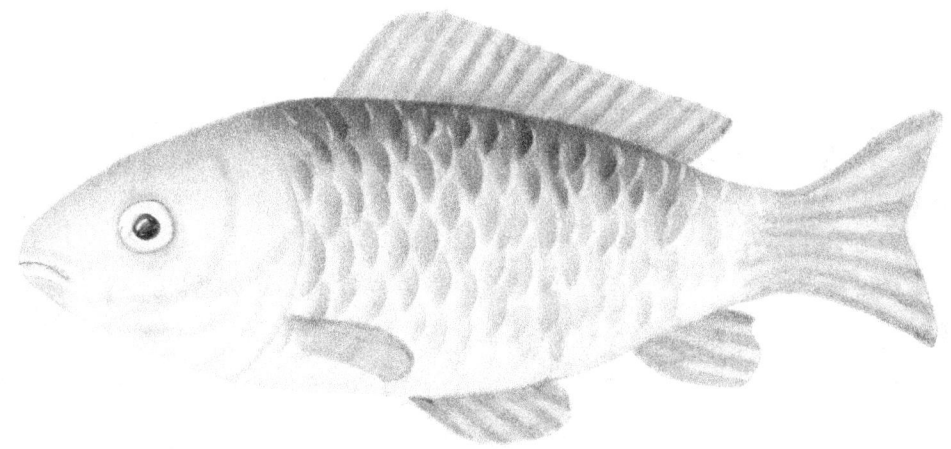

Now you can add some cast shadow under the pectoral

fin to make it stand off of the fish, particularly its top. Use a 2H or a blending stump and shade the tiny area under it as shown in the next image.

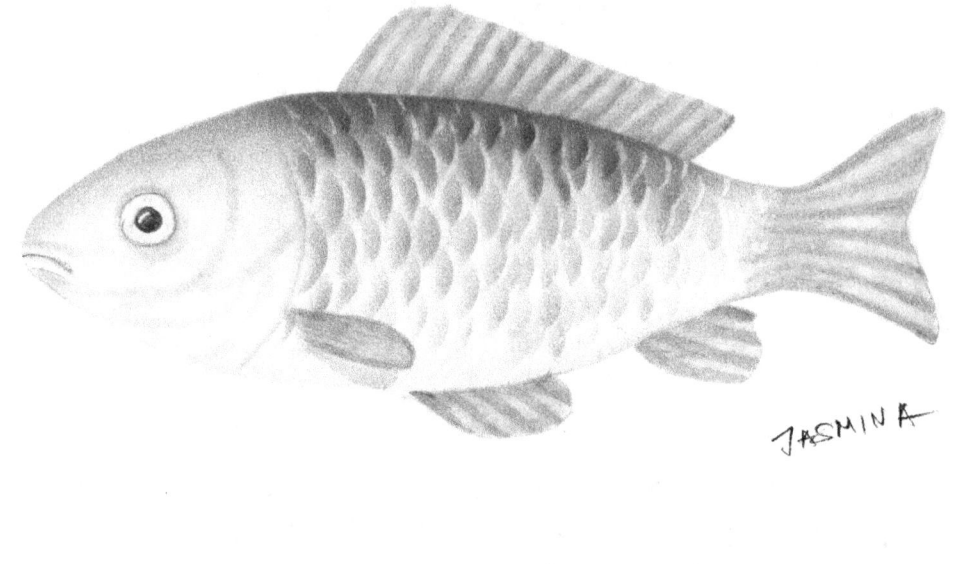

HOW TO DRAW A TEDDY BEAR

After so much shading with graphite powder, let's make one drawing with drawing only.
To draw a teddy bear, we need a few circles, ellipses

and a few other main outlines. Start with one bigger ellipse for the chest and belly, and make one smaller circle above it, for the head. These circles can be whichever size or shape, there's no need to strictly stick to the lines from my sketch. You can see in the next image that the circle for the head of my teddy bears is not a perfect circle, but it is a bit wider in its upper part.

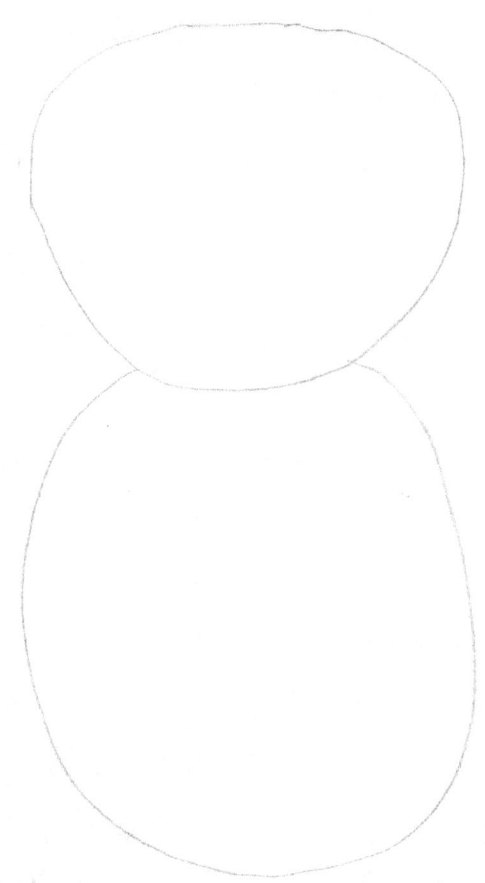

Add the arms as two ellipses attached to the torso of the teddy bear. Also, mark tiny lines for the legs, upper and lower areas of the legs attached to the belly, on its left and right sides. These areas don't have to be symmetrical.

Add two ellipses at the end of the previously drawn short lines, so that the teddy bear appears as if it were sitting. Then add two arches on the left and right sides in the upper area of its head, to create the ears. Take a look at the next image to see these outlines before you start to draw.

Finally, draw the muzzle and the eyes. For the muzzle, just draw a circle, smaller than the whole head by double, and make it "stick" to the bottom of it as shown in the next picture. Draw the nose in the middle of this circle. It is just a tiny circle with two parallel lines starting at the bottom of the nose and ending at the bottom of the muzzle.

Then, draw two circles for the eyes above the the muzzle, on the left and right sides of it. Make about two circles with a wide empty space between them. Of course, these measures can vary, you don't have to place the features in the same places I have.

Let's start with the darkest parts. Use a 4B or darker pencil and fill the circles of the eyes, leaving untouched a tiny area which will represent the reflection of the light. These eyes are mostly manufactured from plastic or glass and they are usually shiny. So, these tiny white dots will make the eyes shiny. If you filled the whole circle with a 4B or darker, you won't be able to erase it to make it absolutely white again, but here you can use white markers, white ink gel pen, or white gouache.

Fill in the area of the nose and the tiny vertical gap under the nose using a 4B or darker. For the nose it is better to make a bit wider highlight, which will make the nose appear slightly rounded. Analyze the next image carefully before you start to draw.

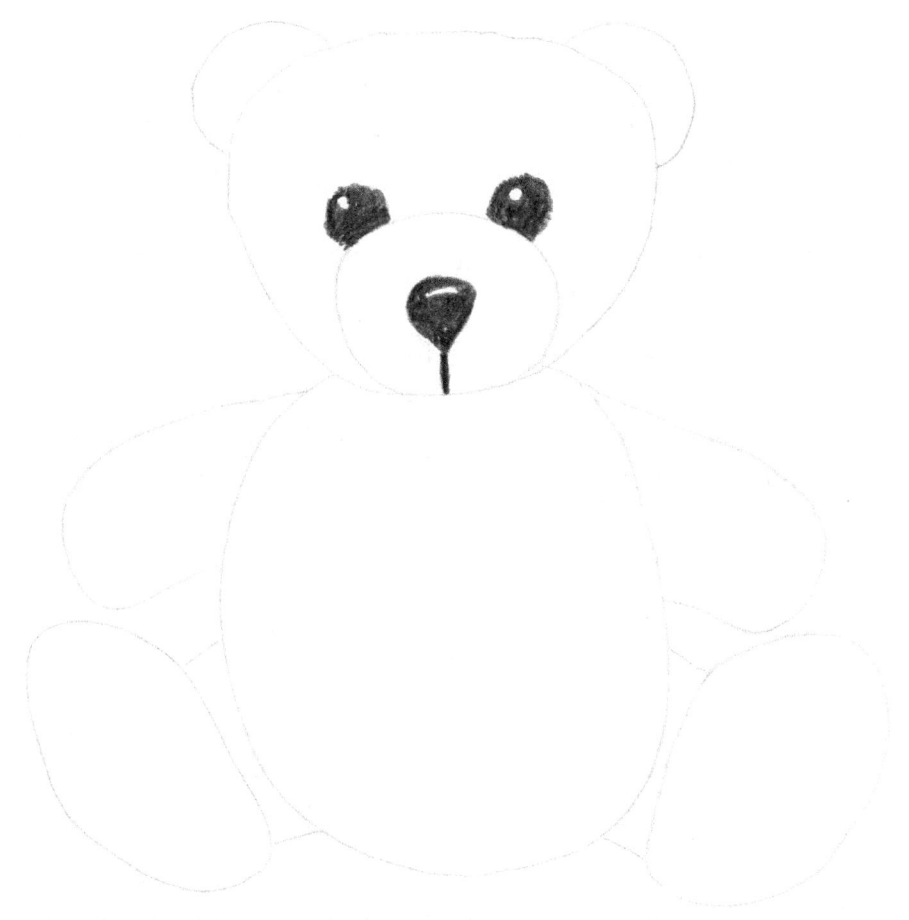

Now we can start to make the darkest areas, which get

almost no light. Use a B or darker pencil for these areas. These areas are in such places where the light hits less or nothing at all. Make circular motions throughout the whole drawing to create the texture of the fleece fabric.

Make smaller and bigger overlapping circles as you go. Alter the pressure constantly to make it less even because this texture shouldn't be smooth, but full of tiny cast shadows and highlights.

Take a look at the next image and practice this kind of shading on a separate piece of paper before you apply it to your drawing.

For making this kind of texture, you should choose the blunt tip of the pencil over the sharp tip. The blunt tip will make the texture appear fluffy and you will be able to cover larger areas and progress faster.
In the next image, you can see where I decided to make the shadowed parts. These are the areas that would get less light.

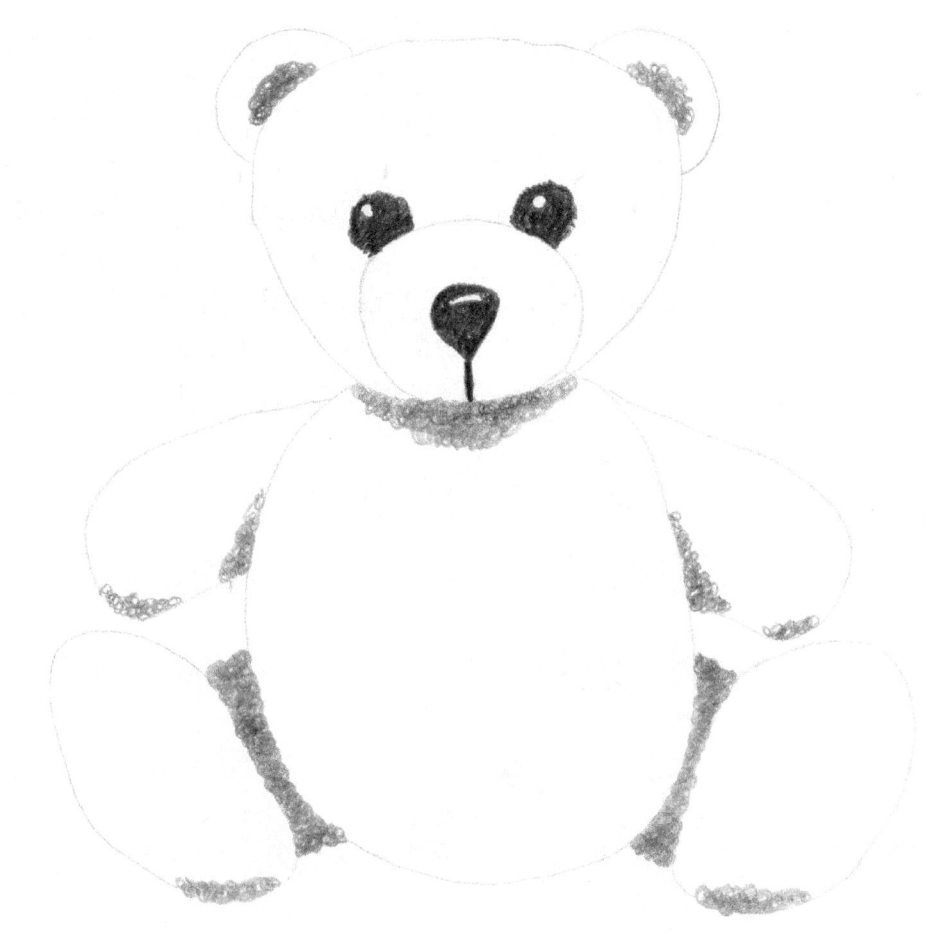

The next step is to create the mid-tone of the fleece fabric that the teddy bears are covered with. These textiles are usually brown, so an HB for the mid-tone is just perfect.

Mid-tone is actually the basic tone which is not affected by the light yet not found in the shadow.

HB is good for this because this is as much brighter than a B as necessary to allow us to make gradient transition between the dark shadows and mid-tone. HB is also perfect for these areas because when we press harder, this pencil is able to create pretty dark tones, yet not too dark. When we press it gently, it creates very bright tones, which are very good when creating the texture of teddy bear's textile next to the highlights on it. Here make circular motions and use the blunt tip of an HB pencil. Take a look at the next image to see which areas I have filled in with this step. When going next to the previously drawn dark areas, go a bit over them, or use a B pencil again if necessary in order to make a gradient transition between these tone values.

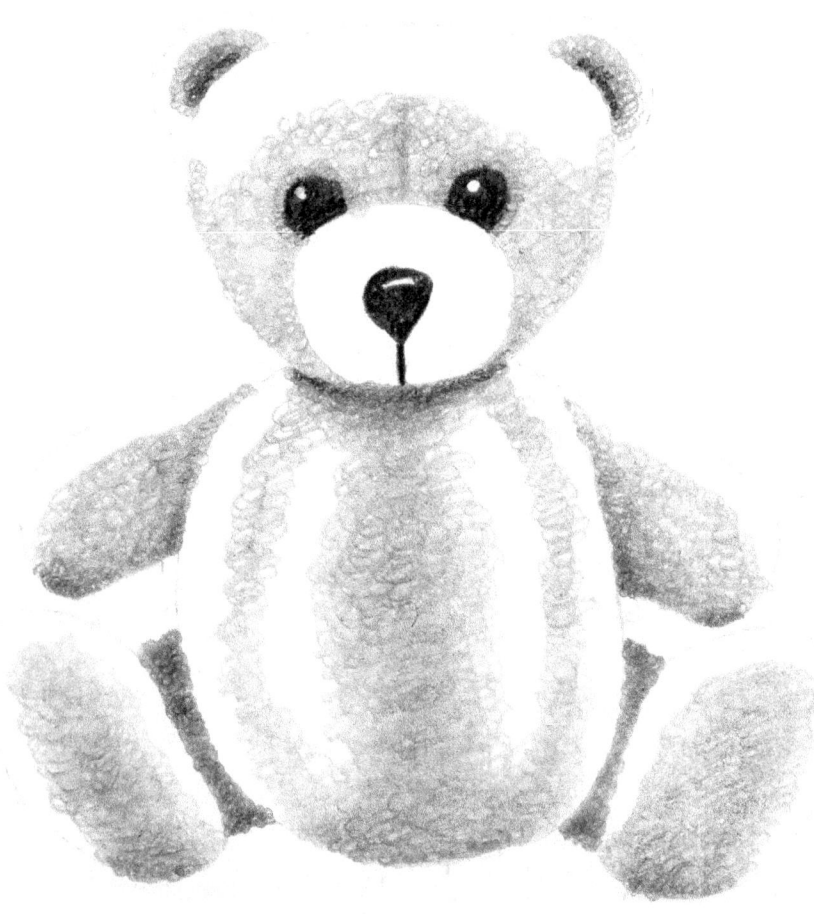

Now you can fill the rest of teddy bear – except for the muzzle - using a 2H or 3H. Here, use circular motions and the blunt tip of the pencil. Press lightly when drawing the edges, and press harder when drawing next to the areas drawn with an HB.

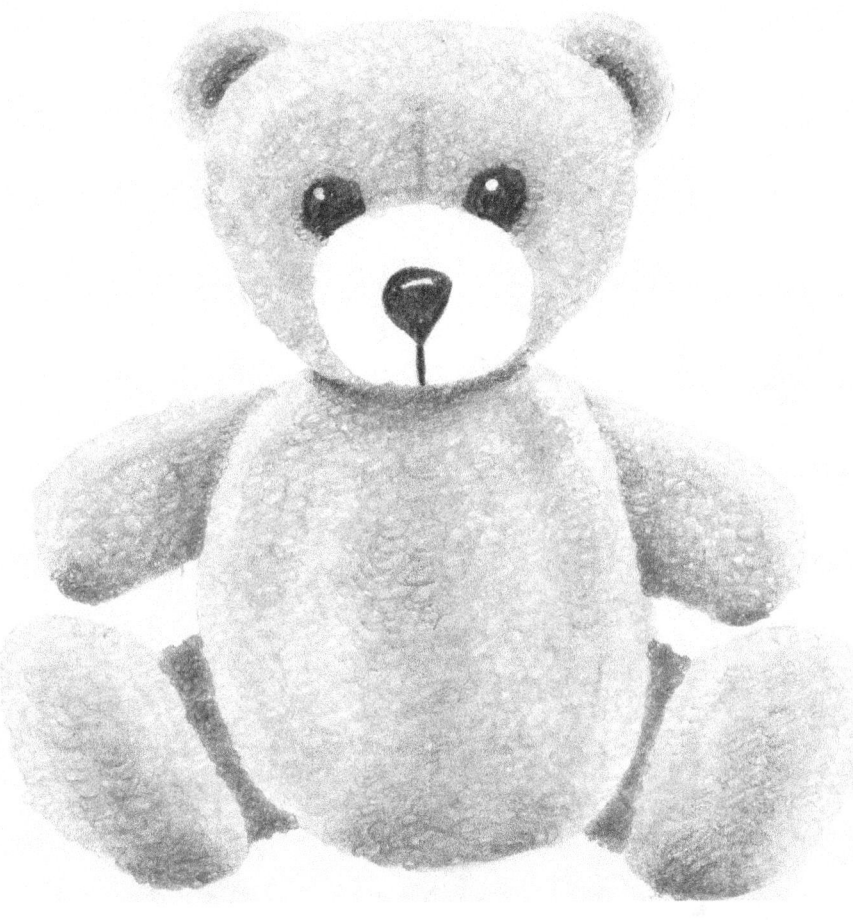

The muzzle of teddy bears is usually made from velvet or plush, so here, we can use a blending stump to shade the muzzle, which shouldn't be too dark because it gets a lot of light from every side. Pick a bit of graphite powder with the tip of the blending stump and apply it in the middle of the lower area of the muzzle, around the vertical, black gap.

Using the blending stump, make the cast shadow under the teddy bear to make it more realistic and three-dimensional.

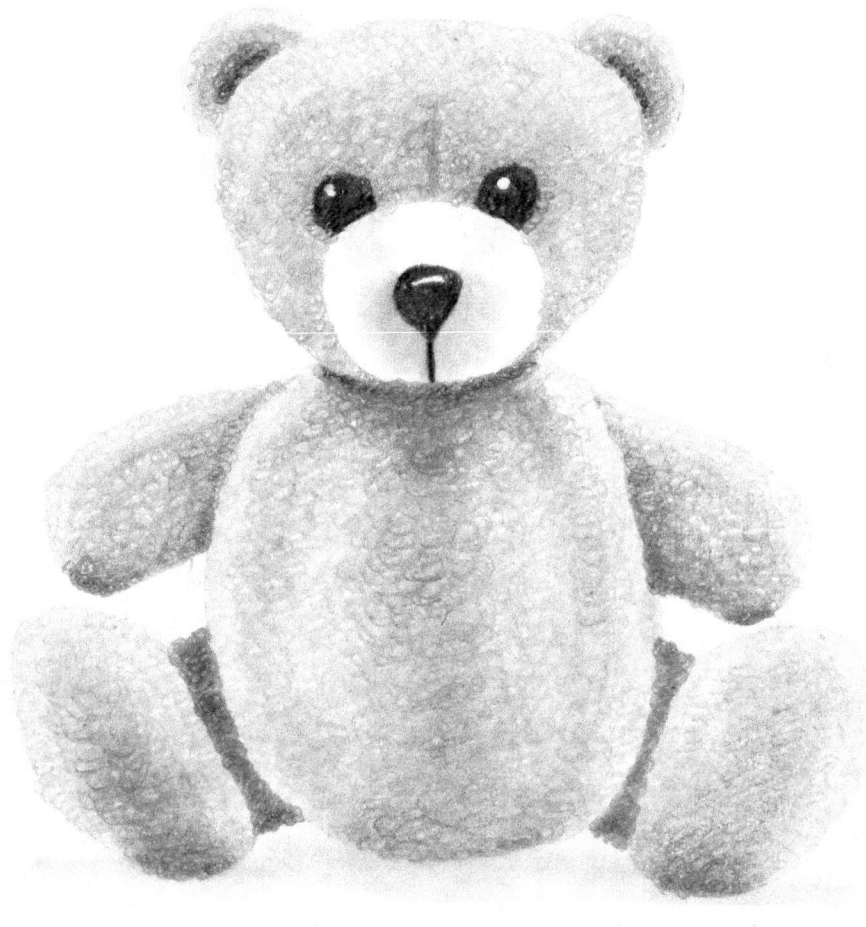

You can fill in the rest of the muzzle using a blending

stump. Press gently and use circular motions. Go a bit over the already shaded darker parts in the middle of the muzzle. Here you can darken some areas and erase the highlights if necessary.

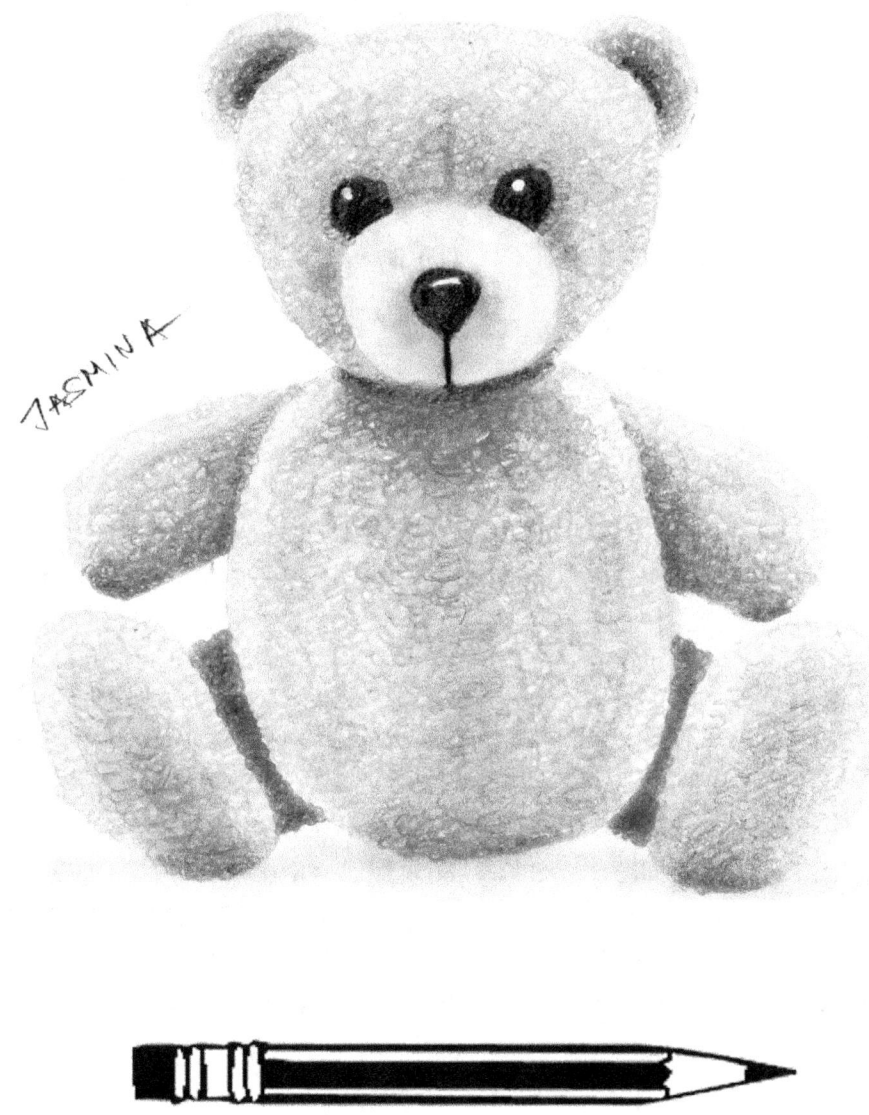

HOW TO DRAW A FLOWER

I want you to draw a simple daisy with me.

Start by creating two circles: one in the middle which will represent the part with seeds and stems, and one surrounding circle, far away from the small one, which we will use to draw petals.

You can use a divider tool for these circles, but it is better to draw them freehand because the flower may seem fake and less realistic if the circles are perfectly round.

In the next image, you can see the two circles I created in the first step, and the distance between them. It should look like the outline of a doughnut. So, try to make similar circles using an HB or brighter nuance. Don't press hard when drawing the outer circle because you will have to erase it at the end and it shouldn't be visible at all. You need this just for orientation .

The area in the middle has to appear bristly, so it has to be anything but smooth. Here we have the benefit of actually keeping those irritating white dots that we usually want to get rid of when we aim to draw smooth textures. Use an HB pencil and fill this whole small circle making circular motions.

Press lightly in the middle because this area is a bit highlighted.

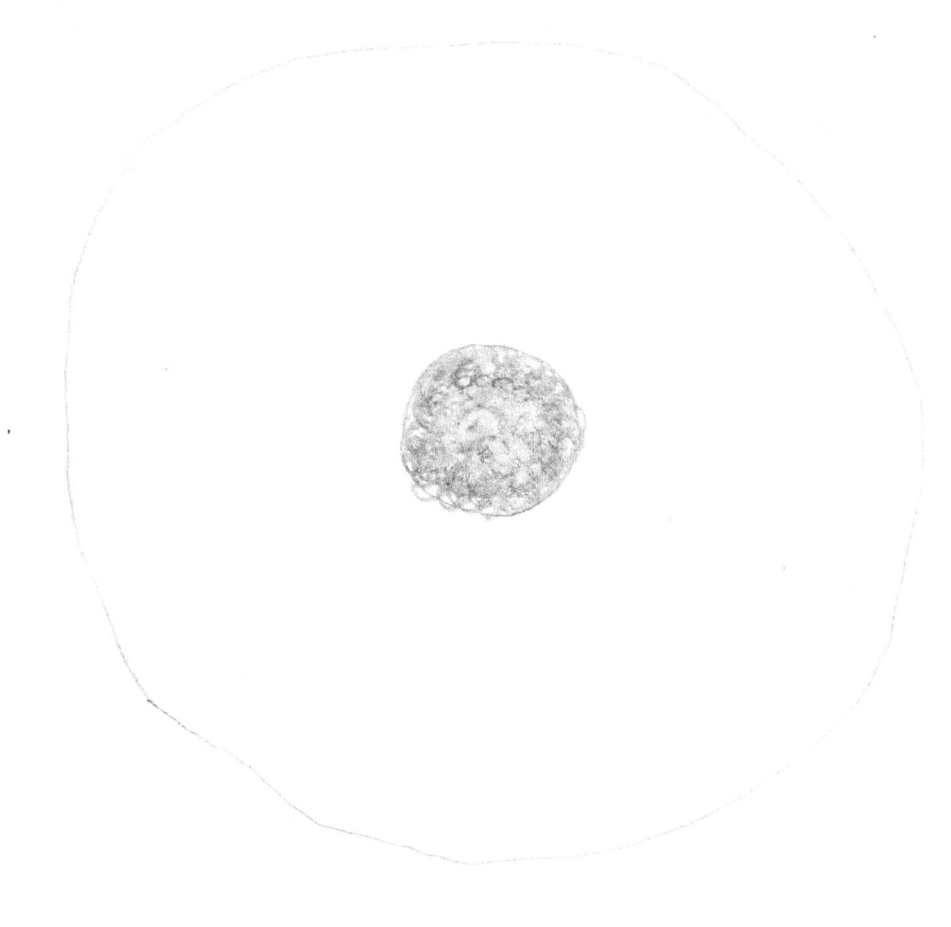

To give this area a slightly round shape, darken the edges all around it using a B pencil. As always when gradual transition is needed, press hard when drawing the edges and release the pressure as you draw towards the center of it.

This is about everything that has to be done with the mid area.

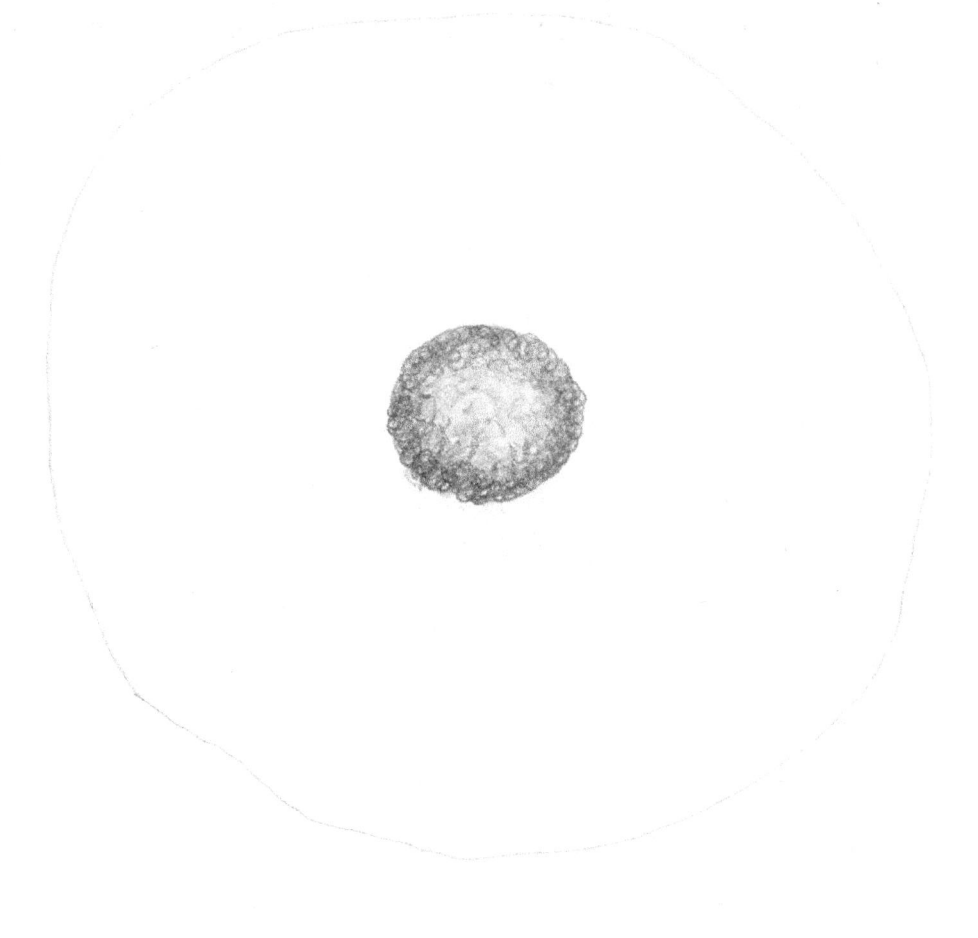

It is time to draw the petals which will take majority of the time spent on this drawing.

Start by drawing the line on the small circle and draw slightly curved lines towards the outer line. There you have to make the shape, something like the half of the circle and to go back to the small circle. The width of the petals next to the area in the middle should be more narrow than the widest area of the petal in order to make all the petals fit equally. Try to make continuous lines without breaking them. To achieve this you have to draw the line very slowly. Examine the next image to see what I'm trying to explain.

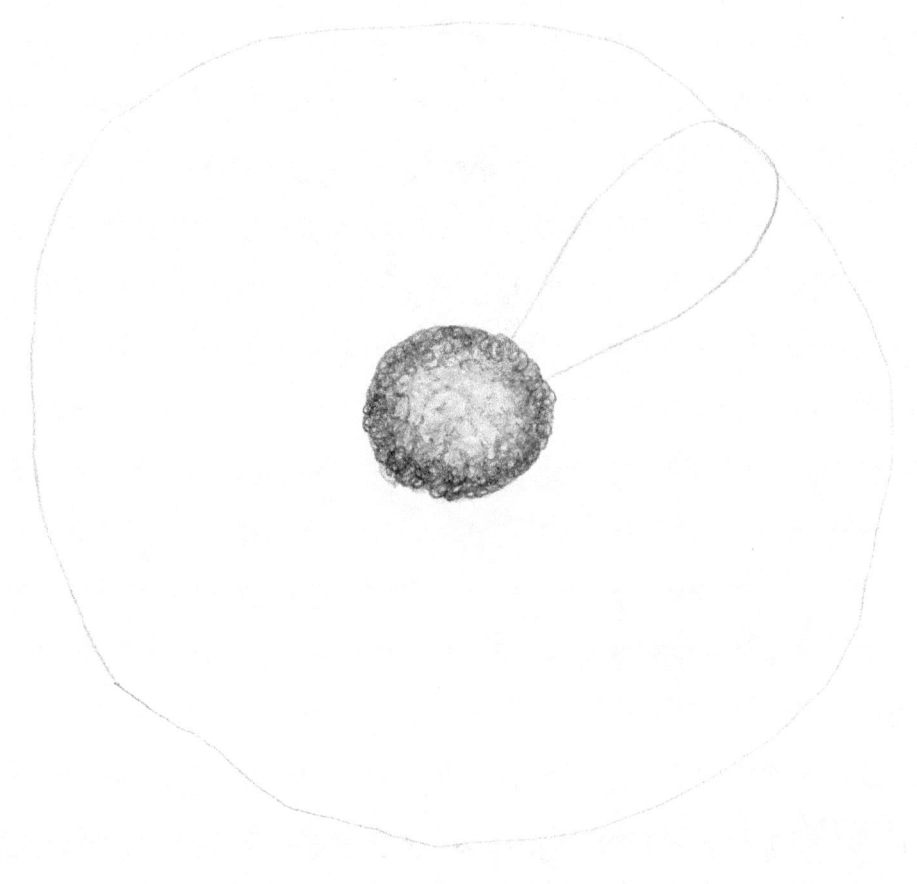

Draw the rest of the petals all around. They shouldn't be all the same. Some of them should be wider than others. Since the outer circle is not a perfect circle, and some parts are further from the center than others, the petals won't be the same length. This is good because it will make the flower more lifelike. As mentioned before, avoid making all the areas the same, otherwise the drawn object would look fake and less natural. In the next image, you can see how some of the petals are stuck together and some have a bit of distance between them. Also, some petals should overlap the others. Draw these petals randomly all around and don't pay attention to the previously drawn petals.

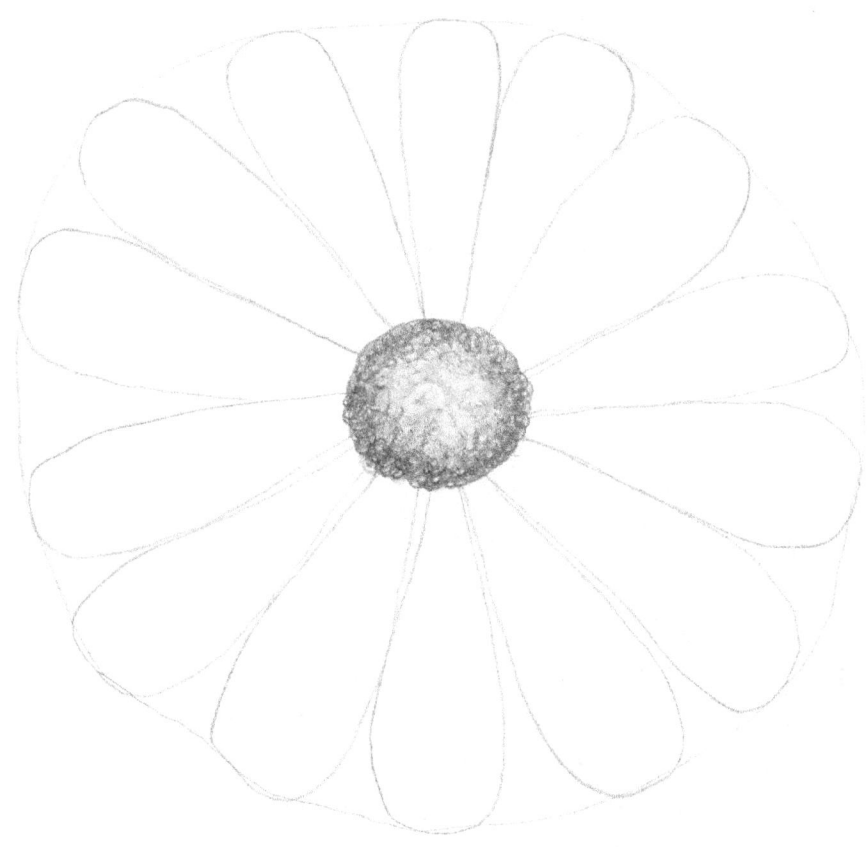

Now you can erase the outer guideline since you don't need them anymore.

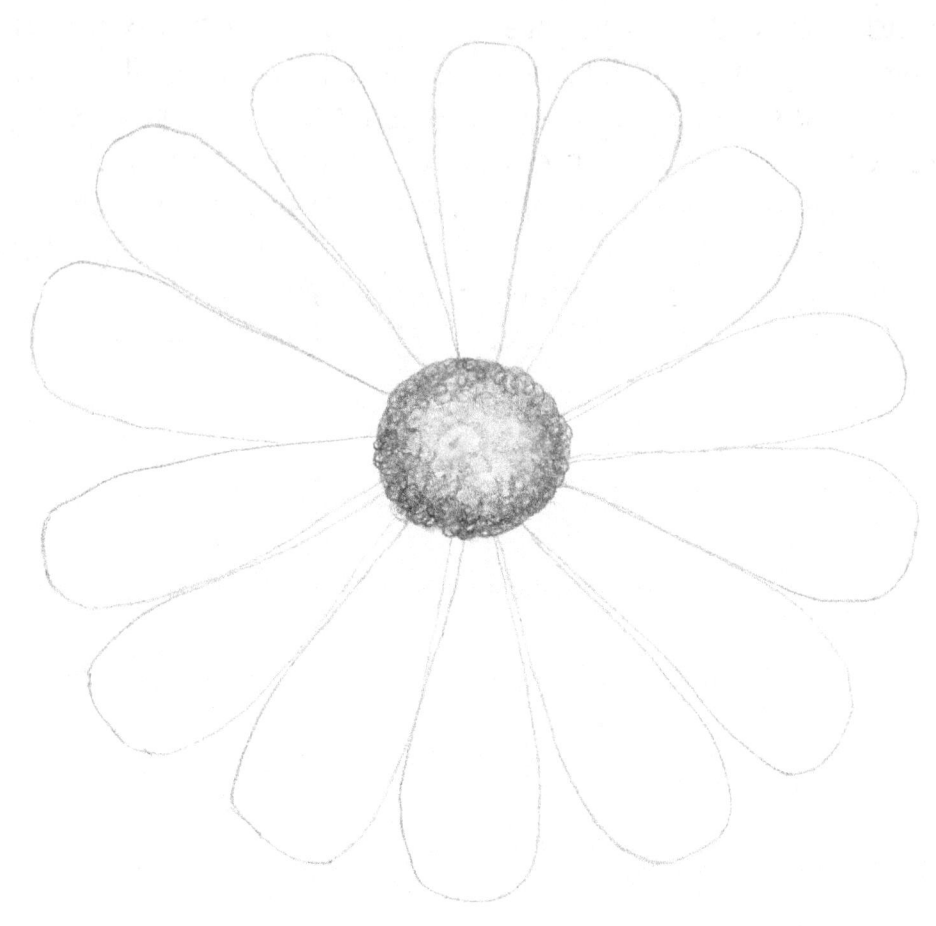

In this step, draw the underlining petals. The top of these petals should be drawn out of the outer line that we had for the guideline. The underlining petals appear longer because they are not allowed to be as bent as the overlapping petals because the pressure of the overlapping petals don't allow them to bend. We have to keep this in mind and to draw petals according to physical rules. That is why the tops of the underlining petals should reach out of the initial outer circle. In the next image you can see how I have added these petals. Draw them differently at random. Some wider than the others, some overlap each other, some longer than the others...

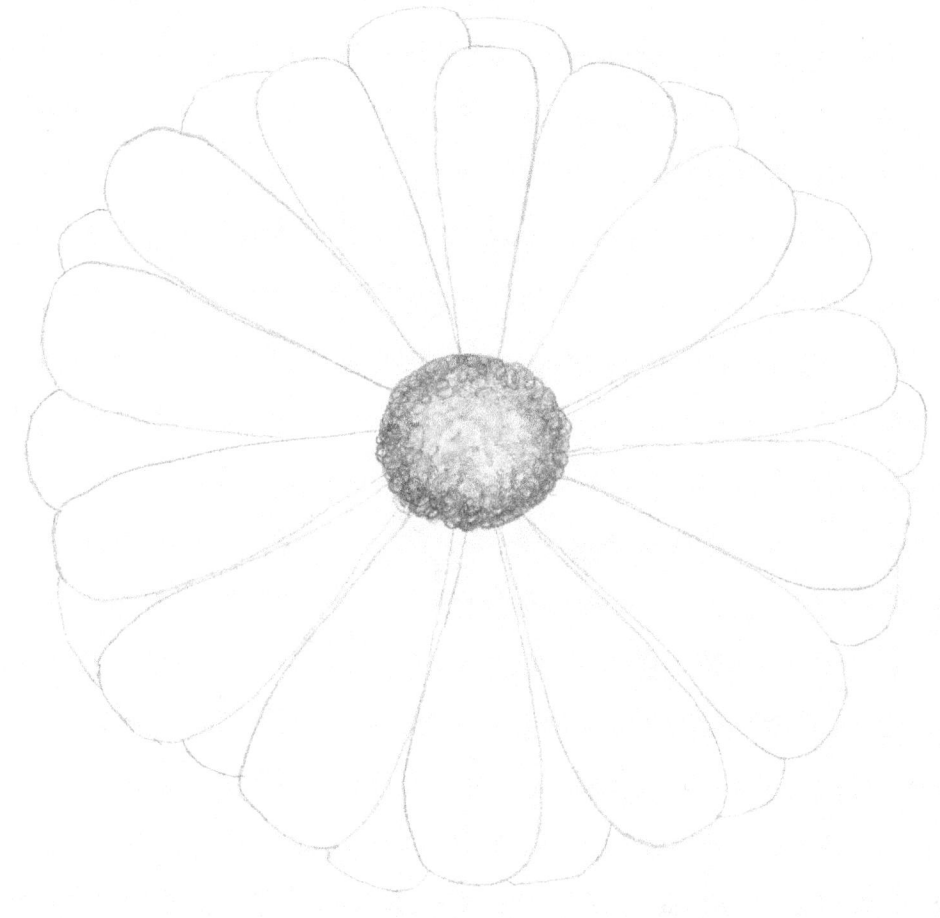

Mark the areas between the petals using a 2B to separate the petals and create the deepest shadows among the petals. This way, you can form the shape of some petals. Draw this carefully because a dark pencil cannot be fully erased. Draw longer and shorter lines among the petals randomly.

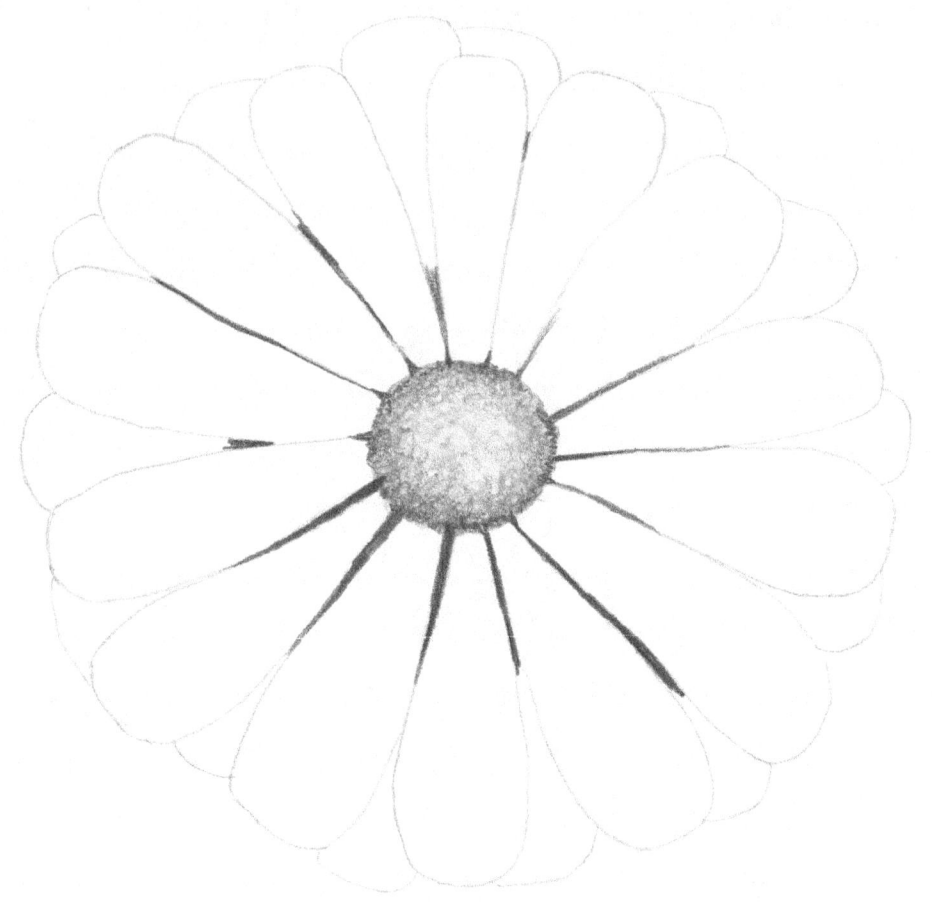

In the case of this flower we have to create a tone gradation on the petals. There are many ways to achieve the gradation of tones.

The simplest way of making a gradient transition is to change the pressure on your pencil. Use an HB pencil and start from the inner ends and draw outwards, towards the center or highlight, applying pencil lines next to each other in the same direction to evenly color the paper. Pressing hard and then gradually releasing the pressure as you work toward the highlight in the middle. You can see this step represented in the next image.

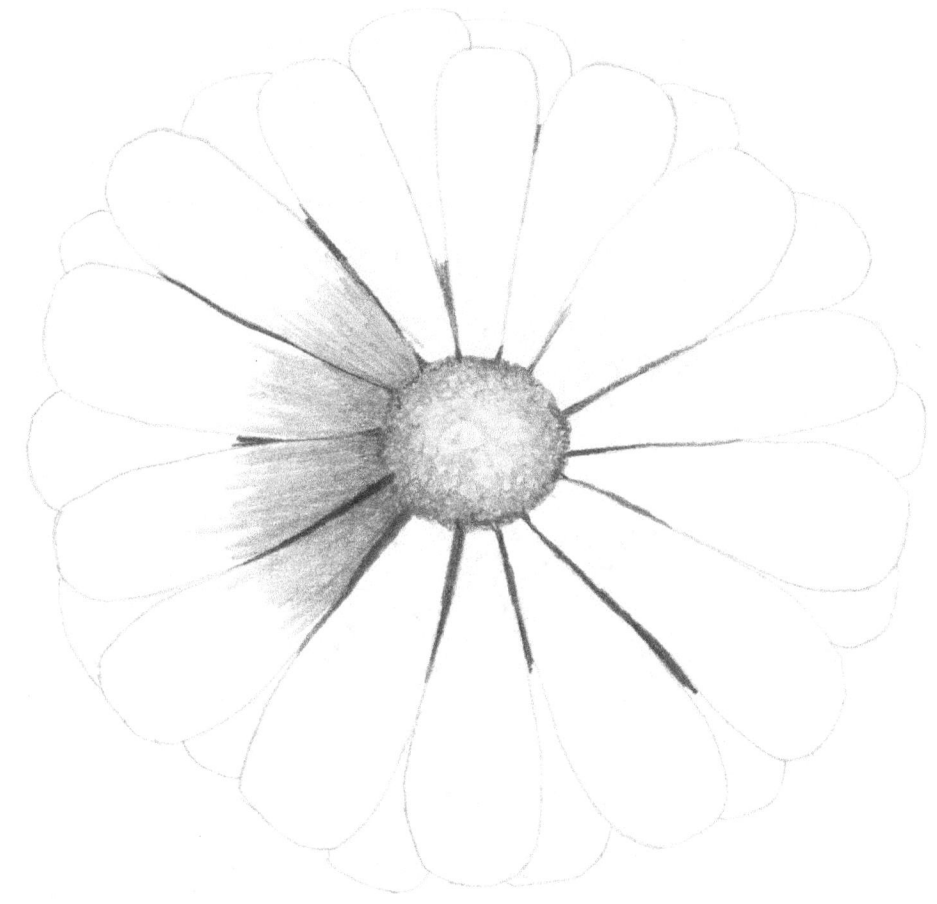

Do the same with the rest of the petals.

Alternately, you can shade the entire area smoothly in the lightest value, then add more layers where it should be darker and blend with a blending stump or erasing the highlighted area if it needs to be brighter. You can fade these evenly into each other or leave a clear line between the areas; it depends on the subject you draw. In the case of these petals, a gradient transition should be as flawless as possible.

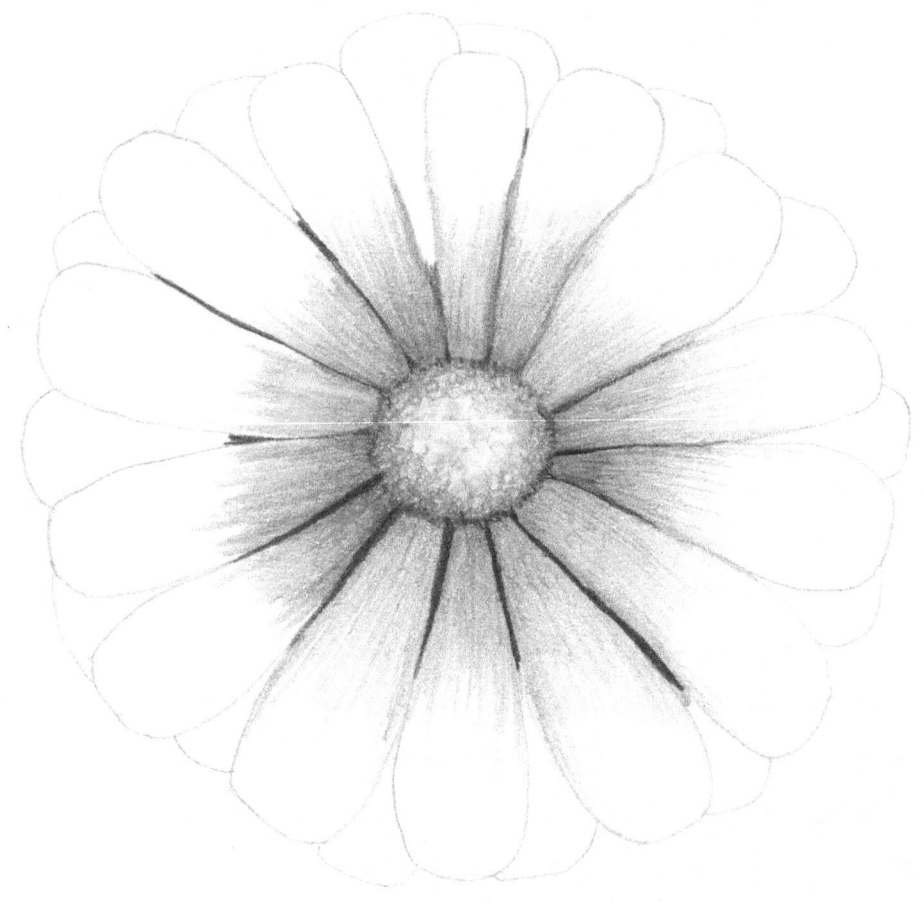

Now do the same with the top of the overlapping petals. Start at the top, pressing hard, and release the pressure on the pencil as you draw the strokes towards the highlight. Examine the next image to see where to apply strokes. Note how the petal with the shaded top looks bent and highlighted with just a single pencil used and different pressure applied.

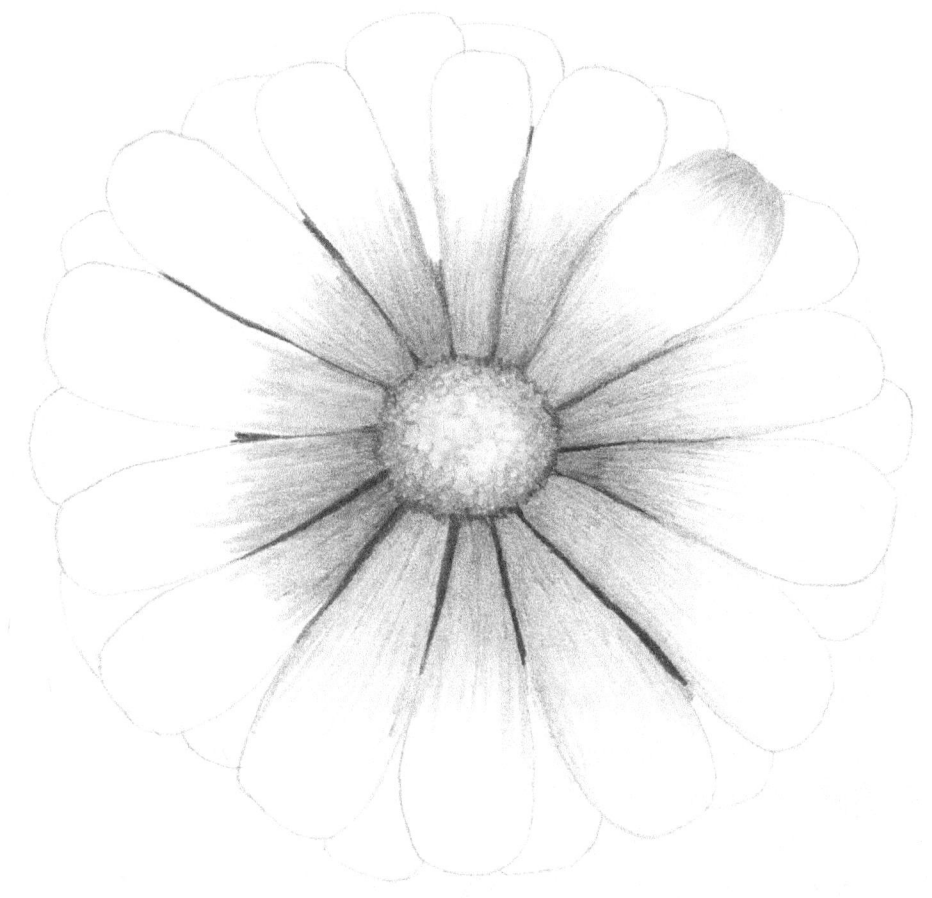

Do the same with the rest of the petals, and also with the underlying petals. This is a time-consuming step, but after having it done, almost the whole drawing is finished.

Here you can see how the gradient transition is important in every drawing. That's why it is good to practice it a lot through these tutorials.

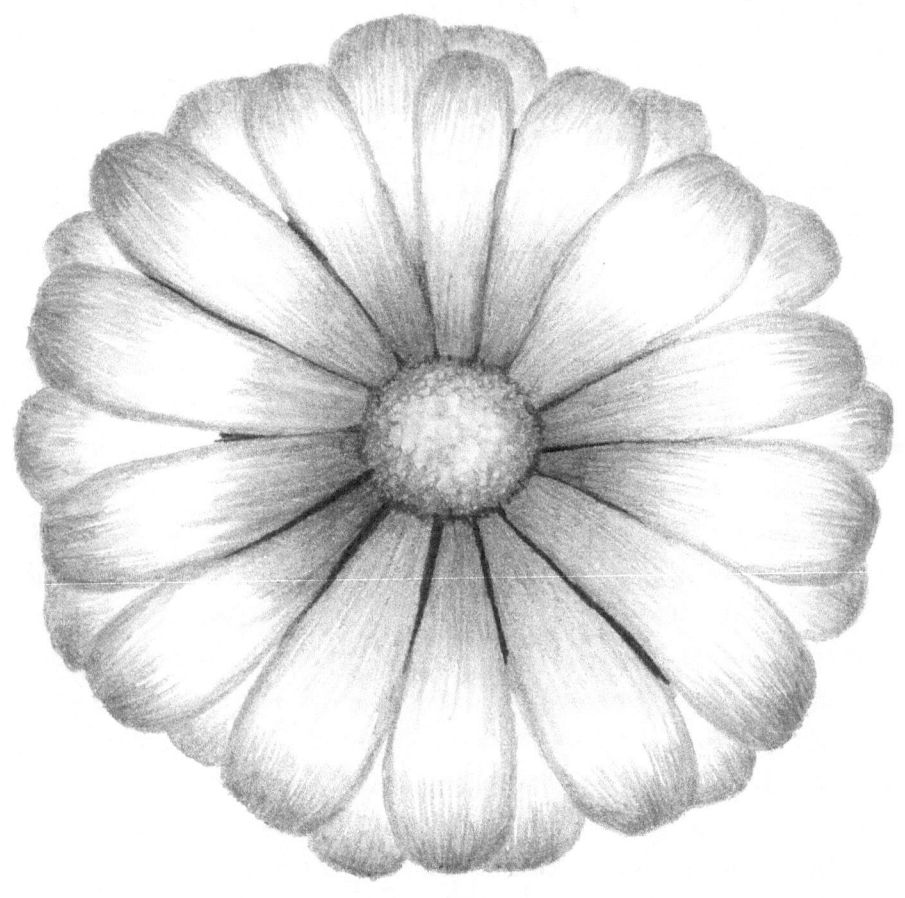

Here you can see how the petals appear shiny, which is not good because – as you may know - this flower has a matte texture of the petals. To make the petals look matte, yet to keep the highlights in the middle, we have to blend it with blending stump, pressing lightly in the middle of the highlight, and pressing harder next to the edges of the petals and the ends of the drawn gradient tone. But let's blend the underlying petals first. Here you have to make the edges between the highlights and the tops of the petals invisible. Darken the highlights of the underlying petals using a blending stump, yet make them much brighter than the edges of the overlapping petals. Go all around the flower and do the same with the rest of the underlying petals. Now they shouldn't appear shiny anymore.

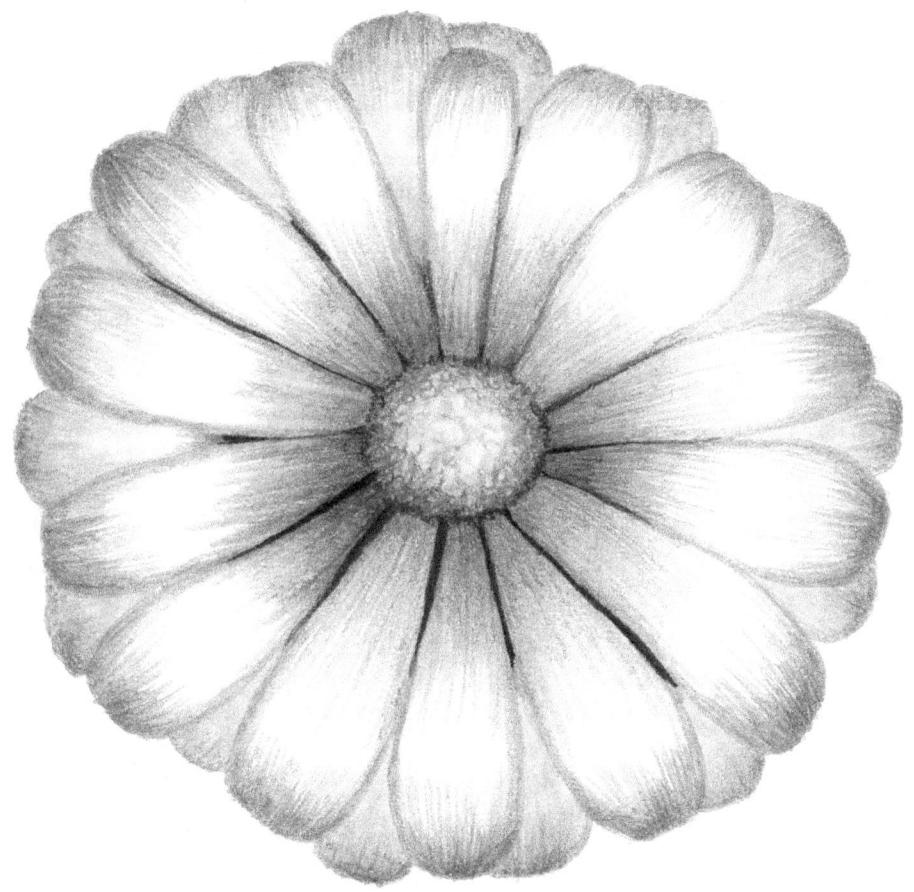

Do the same with the overlapping petals. Make 2-3 lines along the length of the petals with blending stump in the middle of the petals as shown in the next image.

Press hard with a blending stump when creating these patterns, and press gently when shading around them. The point is to cover all the white color of the paper, yet to leave the highlights bright enough. Here you can darken some shadings if necessary.

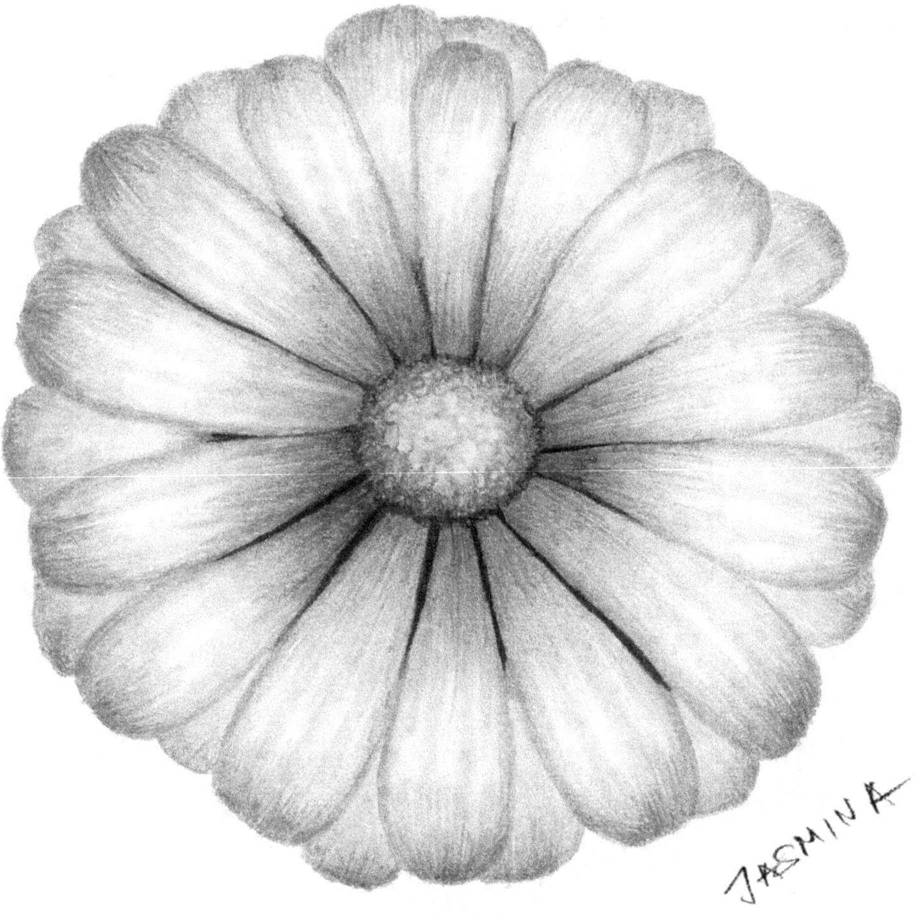

HOW TO DRAW AN ANAMORPHIC 3D W LETTER

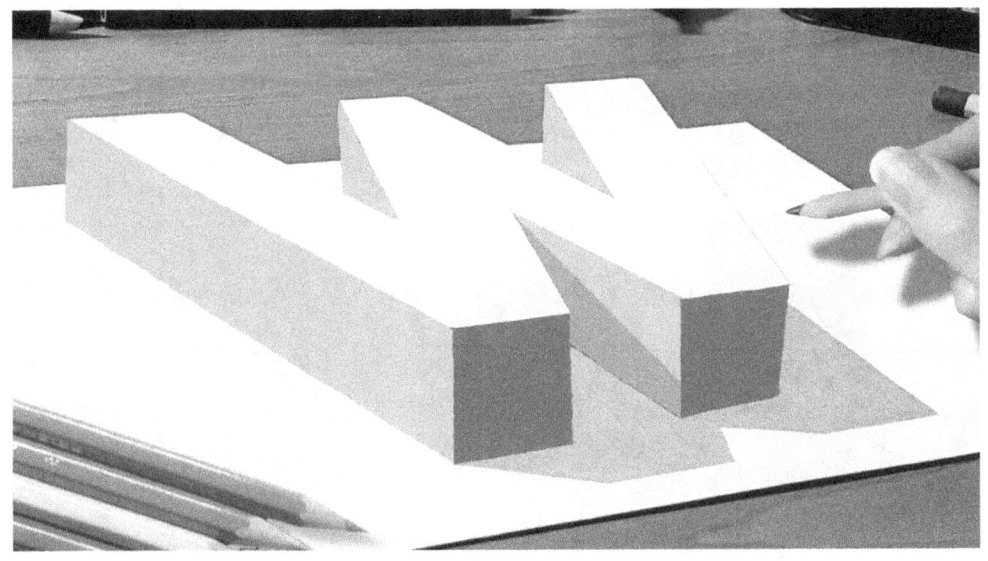

Let's make something a bit different and what many people find interesting and want to do themselves.

Using an HB graphite pencil, draw any letter in the upper right corner of the paper. For now, you can choose a "W" letter like me, and after you have tried this one and figured out how it has to be done, you can experiment with other letters and numbers, or even objects. Note, in the next image, the position of my letter. You don't have to draw exactly the same or a proportional letter. It can be thinner or thicker, doesn't have to be the same as mine.

Use a ruler if you want to make straight lines for the letter.

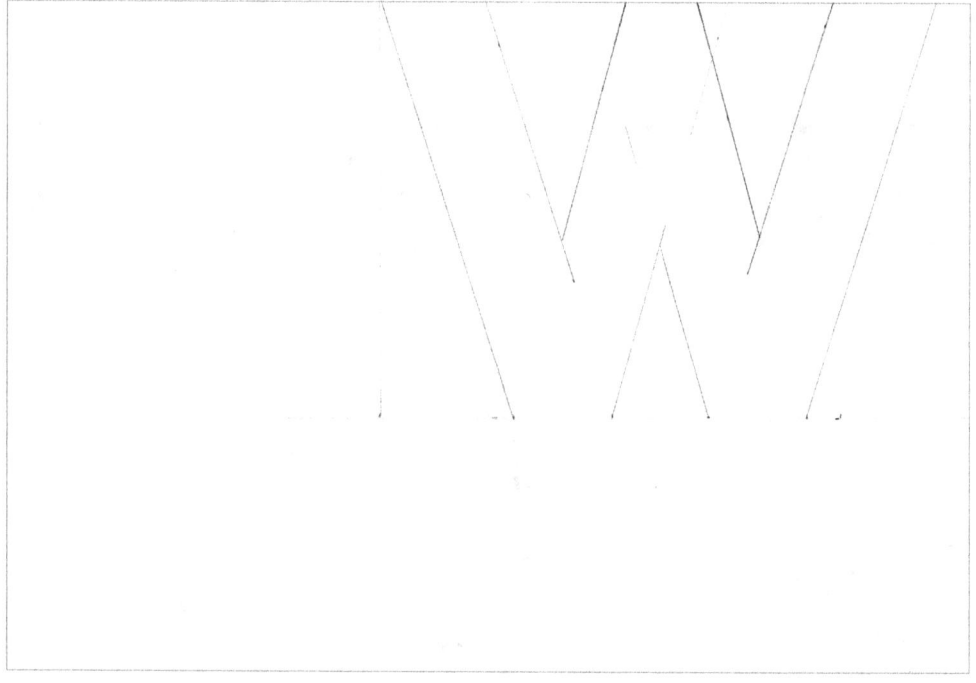

In this step, we are adding the third dimension to the letter.

Draw the lines starting over the corners on the lower left side of the letter. Examine the next image to see where I have placed the lines and how. Don't make these lines parallel to each other, but make their ends a bit closer to each other.

I suggest starting with the (A) corner as it's marked in the next image and then make the other ends closer to the lower end of this line. This is important because we want the upper surface of the letter to be closer to the viewer's eyes, and the bottom to be further, lower. The length of these lines can be almost the half of the total height of the letter, and every line should have the same length.

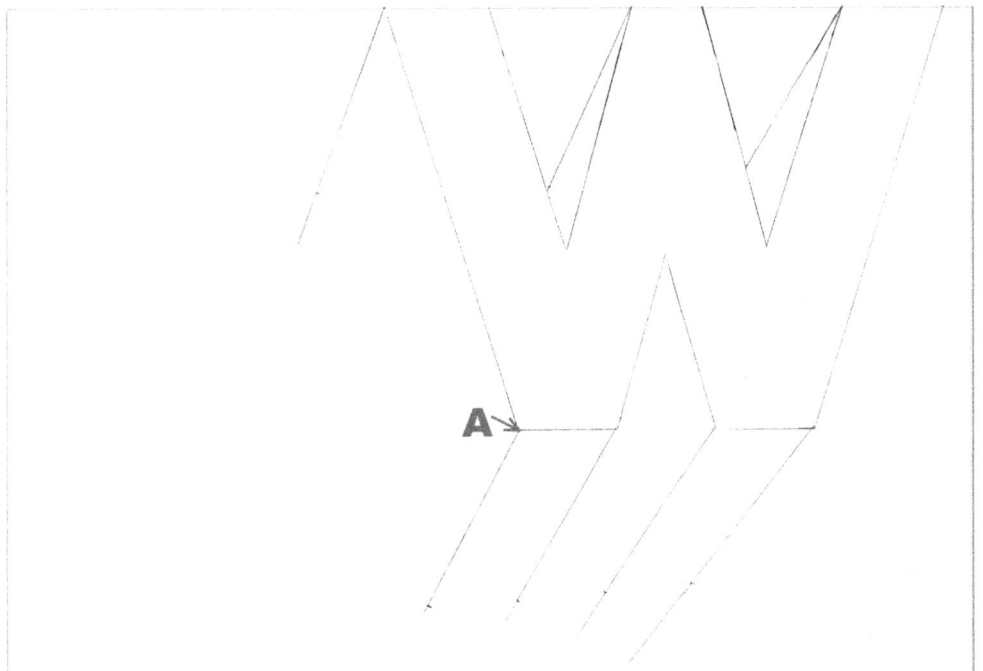

Now connect the ends as shown in the next picture.

You should often check the drawing from the point of view that you want it to be seen from at the end of the drawing.

Check out the image at the beginning and the end of the tutorial to see how my drawing appears from that specific angle, and yours will be similar to this one, so you can have an idea what it will look like at the end.

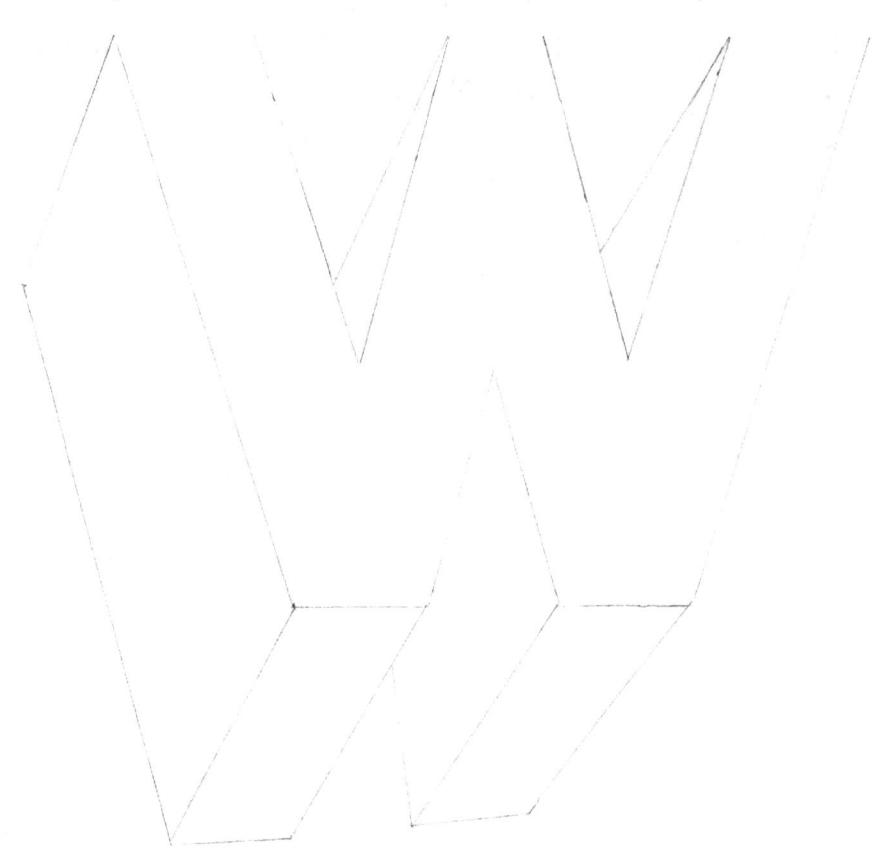

Now, imagine that the light source is found at the upper left corner, but much higher above the paper, and according to this, draw the cast shadows. Namely, fill the previously created three-dimensional areas with a 2B or even darker nuance, and try to make the surfaces as smooth as possible.

So, in this step, shade the most shadowed area, which should be found under the letter. Analyze the next image before you start to shade.

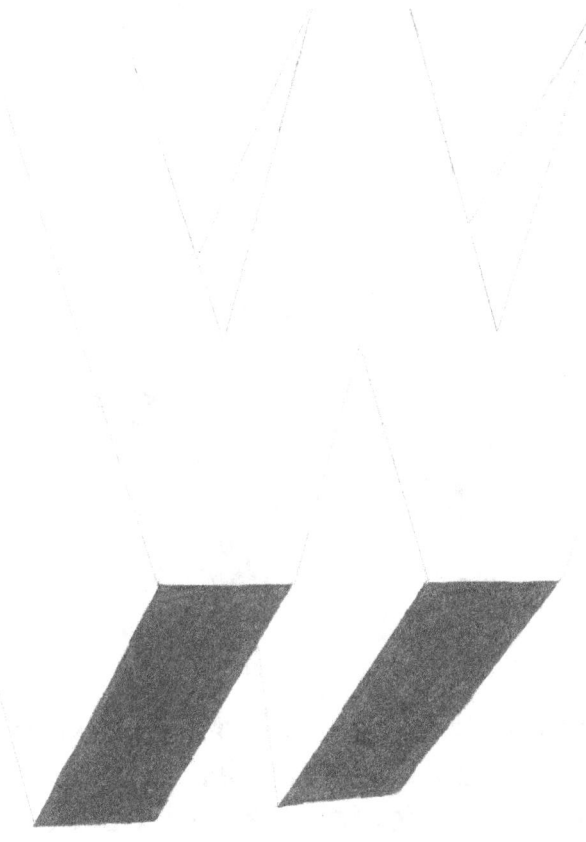

Now, in this step, create the shadow that the letter casts on itself. Use a HB to fill in the area where the shadow falls over the letter, keeping in mind where the imagined light source is coming from.

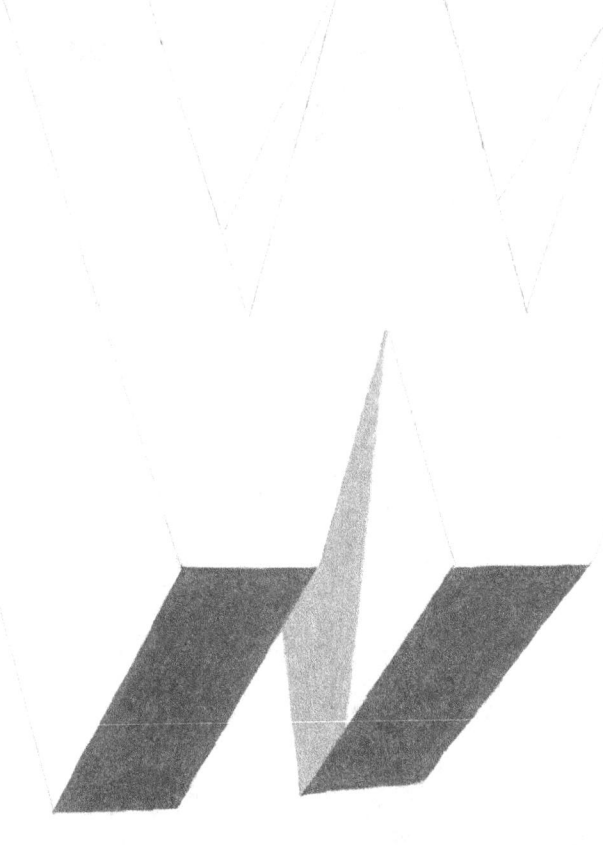

Now you can fill in the rest of, so to say the third dimensional areas, using a 5H or 6H, using small circular motions in order to make the surface even.

As you can see in the next image it already appears three-dimensional.

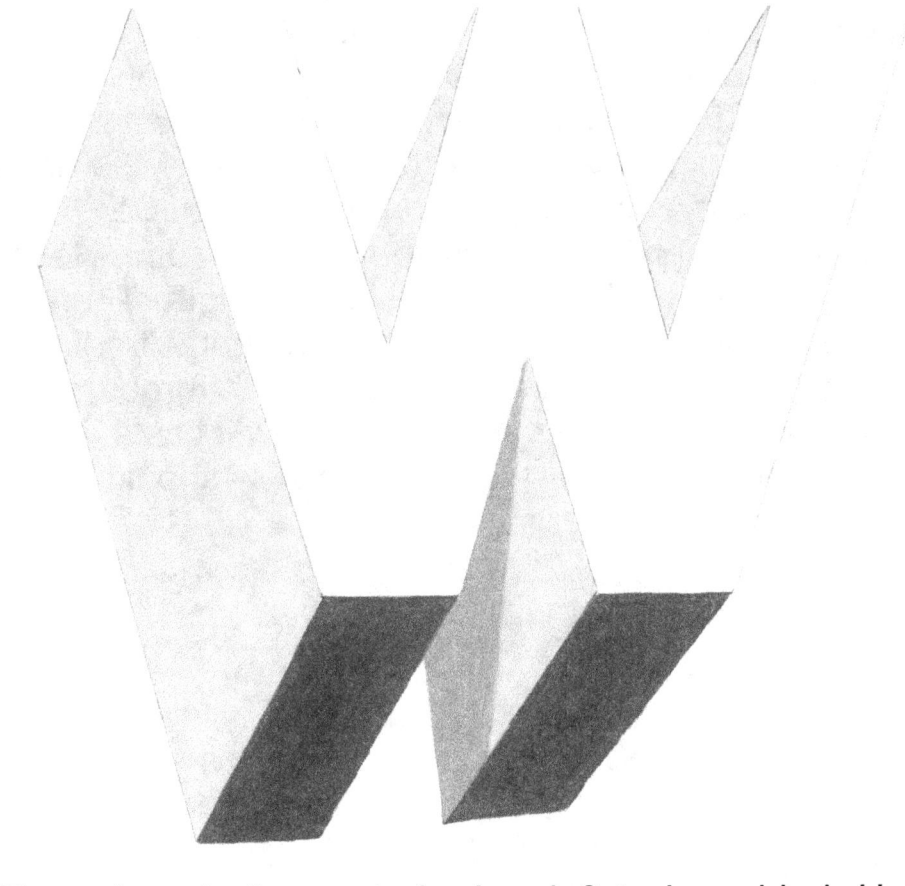

There is only the cast shadow left to be added. Use a 2H for this. As you can see, I suggest you use different nuances in these areas to make them look as if they were different dimensions. This kind of coloring will add a lot to the 3D effect. Here is the most difficult and tricky part where you have to use your imagination. You have to determine where the letter would cast the shadow underneath itself. Still keeping in mind the direction of your light source, create the edges of the cast shadow. As a help, you can examine the next image to see how I have placed the lines and colored the shadowed area. The shadow I drew is close to the letter, which means that I have imagined the light source being much further above the letter. The closer the light source to the upper left corner of this surface, the longer the shadow would be. Use a 2H graphite pencil for the edges of this shadow and experiment with the positions of the lines until you find the most appropriate place. It is easier if you drew the same letter as me, but any other letter would also cast a shadow of a similar length. There is only the shape that you have to experiment with. If you draw "R," "O," "P," or similar letters, don't forget about the "hole" in these letters and the shadow it casts. In the case of these letters, the self-shadow should have gradient tone value.

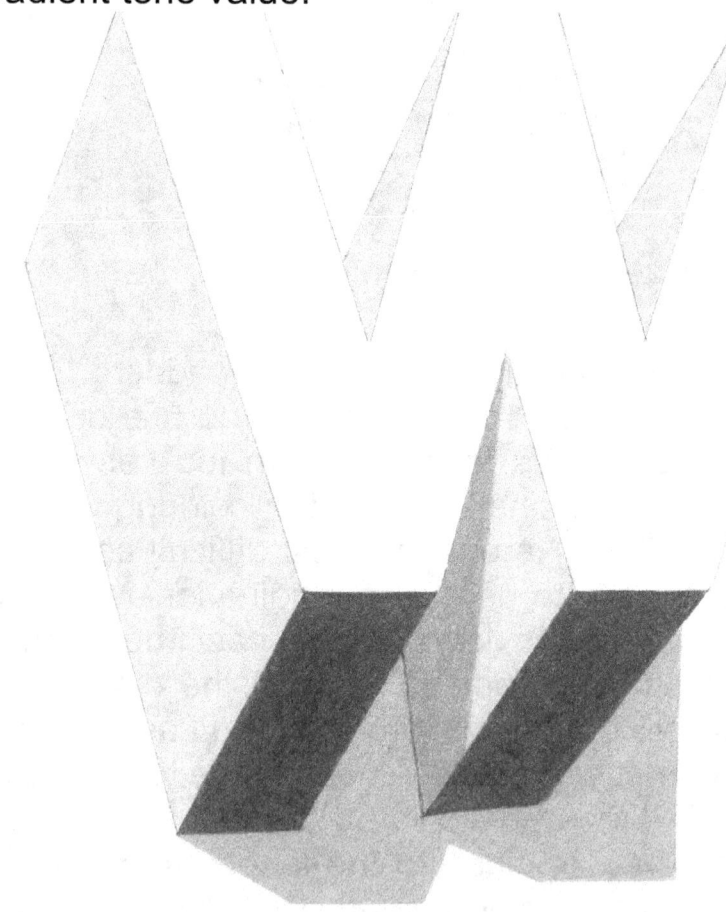

Now you can cut the upper area of the paper, outside the letter to make it even more three-dimensional.

In the next image you can see where to cut the paper.

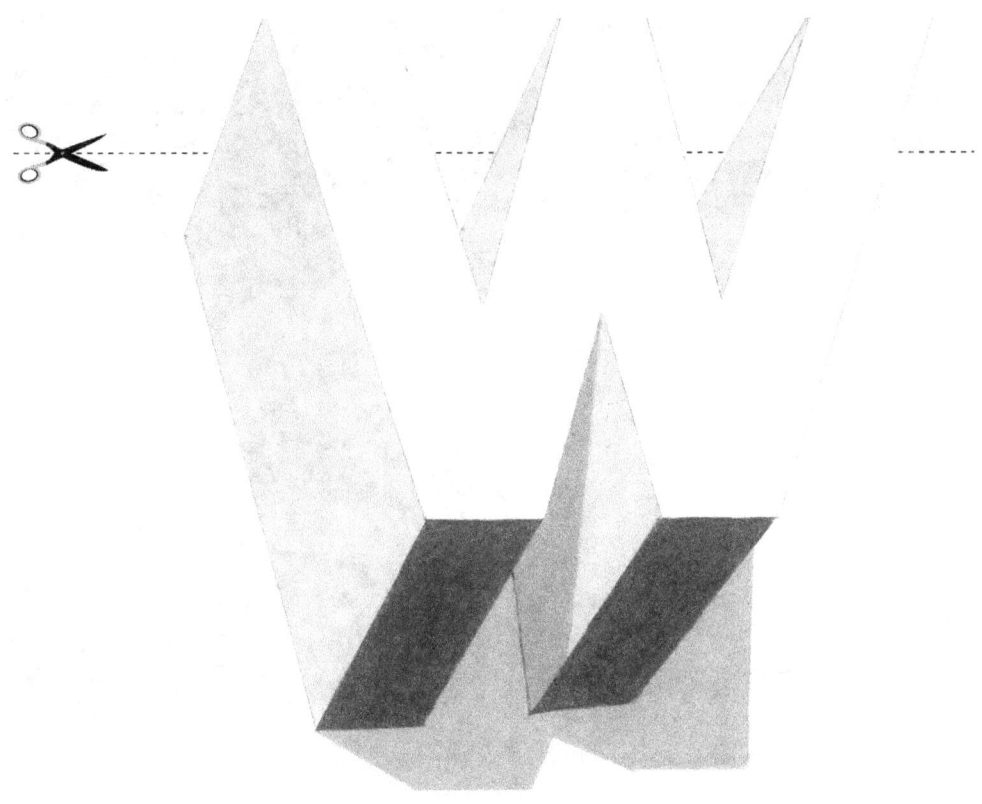

When you place the cut drawing on the table and look at it from a certain point, it will appear as if it were standing out from the paper.

Here you can see any final mistakes. Correct them or make a new drawing.

You are now enriched with more experience and knowledge of how to do better next time and on your future drawings.

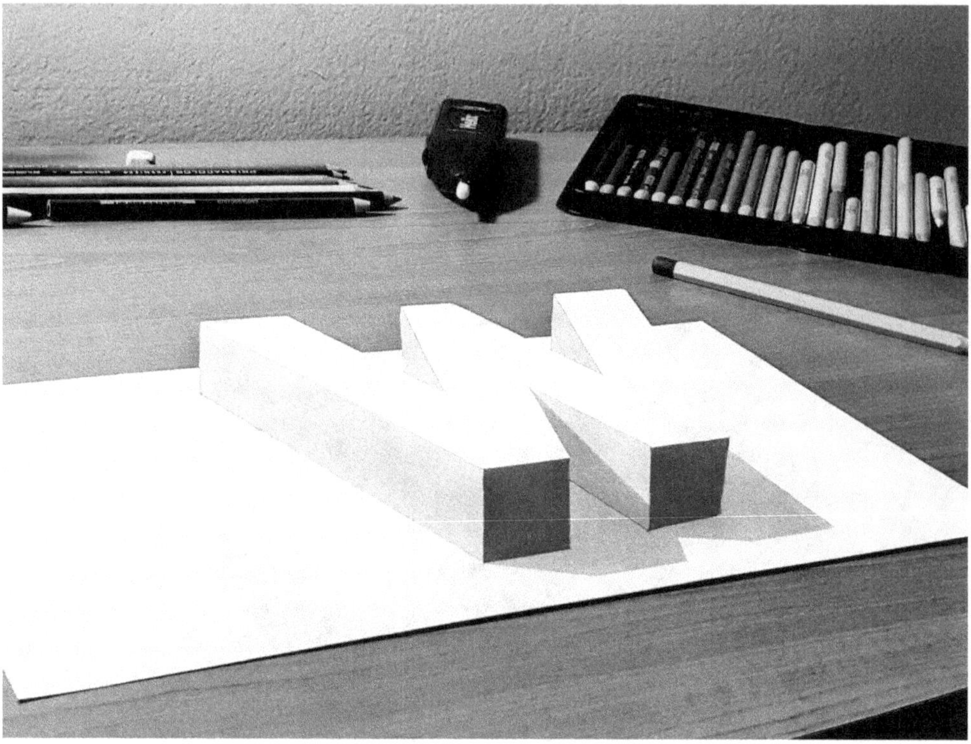

HOW TO DRAW A PORTRAIT
PART I SKETCHING

If you want to draw a portrait in a realistic style, you may want to be as lifelike as possible, and to catch the likeness of the person you want to draw. The proportions are the most important when creating the outlines for a realistic portrait. To achieve an accurate proportion you have to follow some commonly accepted guidelines for the placement of the facial features. The more measurements you make and the more drawing you do, the more you will acquire the successfulness of the final outlines and in creating the similarity of the person.

It is common that people draw portraits from photographs – as I do myself – because it is not easy to have someone sit there for you for many days; particularly, if you want to draw a celebrity, or someone you know, but you want to surprise them with your drawing. For drawing from photos, the best is to use the grid-method. In this book, we won't use either reference photos or the grid method, but we will draw a random face according to well-known proportions. But let's have a look at this method so you can use it for your future drawings when you want to draw from photos.

Many people consider the grid method as copying the picture and doing nothing new. Others - including me – see this method as a little help to create our outlines faster and with less erasing. You can use this method, or decide not to, it's up to you. The grid method has been used by most popular artists since the Middle Ages: Vincent Van Gogh, Albrecht Dürer and even Leonardo Da Vinci. Nobody disclaims their art because they used of this method. In the next picture, you can see Albrecht Dürer using the grid method with the model laying in front of him, looking at her through the grid and creating the outlines on his gridded paper.

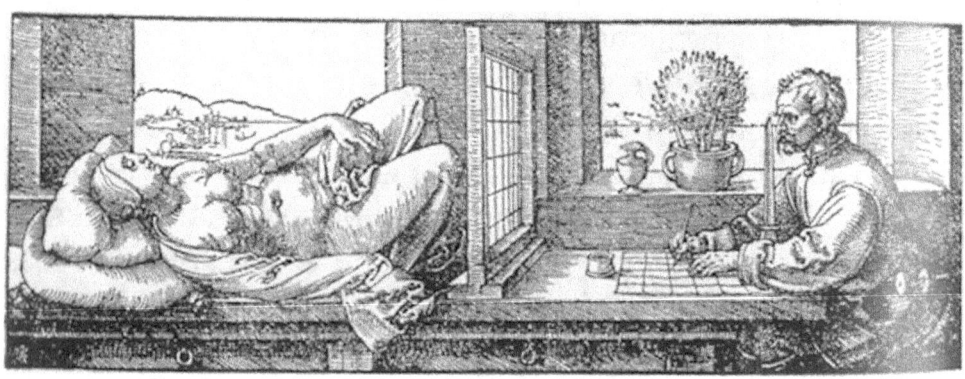

You *can* create a good sketch without using the grid method, but it would take you a lot of time and your paper won't be smooth anymore due to a lot of erasing. The grid-method helps you learn to draw freehand. As you decrease the number of the squares of your paper with time, and use only 1-2 squares, eventually, you will be able to sketch without using this method at all.

To use the grid method, draw a grid over your reference photo, and draw a grid over your blank sheet of paper. The more squares you draw, the easier it will be to create accurate outlines, but don't forget that you will have more to erase, which will damage the paper. You can label the rows and columns with numbers and letters, each box on both your reference photo and your paper. You can see in the next image the reference photo with the grid and labels in the squares I've created to show you how it works.

After using the grid method a few times, you won't have to label the squares because you will be able to sketch with more confidence. Press lightly when creating the grid and labeling the squares, using an HB, so that you can easily erase the numbers at the end. Don't use harder pencils, 2H or harder, because they are so hard that they would leave dents and they would be visible after applying graphite over it. Softer pencils than HB are just too dark for creating the main lines.

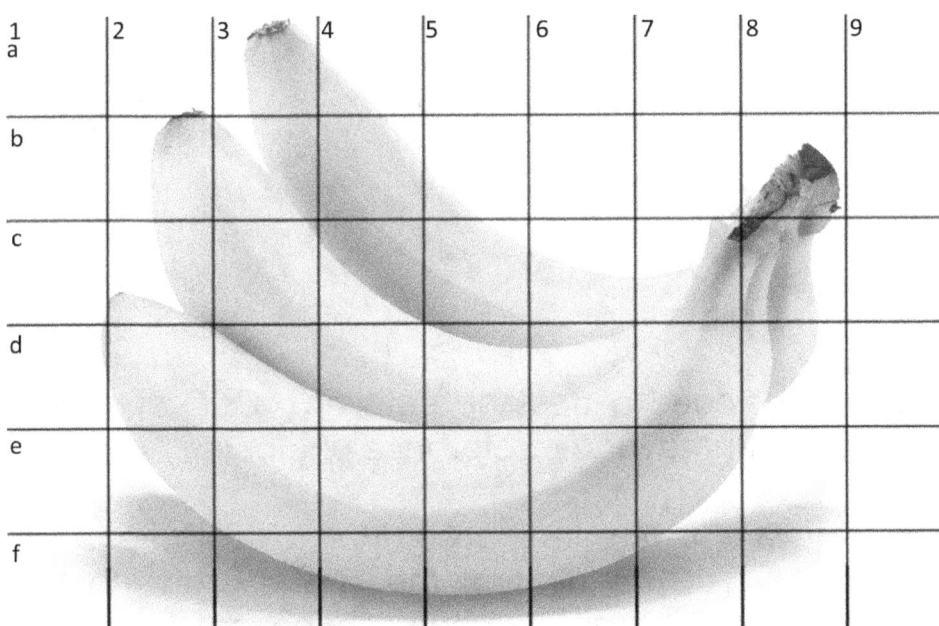

Now draw the same numbers of rows and columns on a blank sheet of paper. You can use the same size of the paper as the reference photo, bigger or smaller, the point is to create the same number of the squares.

Once you have your grids, copy the main lines from each square of the reference photo to the corresponding square on your own grid.

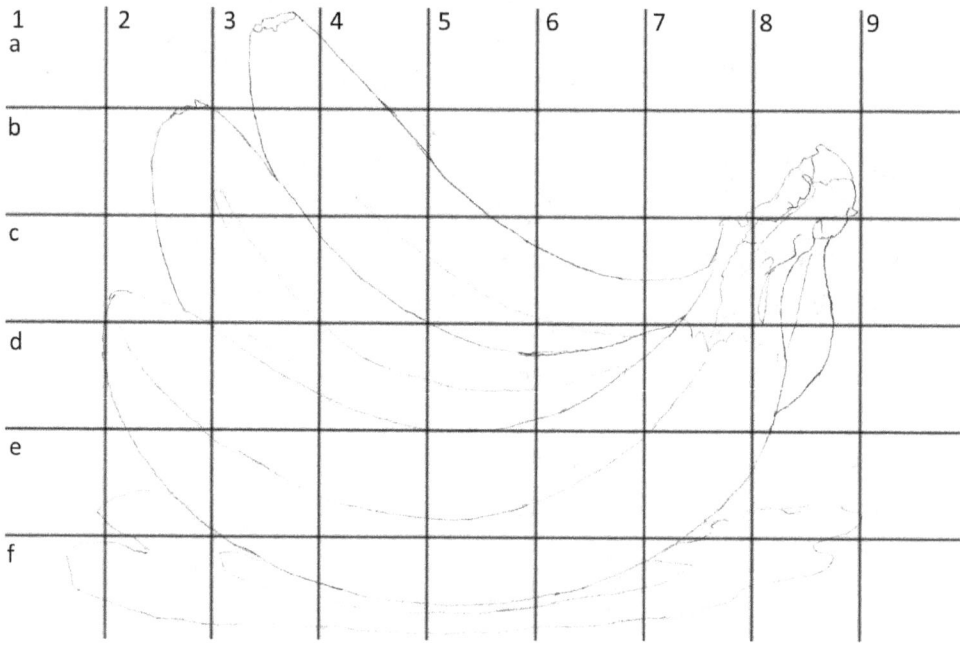

I have developed a desktop software, GriDraw, which creates the grid over the reference photos.

This software is created according to my needs and experience. The features of the GriDraw on the right side meet all the requirements of the artists when it comes to placing the grid over the reference photos even the labeling and diagonal lines. The created grid is movable so that it can be placed in the desired position over the reference photo.

The color, thickness, and opacity of the grid lines can be set to the artist's needs and desires. This software supports cropping, resizing, transparency, saturation, brightness, contrast, hue, color temperature, flipping, and rotating. It also has Save and Print features even without the placed grid. Therefore, GriDraw can be used solely as an image editor. With this software you can create the perfect grid within a couple of seconds.

You can get this software for yourself at
www.gridraw.net

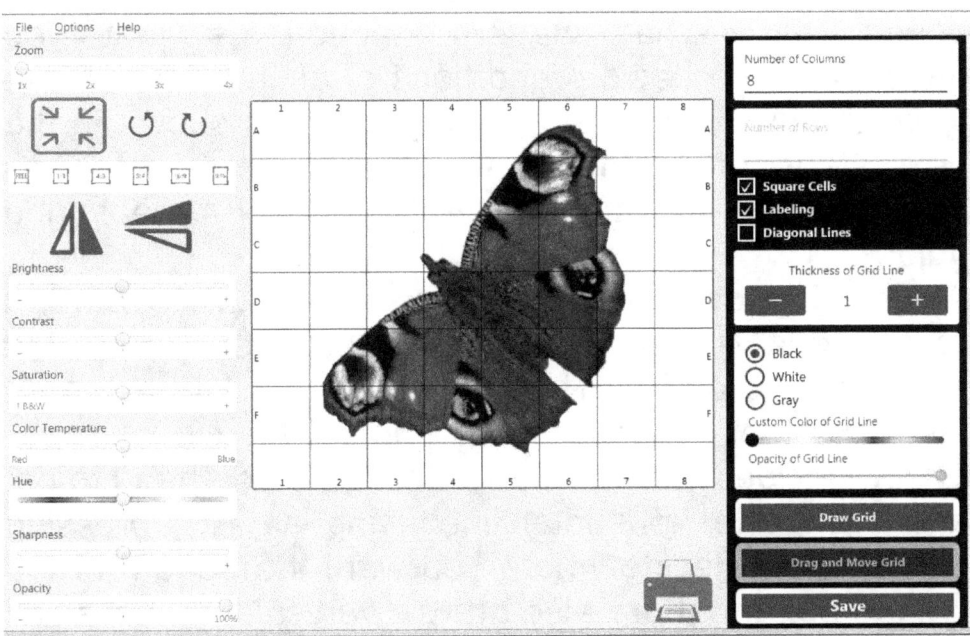

But the sketching is not the most important part of the drawing. You can have a good sketch and end up having a drawn portrait that looks nothing like the person you used a reference photo of. Also, you can have an inaccurate sketch (which often happens to me when sketching freehand) and make it right by adding certain tones, shadows and highlights in the right places. Think just of the make-up artists who make the face or nose look thinner, the lips or eyes bigger, etc. by creating the shadows and highlights!

So, let's draw our very own portrait from scratch!

Remember that proportion is relative. Each face is different. Some people, for example, have higher foreheads than others. They may have close-set eyes, narrower nostrils, thinner lips, smaller chins, protruding bones, etc. What matters, though, is that you understand the basic proportions of each face and use them to build your image. The guidelines shown in the next steps are general. I will give you some tips regarding how to draw a portrait by using a measuring guide.
At first, decide how big a face you want to draw. I recommend an A4 paper format because it is not too small yet not too big. The first thing to do is to establish the position of the head on the page
Firstly, decide where you want the top of the head to be, and draw one horizontal line using an HB, pressing lightly. Then, decide where you want the bottom of the face to be, and there also draw a vertical line. Let's call them A lines so that you can better understand which lines I mean when you look at the images.

The next step is to place the horizontal line exactly in the middle between the two A lines. This is the line B that you can see in the next image. On this line, we will draw the centers of the pupils in the following steps. The eyes are placed just about in the middle of the height of the head (height including the hair), so in this step we will establish the position of the eyes.

———————————————————— A

———————————————————— B

———————————————————— A

The next step is to determine the width of the face. It should be a bit wider than the length between the A and B lines, in the next image you can see the F line that I have placed digitally to show you the length I mean. So, the length between my A and B lines is about 4 inches (10 centimeters) so I have decided to make the width of the face 5 inches (12 centimeters). Of course, these measures differ from face to face, and you don't have to strictly stick to my measures, but to make it wider or narrower. A little difference doesn't matter.

Since we have determined the length and the width of the face, and have created the frame for our portrait, we can make the outline of the head. This is basically an oval shape. Here you have to decide whether you want to draw a male or a female portrait because females have finer contours and male have stronger jawbones and so on.

Firstly, focus on the upper half of the outline, between the upper A and B line. You can see in the next image how I have outlined it. This upper half is basically the round shape of the upper area and just following the C vertical lines in the lower area.

Now you can move to the lower part, which is a bit more complicated. Here you have to create the shape of the jaw. I have decided to make an oval-shaped female face. You can draw like this or create different shape, as in every step in these tutorials, it is also arbitrary. You don't have to do exactly the same thing.

When you start to contour the upper area of the lower part of the face, follow the C lines, and draw over them, next under the B line. Then draw the lines towards the face, and draw a certain width over the lower A line, which will represent the bottom of the chin.

Thoughtfully examine the next image before you start to outline.

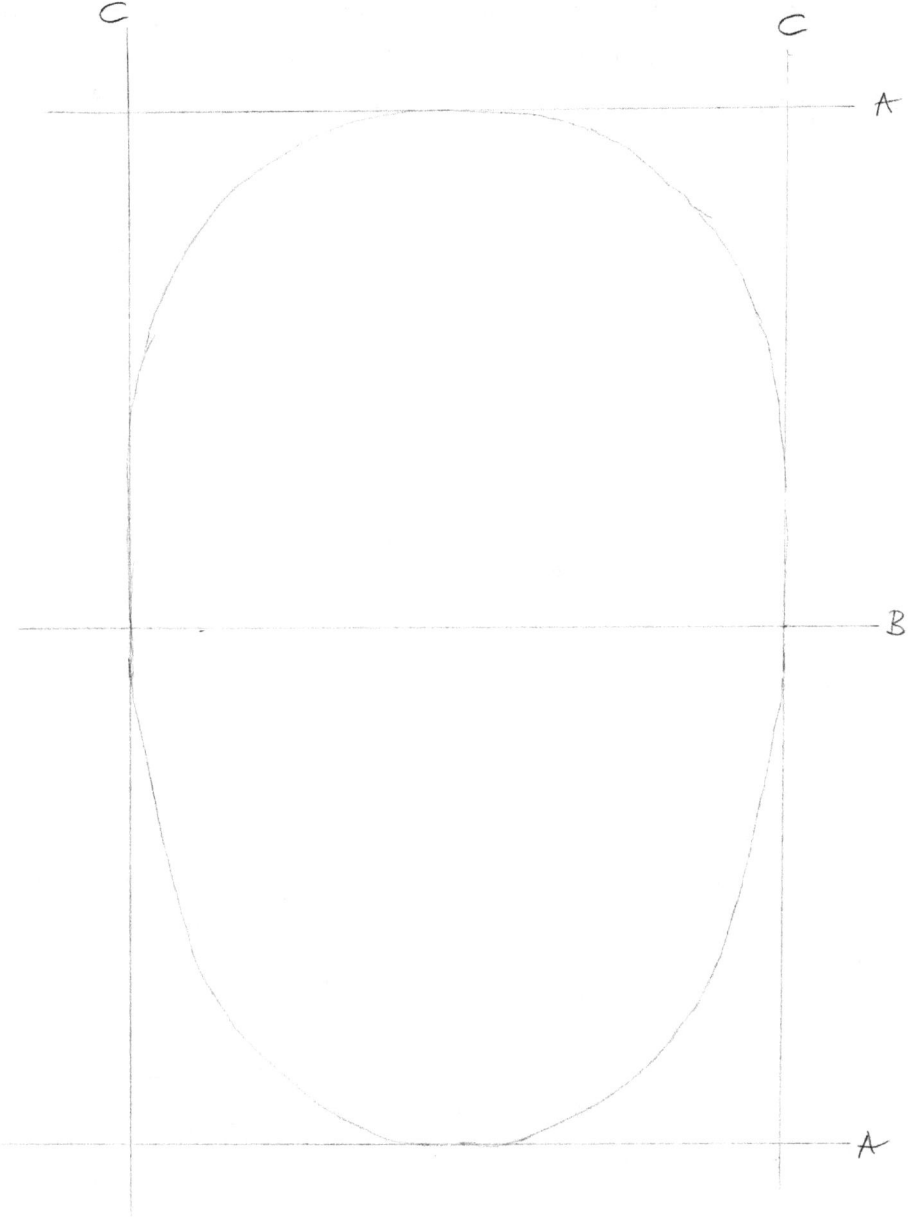

To be able to determine the position of the facial features, let's firstly determine the position of the hair. This is only the area of the skin where the hair grows and not the whole area that the hair will take. We need to determine the hairline between the forehead and head, and in the next step you will see why. In the next image you can see the area that I have reserved for the hair.

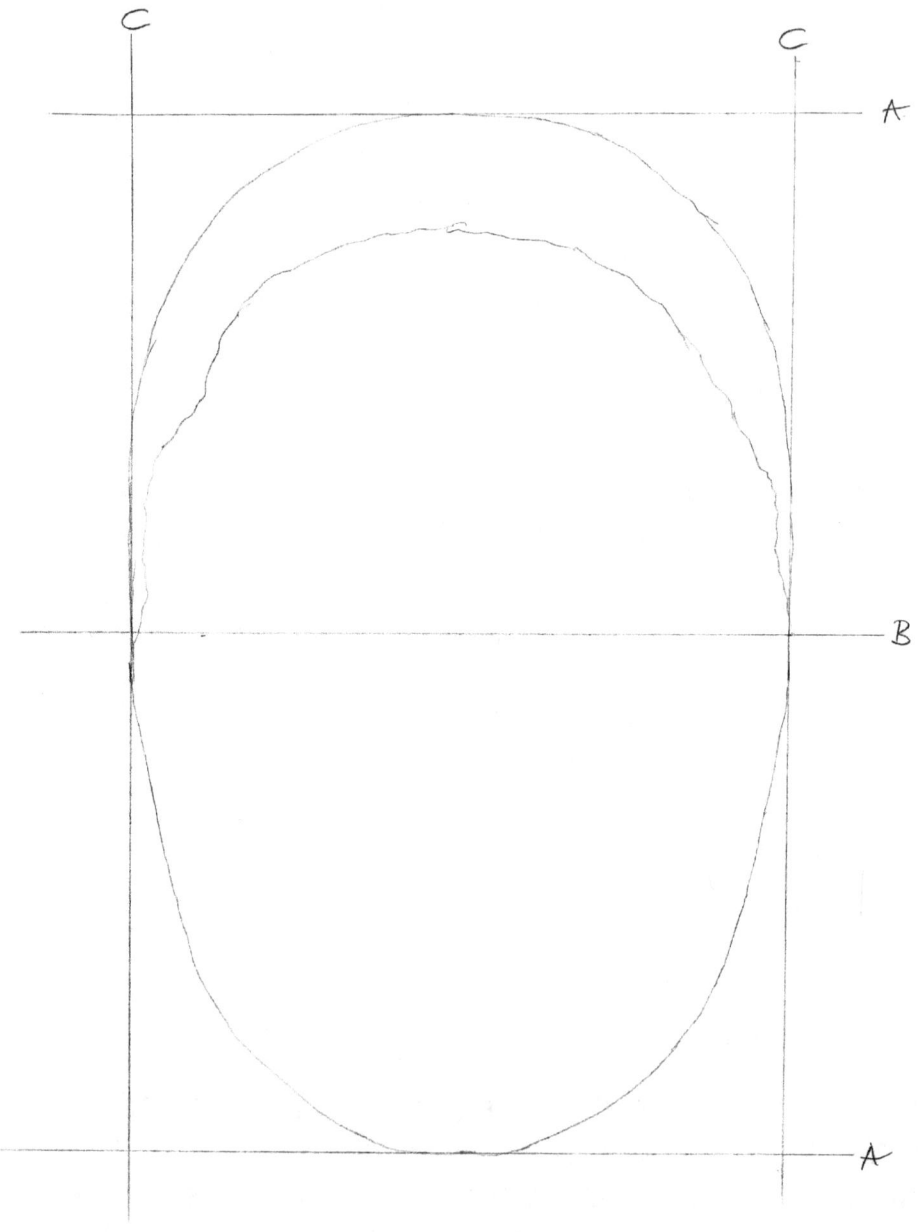

Now we are able to divide the face into three fairly equal parts.

I have drawn the dashed lines G so that you can see where to place these lines. We have to place four lines in order to create three areas. The first line (starting from the top) G1 is horizontally placed over the edge between the hair and the forehead.

Now you should measure from here to the bottom of the chin, and if this length is say 9 inches, then you will have to mark the next line (G2) 3 inches lower. This line determines the positions of the upper edge of the eyebrows. Now, the third line (G3) should be placed again 1/3 length lower. This line determines the position of the bottom of the nose. The fourth (G4) line is the same as the lower A line.

I have placed arrowed lines digitally in the next image, so that you can see these three equal areas and where to draw the G dashed lines.

If you have drawn all these guidelines, you can start to draw the ears and facial features.

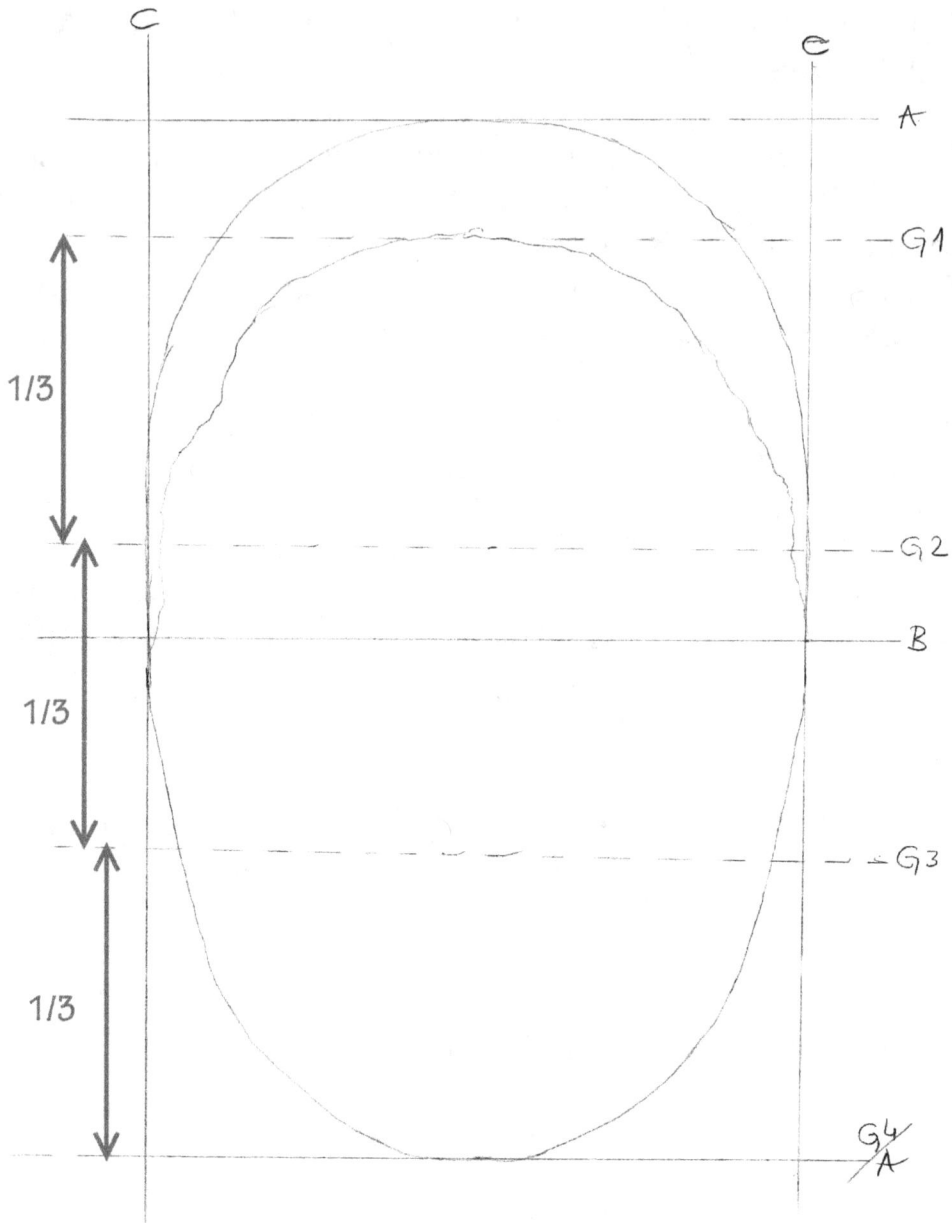

Let's start with the ears. The ears will equal the center third length of the previously divided area, from the G2 line to the G3. Here also it is arbitrary how far away from the head you draw the ears. The point is to make the upper area a bit further from the face, and a lower area closer to the face, and of course to keep the top and the bottom of the ears exactly over these G lines. The ears don't have to be symmetrical, so don't focus on this, but on the things that I have previously mentioned.

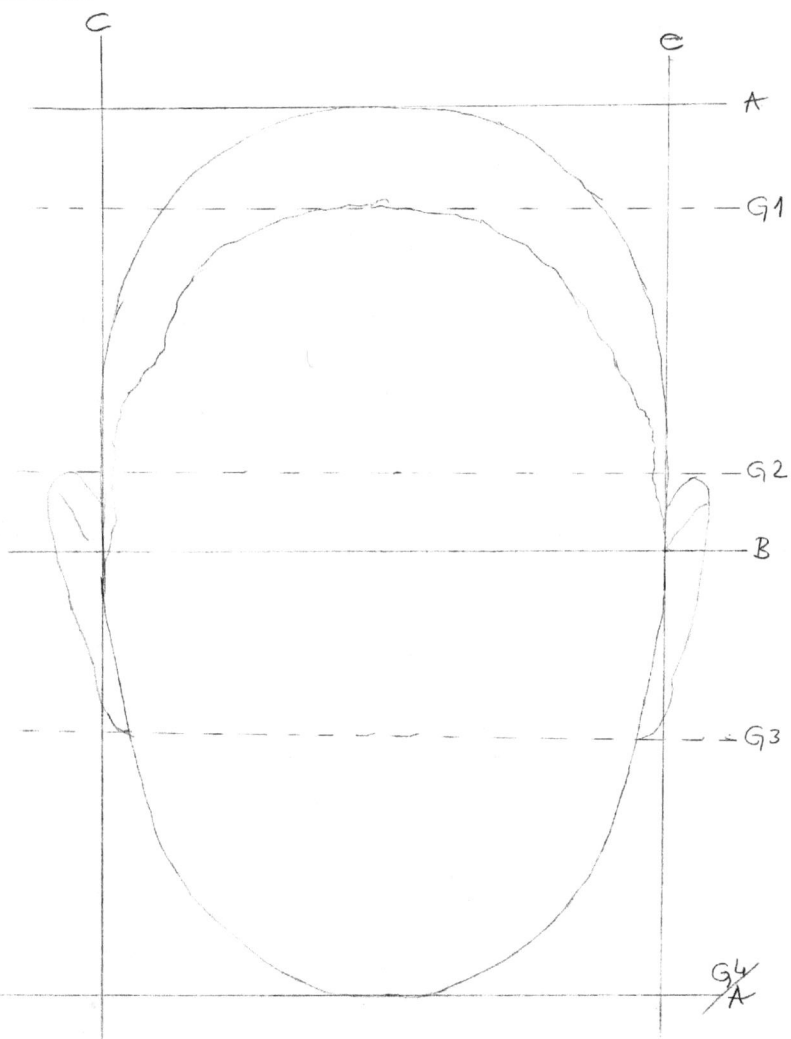

In order to draw the eyes, divide the width of the face, somewhere on the B line in 5 equal parts. Draw 4 vertical lines as you can see in the next image, so that you will have the areas that I have marked as H1, H2,

H3, H4 and H5. The area between the two eyes is always about an eye wide. As mentioned, the pupils will be placed on the B line, and now we have determined the position of the corners of the eyes, we can outline the eyes in the following step.

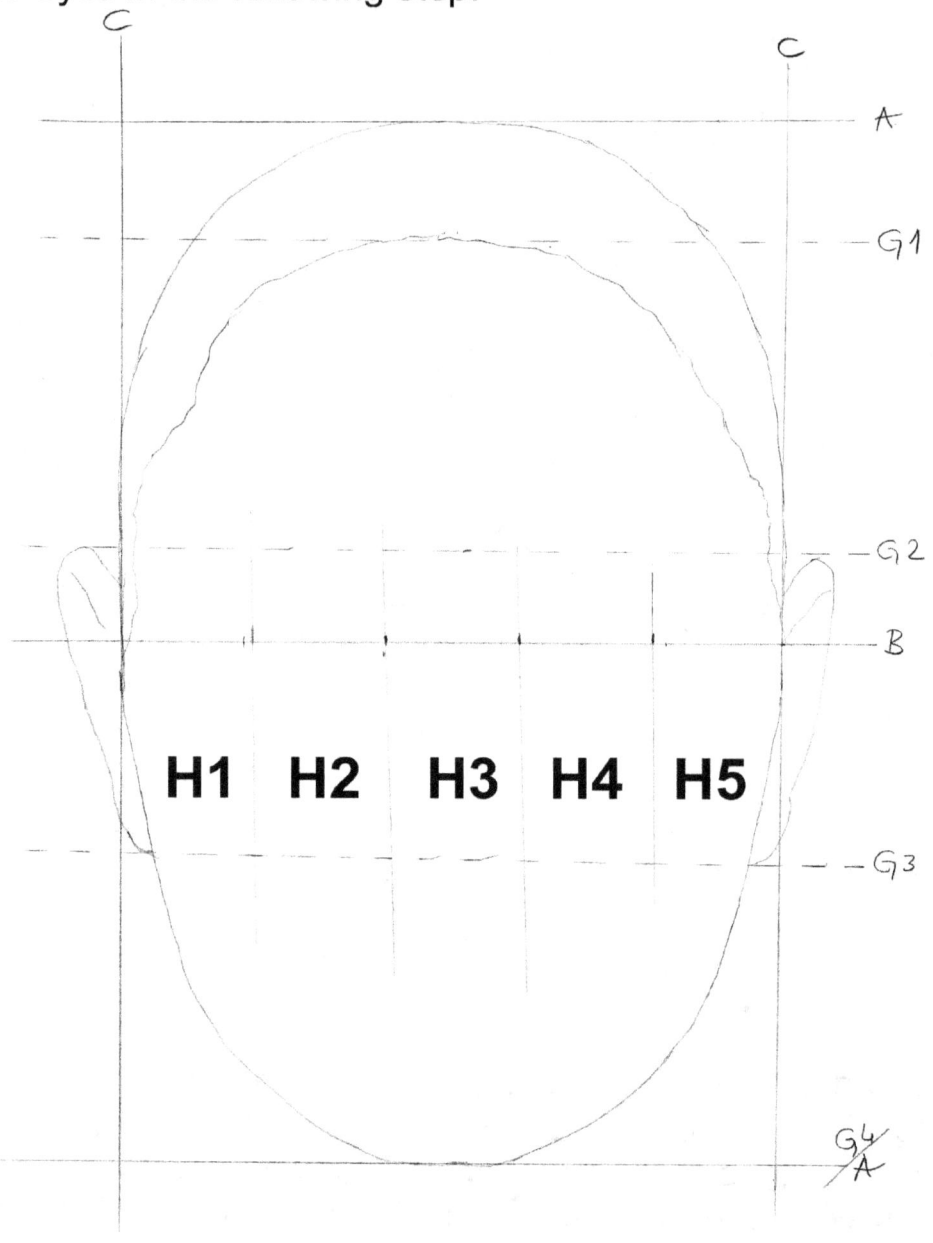

Before we start outlining the eyes, it is good to know a few rules in order to create a more proportional, realistic portrait. The pupils and irises are always circular in a front view. Under normal circumstances, the upper eyelid always covers the upper part of the iris, and the lower part of iris lays just over the edge of the lower eyelid. The untouched part of the paper, usually dot or tiny square, should be left which will represent the reflection of the light and make the eyes shine.

Start with an HB pencil to outline the shape of the eyes. This outline should not be too dark, so a B or darker pencils are not good for sketching, unless you press really lightly. Here we need just the basic shapes outlined.

Start with the pupils, exactly in the middle between the previously drawn vertical lines, over the B line. So, left eye should be drawn in H2 area, and the right eye in H4 area. Draw both pupils the same size. Then outline the irises and create the upper lid. I have placed a double line for the upper lid because of the thickness of the upper eyelid. Also, draw the creases above the upper eyelid following the same shape of the upper eyelid. After that, draw the lower eyelid, next under the irises and connect the lines of the eyelids in the corners somewhere on the B line. Examine the next image to see the placements before you start to sketch.

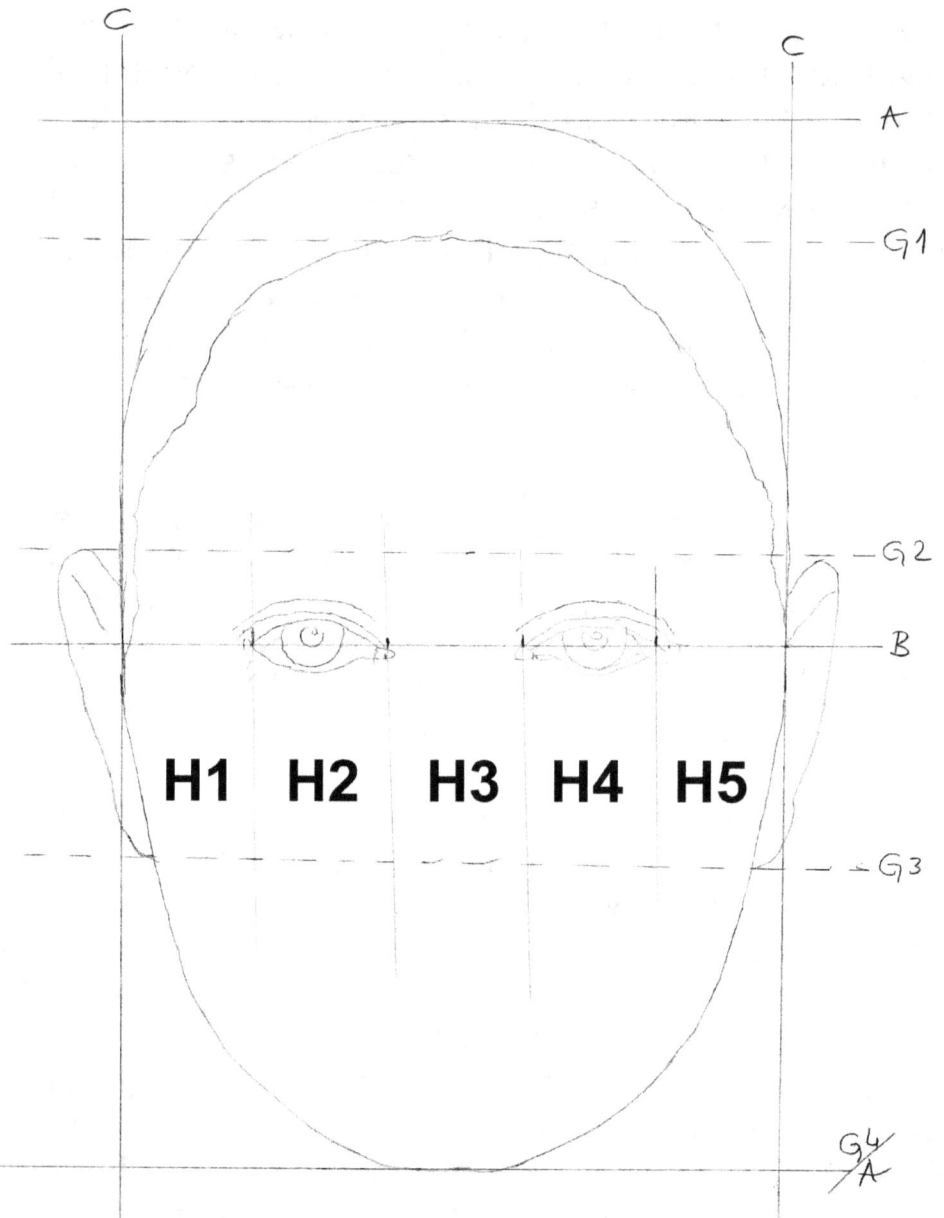

Now you can draw the eyebrows. This is also arbitrary. I have chosen to draw classic female eyebrows, which are slightly curved on closer to the sides of the face. Male eyebrows should be drawn straighter and a bit thicker. Here we have to determine the position of the eyebrows, but the raw lines should be deleted later because the eyebrows should be drawn with tiny lines and not outlined like this. These lines (for now) are just necessary for the orientation.

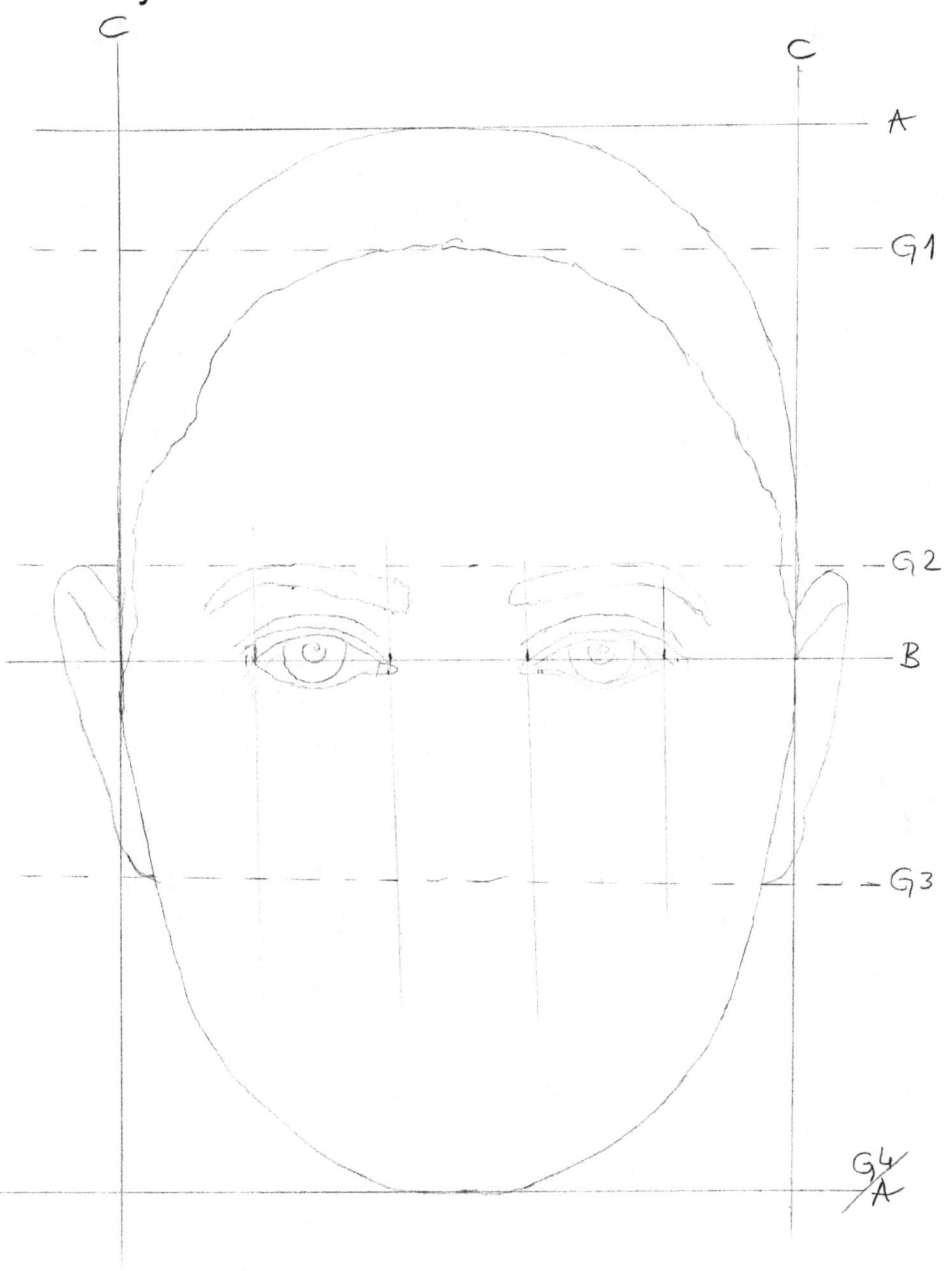

You can outline the nose, whose bottom should be placed over the G3 line, and the whole nose should be positioned within the H3 area (I haven't marked H areas here, check out in previous images). So the outer edges of commissures should be placed exactly under the inner corners of the eyes.

It is pretty difficult to outline the nose from the front view because there are just few outlines to be drawn, and the nose mostly should be shaded and not drawn.

Start by drawing the outlines that can be seen, namely the edges of the nostrils, the round outline in the middle of the bottom of the nose, two nostrils, and everything else that you may find necessary.

I also marked two dashed, vertical lines for the plane of the nose, and the cast shadow under the nose. The nose – as everything else – will cast the shadow with sharp edges in direct sunlight or under a lamp, but will cast the shadow with blurry edges in enviorments that are not strongly illuminated. If you also need these lines, draw them lightly as you want them to disappear under your shading at a later stage in the drawing process.

Examine the next image and outline the nose.

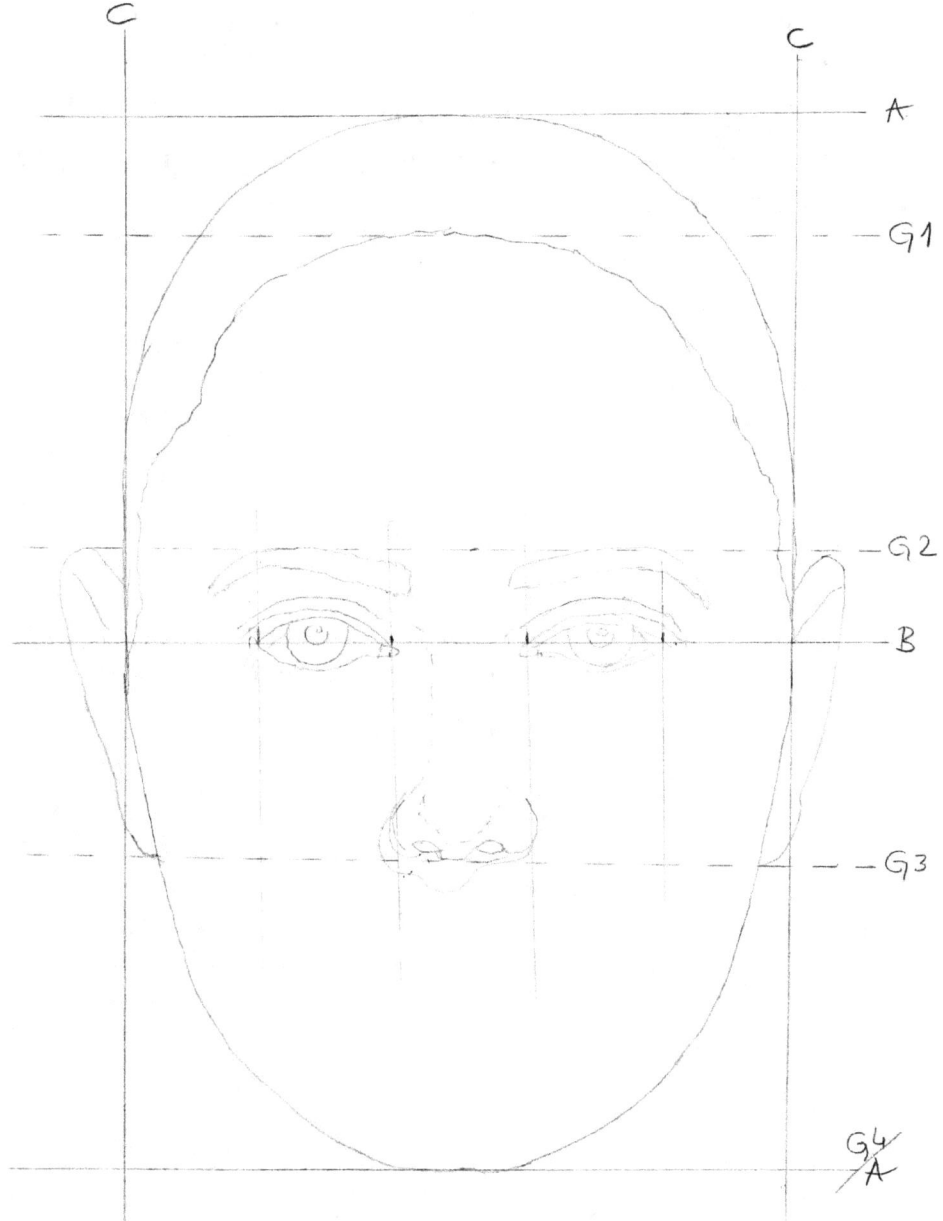

There's only outlining the mouth left. The corner of the mouth should be placed exactly under the pupils. You can see in the next image two vertical lines that I have drawn, and I have deleted all the guidelines since I don't need them anymore. I have drawn the female, fleshy lips, but you can draw them otherwise. If you draw a male, you can draw a bit thinner lips, but that's also not the rule. The upper lip is almost always a bit thinner than the lower lip, and don't forget about the cupid's bow over the upper lip.

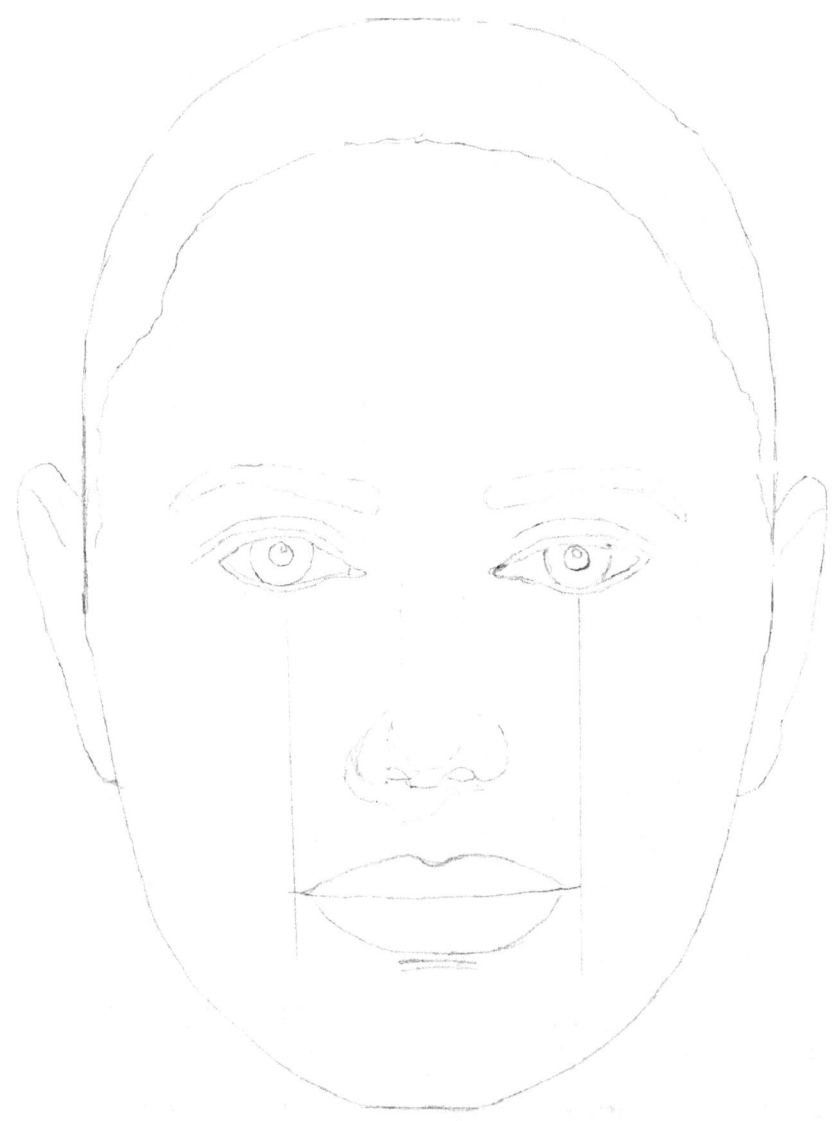

So, this is how my final sketch looks. I hope that you

also created a proportional sketch and now we can start to draw and shade the facial features. After that, we will shade the skin of the whole face and neck. As the final step, in the last part of this tutorial, we will draw hair.

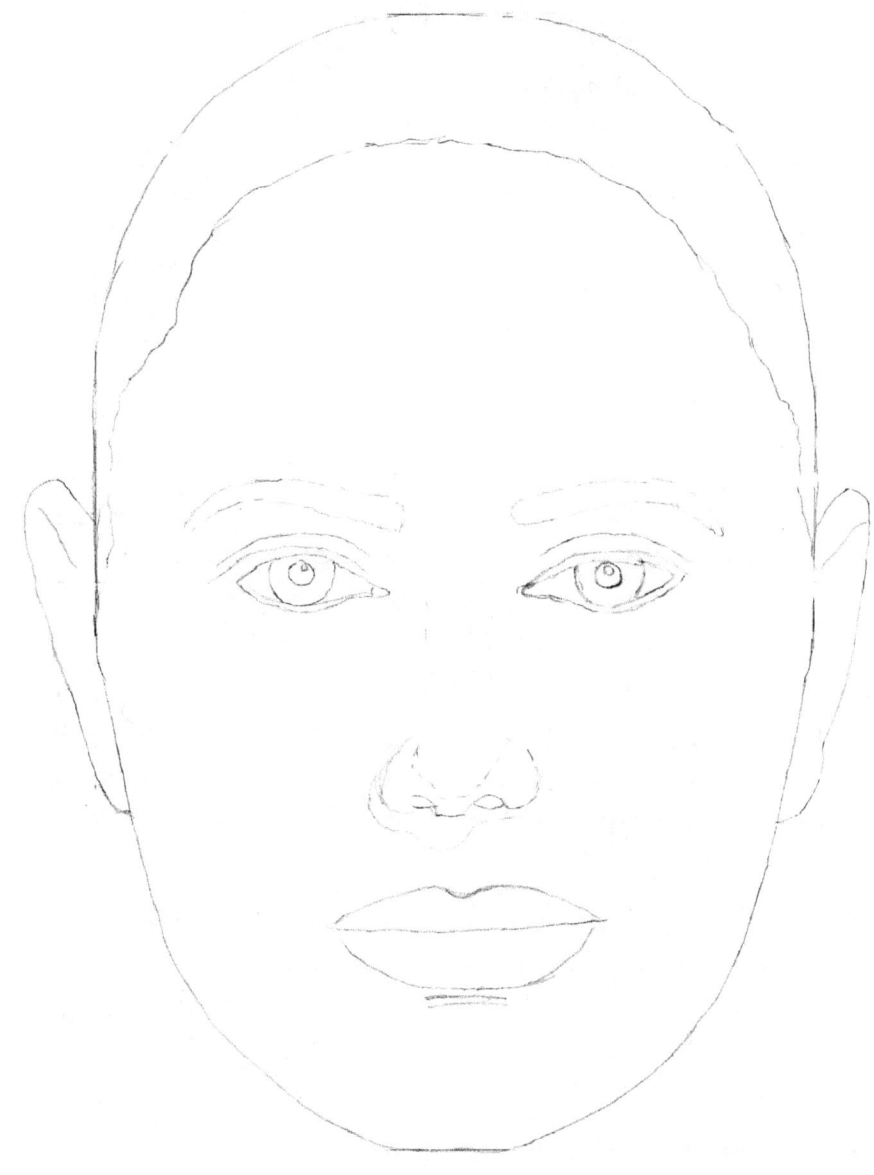

HOW TO DRAW AN EYE

You should begin to draw a portrait with the eyes as they are the most important.

You can draw the eyes one by one. I will give instructions for the left eye, and you can apply the same for the right eye, but flipped (except for the reflection of the lights, they should be on the same side).

Using one of the pencils from 4B to 9B, fill in the pupil. Don't use HB or softer as they won't produce absolute black color and the eye will appear unnatural. If you have drawn perfect circles, you can press hard, but if unsure, press lightly as you may want to erase something if you need to make corrections. This is why the initial sketch is important. You can go over this area again to achieve a darker tone and to fill in the tooth of the paper. Hopefully you have marked the tiny dots as a reflection of the light while outlining, so that you can now just draw around them. And leave them white.

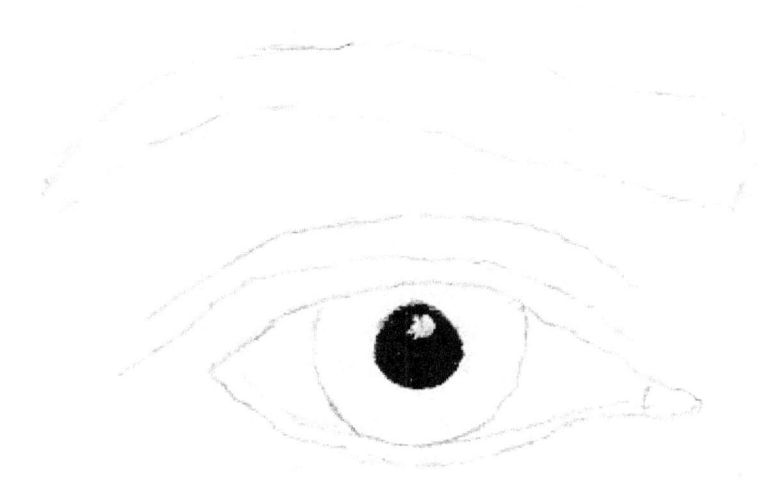

As a next step, outline the iris using a B or brighter pencil. If you draw a brown eye, like me, use a B or F pencil, but if you want to draw blue or green eyes, use HB or a harder pencil to outline the irises. This outer area of the iris is called a limbus, and its edges should be a bit blurry; from the outside because the edge between the eye-white and limbus is not really sharp, and the inner edge should be even more blurry because we will have to blend it with the main tone on the iris that we will do in the next step. Do this step carefully and press lightly until you achieve the desired tone. You can blend it with a blending stump if you find it too sharp. Next, press harder under the upper eyelid because it casts a shadow over the iris and limbus.

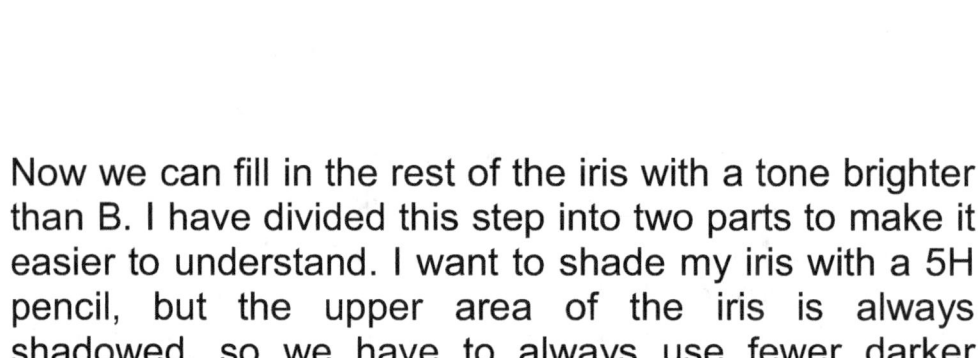

Now we can fill in the rest of the iris with a tone brighter than B. I have divided this step into two parts to make it easier to understand. I want to shade my iris with a 5H pencil, but the upper area of the iris is always shadowed, so we have to always use fewer darker nuances for this upper area. The shadow is even darker if the woman wears heavy make-up.

There can be even more reflections of the light over the whole eye, particularly if there are more light sources or bulbs. To show you how it looks, I have left untouched the rectangular shape of the upper-right area of the iris. The right eye has to have this light reflection in the same position, so if you flip the pictures of this tutorial when you draw the right eye, keep this in mind. I also wanted to create more light reflection because it has

made the eye even shinier, hence more lifelike.
Since the iris contains a variety of tones and flecks which radiate to the center of the pupil, draw the tiny lines starting next to the pupil and move outwards towards the limbus. In order to make the iris even more lifelike, press differently when drawing these lines to get the patterns of the iris. You can use a blending stump to blend this area, but if you have drawn your strokes next to each other and filled the paper totally there's no need for blending it.

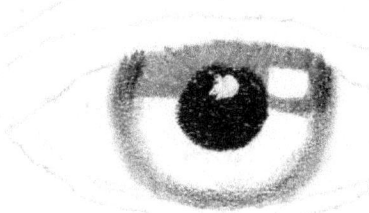

In the second stage of coloring the iris, fill in the rest of the whole lower area, also drawing the spokes going outward from the pupil. Overlap some of the spokes randomly to create thicker lines. As mentioned, the lines radiate from the pupil radially, so draw straight lines towards the limbus. I used a 2H for this.

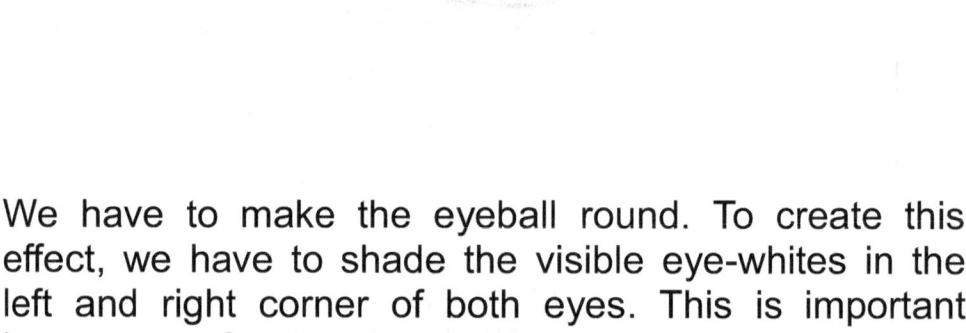

We have to make the eyeball round. To create this effect, we have to shade the visible eye-whites in the left and right corner of both eyes. This is important because so far the eyeball looks flat instead of round, and this shading will add depth to the whole eye.

You should leave the eye-white absolutely white only in the middle, next to the irises. To shade the corners of the ball, use a 4H or graphite powder from a 4H or brighter nuance. Never use darker nuances for these areas. When shading the eyeball, start in the corner and press harder. Then, as you go towards the center or iris, release the pressure and eventually don't shade at all. Also, create the cast shadow under the upper eyelid using a bit darker nuance, a HB for example, and blend it with a blending stump.

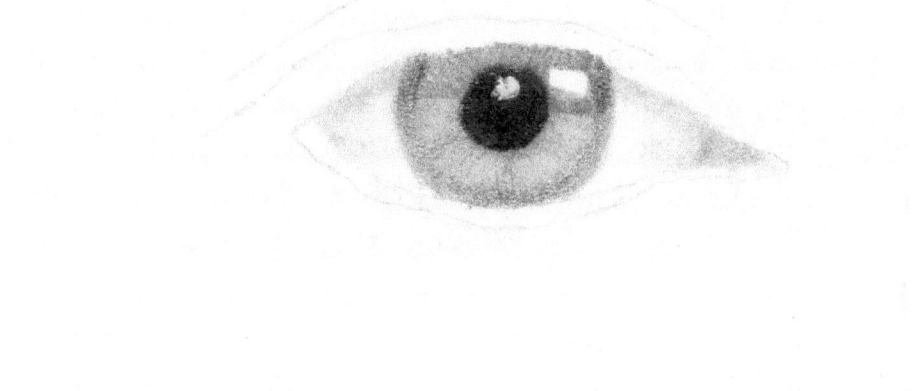

Darken the creases using a F or H pencil. Also, create a bit of a shade over the lower eyelid, under the root of the eyelashes using a blending stump.

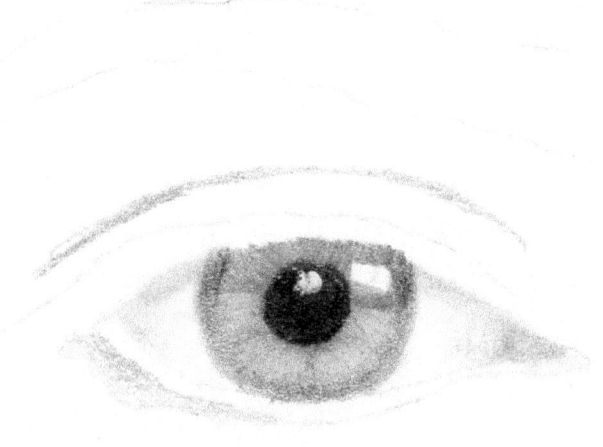

You can start to shade the skin around the eyes. Let's do it area by area to make it easier. As already mentioned, I use to put the cut piece of paper over the area that I don't want to shade. This is what I have done here, I have placed the paper over the area under the crease, and I have shaded the area above the crease. Pressing harder next to the crease, and releasing the pressure as I shaded towards the eyebrow. This gradual transition is important here to give the eyelid its shape. You can do it with a tissue or cotton pad. The blending stump is not that good here because you have to shade a larger surface which has to be smooth.

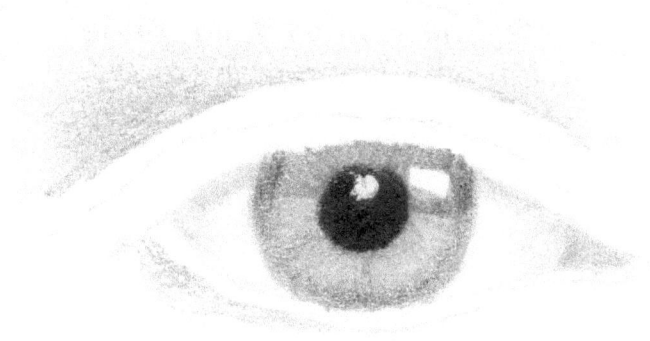

Do the same in the area between the crease and the eye, but leave the skin in the middle untouched. This will give the round shape to the upper eyelid. So, shade only in the corners and release the pressure as you shade towards the highlights.

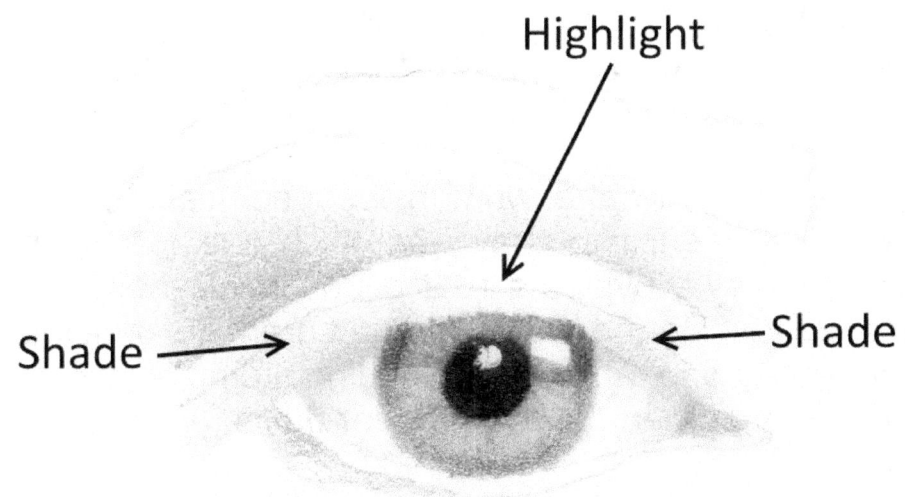

Do the same under the eye, shade the lower eyelid the same way: press stronger under the root of the eyelashes and lighter as you shade downwards.

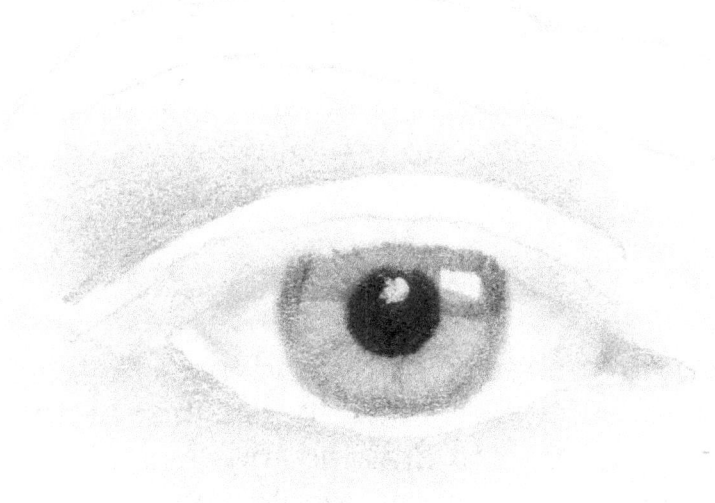

Leave the upper edge of the lower eyelid, above the root of the eyelashes untouched. This way you can establish the thickness of the skin.

I wanted to draw the woman wearing make-up, so I used a 4B pencil to draw the thick line for eyeliner above the eye, over the root of the eyelashes. If you don't want to do the same thing, use an HB pencil and draw a tinier line, and use a blending stump for the area in the inner corners, above the tear duct.

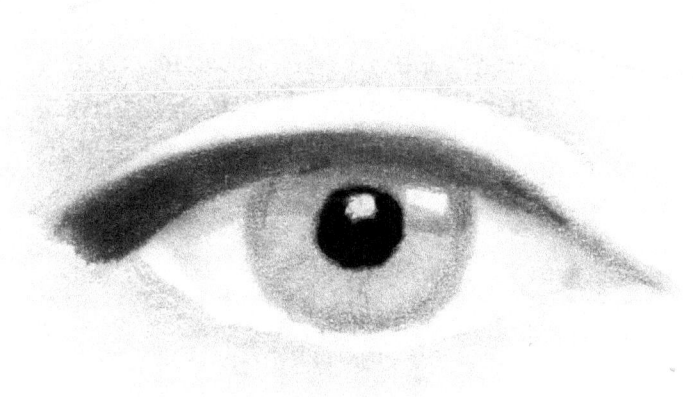

Since we have shaded all around the eye, we can draw the eyelashes. It is better to do this at the end of shading, compared to drawing the eyelashes first, and then shading because you would smear the eyelashes and they wouldn't appear clean.

Eyelashes should be drawn using curved lines, not straight lines.

Use an HB or darker pencil for the eyelashes. I used a 4B because I wanted to add the effect of mascara. Draw longer eyelashes starting at the outer corner of the eye, and make them smaller and smaller as you go towards the tear duct.

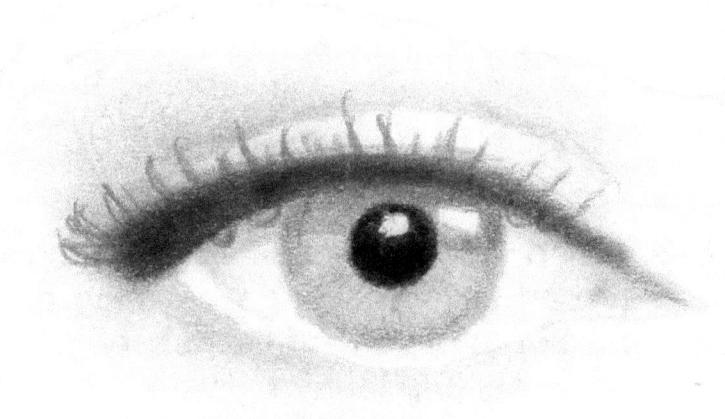

The same applies for the eyelashes on the lower eyelid, but draw those shorter and a bit brighter. Some of their ends can stick together and try to draw their length randomly.

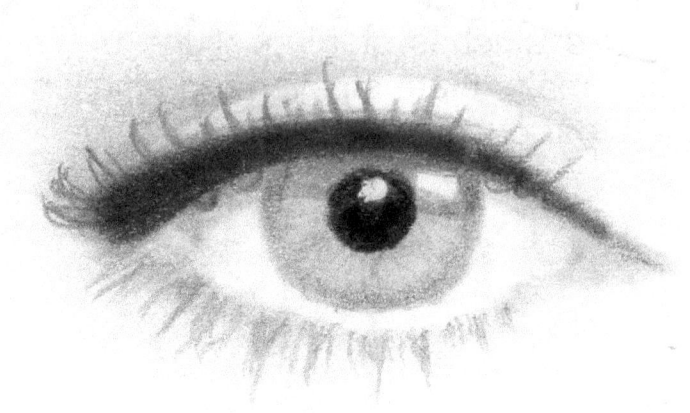

If you are satisfied with your result, you can move to the eyebrow. You can always change anything during the drawing process or at the end, if necessary.

To create the eyebrow, I have divided this into two stages. The first stage is to shade the whole area that you have supposed to be the eyebrow. This is good firstly because this will lessen the contrast between the hairs and the skin, which will make it look more lifelike, and the second because the hairs of the eyebrows cast some shadow over the skin, so it would look really unnatural to just draw the hairs without shading the area. I used blending stump for this. Examine the next image to note the mentioned things before you start to apply it to your drawing.

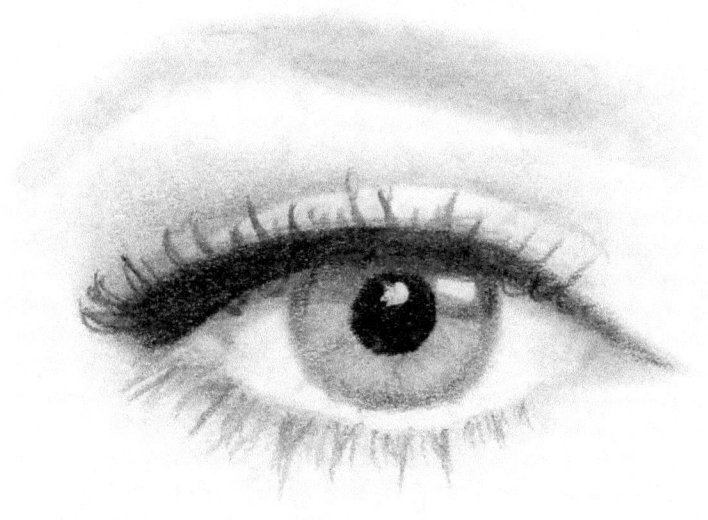

Now we can start to draw the hairs in the direction of the hair's growth.

I used HB for the whole area and pressed harder above the sclera on the right side of the iris. This area is under the bone and the skin itself is shadowed, so the hairs will be darker too. The opposite applies for the hairs over the highlighted skin, these hairs should be drawn with less pressure.

If you draw male portrait, you shouldn't draw the finely shaped eyebrows as women have, and as I have drawn, but to add the hairs randomly around the eyebrows. Before you start to draw, you can examine the photos of people, or the people around you in order to make your portrait more realistic.

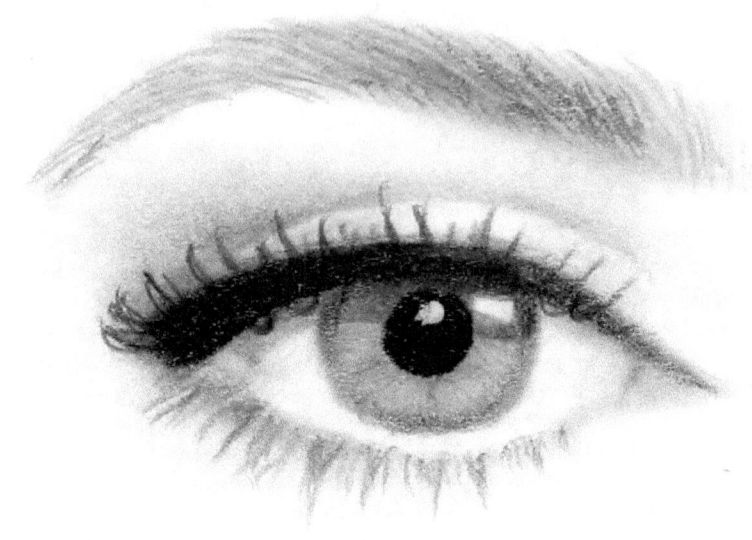

Now you can draw the right eye, using the same tutorial.

To draw the right eye, just flip the images or look at them in the mirror if you find these tricks helpful. The point is to avoid making the eyes symmetric because they would look fake. The right and left sides of the face are never symmetric in real life, so keep it in mind when drawing portraits.
In the next image you can see both eyes that I have drawn.
You can draw your next portrait by drawing both eyes at the same time to try out different approaches and to see which one you enjoy more, and which one brings you more success.

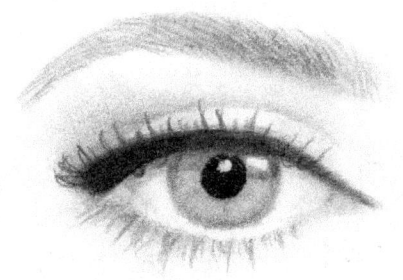 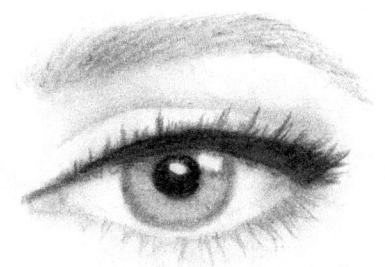

HOW TO DRAW A NOSE

If you have outlined the nostrils and the sides of the rims, you can now draw and shade the nose. The nose basically consists of shades and not lines.
At first, fill the nostrils with 4B or darker.

It is difficult to draw the nose observed from the front view because there are no lines to be drawn, but you have to play with shading the tones of the nose to create its form.

Since you have drawn the nostrils, start with shading the whole bottom of the nose. You should also cut a piece of paper and put it all around to get the powder only over the nose. Here press harder on the edge and release the pressure as you shade towards the top of the nose. You can even use a blending stump or a cotton swab for this, and if you get some powder around, you can erase it.

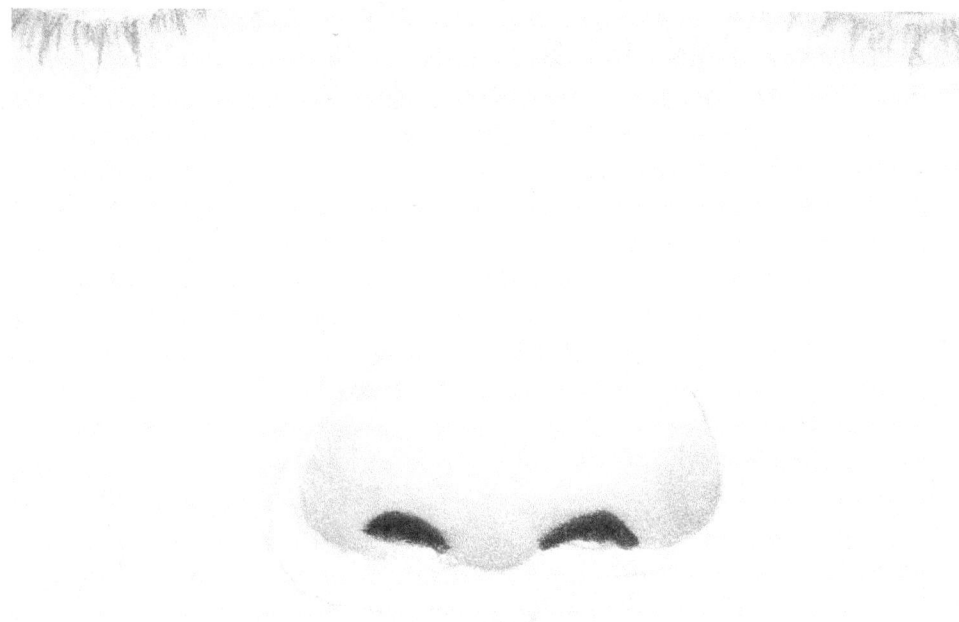

The next step is much more delicate and crucial, so before you apply the graphite powder on your drawing, practice the motions with your hand and a tissue or cotton pad on a separate piece of paper.

Here you have to shade both sides of the nose and create the gradient transition between the shade and the surrounding areas. The bridge should stay untouched because it is always highlighted.

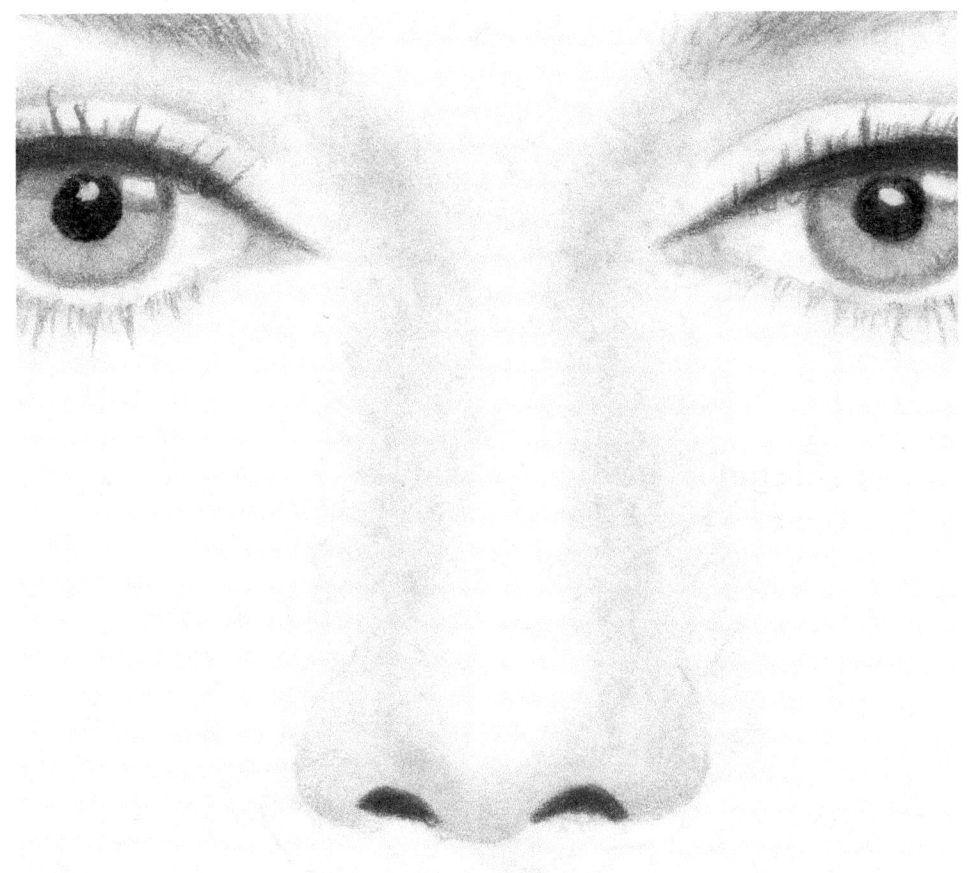

You can erase the reflected light on the outer sides of both rims, and on the top of the nose as shown in the next image. You can draw a cast shadow using a HB, drawing the area evenly and blending it with a blending stump.

The cast shadow will make the nose pop up off of the page. If the light source is strong, as in the case of direct sunlight, the edges of the cast shadow should be sharp, and if the light source is weak, the edges of the cast shadow should be blurry.

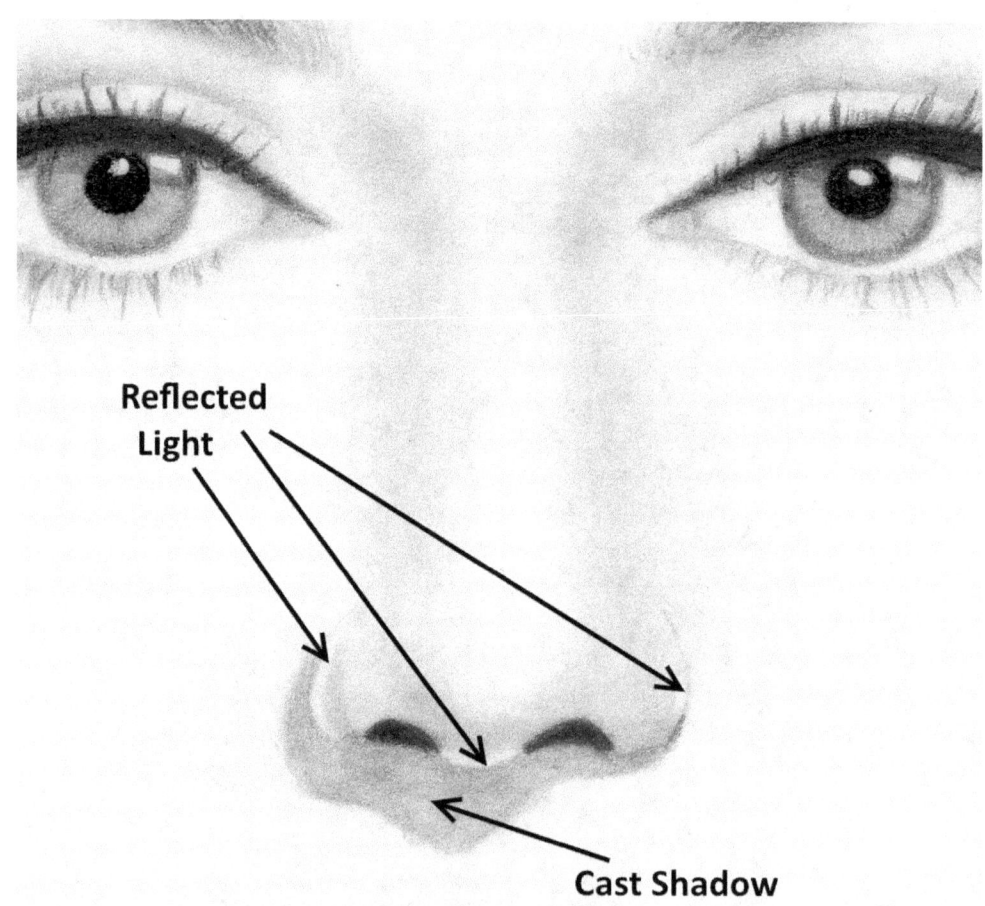

HOW TO DRAW LIPS

Basically, drawing the lips and making them round will contain three steps of shading, whether with pencil or with graphite powder, but I recommend shading with graphite powder first, and later we will add the details.

So, let's go through these three steps before we make the details and cast a shadow.

Firstly, make sure to erase the initial sketch and to make it hardly visible, particularly over the cupid's bow.
As a general rule, the lower area of the upper lip is darker because it usually gets less light. The upper area of the upper lip is almost as bright as the skin above it, unless a woman is wearing lipstick.

So, now we can shade the upper lip. As mentioned, cut the piece of paper to cover the lower lip and to get stronger shading over the lower area of the upper lip. Here you have to create a flawless gradation, so release the pressure with your tissue or cotton pad as you shade upwards. You can see in the next image how I have created the upper lip only with shading.

The lower lip is usually brighter and fleshier, and it gets more light.

You can cover the upper lip and shade the upper area of the lower lip the same way. It also has to have gradient transition. Examine the previous and the next image to see the difference after the added shade.

You have to shade the lower area of the lower lip the same way. Also, cut the piece of paper in the shape of the lower outline in order to cover the skin around the lower lip. I want the woman to be wearing a bit of lipstick, so I have shaded it harder, but if you want to draw the lips without lipstick, press lightly. This same technique and instructions apply for any tone of the lips. Press harder over both sides of the lower lip and the bottom, and leave it untouched in the middle (approximately the middle third of the width of the lower lip).

Create some vertical lip wrinkles using a HB pencil. Draw them randomly because it will create a natural look. Press harder when you create these wrinkles in the shadowed areas (or use a B pencil), and press lightly when you draw them over the highlighted areas. The upper area of the upper lip should still stay untouched because it hardly has any wrinkles, and those are highlighted so that they can't even be seen.

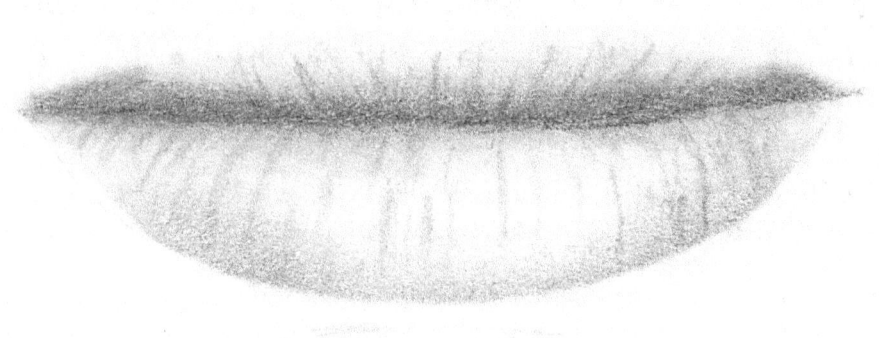

Since I want to draw a woman wearing lipstick, I have filled the upper lip completely with a blending stump. If you find this area too dark, you can always erase it at the end of the drawing when you will see how the lips appear as a final product.

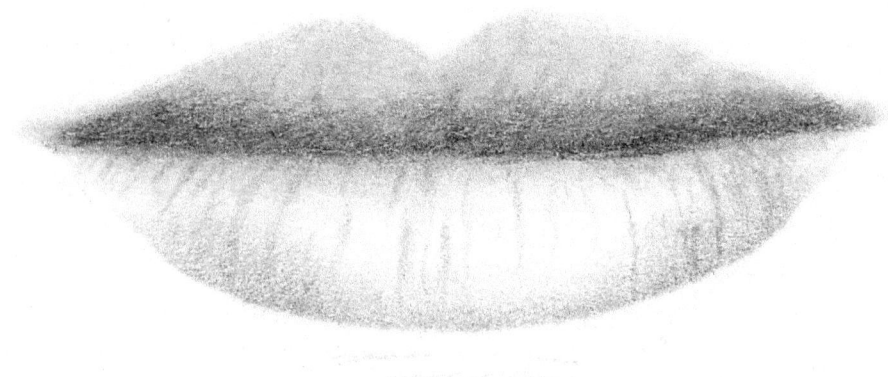

Using a blending stump, smooth out the wrinkles on both lips. Add more shade to both sides of the lower lip using 2B and blend it with a blending stump.

Add some highlights over the highlight on the lower lip among the wrinkles by erasing the powder if you have applied any over this area.

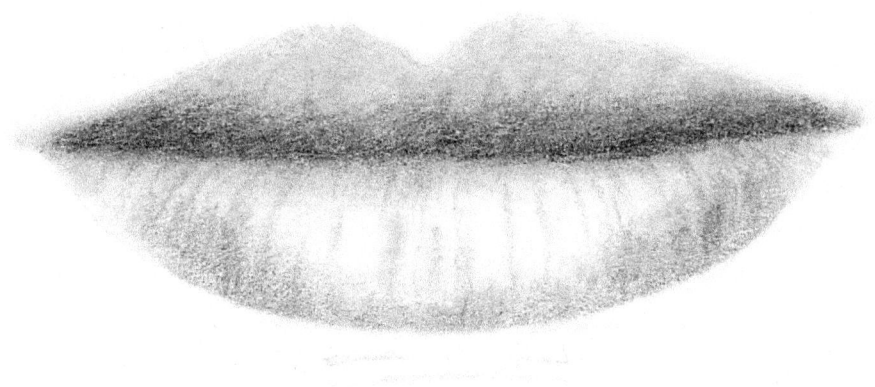

You can add the cast shadow which will make the lower lip pop up off the paper and give it an even rounder shape. Cover the lips with a piece of paper and shade starting next under the lower lip, releasing the pressure as you shade downwards.

There should be much more detail for intermediate and professional artists, but for the beginner, this much is just enough.

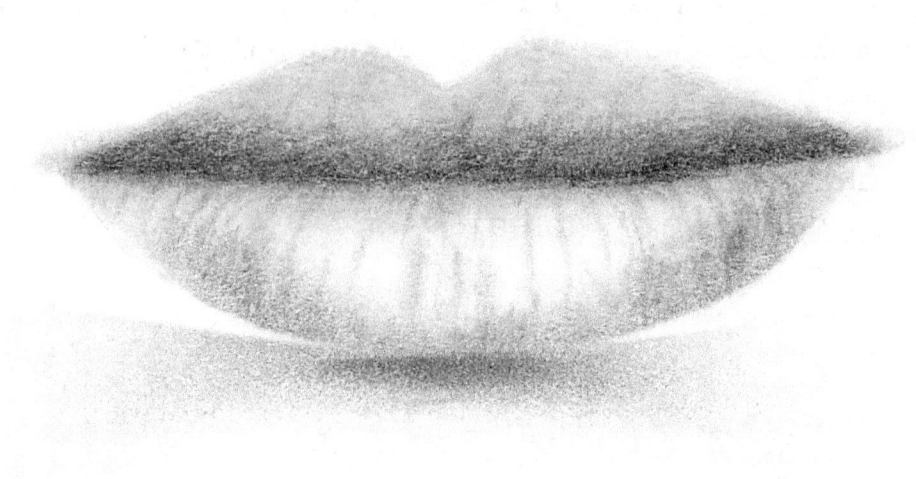

HOW TO DRAW PORTRAIT PART 2 SHADING THE SKIN OF THE FACE

When shading the larger areas of the skin, it is important to make an even, smooth texture, which can be achieved – in my opinion - only by applying graphite powder with tissue or cotton pads. You can use a 5H and draw it with strokes, but the areas between the ends of the lines will remain visible, as shown in my example in the next image.

You can use a blending stump for the skin, but the problem will be the same. The area won't be even and smooth. Even the experienced hand can't apply the graphite evenly over the larger area.

When you apply graphite powder with tissue or cotton pads, using small circular motions, and pressing lightly, you will create the perfect texture for the skin.

Make sure that you keep your piece of drawing paper clean all the time because if you touch the paper, particularly with your fingers, it will be visible after applying graphite powder. As you may know, a similar method is used by crime investigators to find fingerprints. So, no matter how clear your fingers are, they will always leave a print which will be visible after shading with powder. Always hold your hand on a tissue or a blank piece of paper, and use a large brush for cleaning the drawing paper, and eliminating the powder and other dirt.

For the previous image and sample I used graphite powder made of the 2B progresso, but for the pale skin we have to make the powder from a 5H or even brighter pencil.

But how do you choose the right tone for the skin? And how can you do it when you want to draw from your reference photos? There are many methods to determine the right skin tones.

The first: you can draw the swatches with your pencils, and compare their values to the value of the skin on the reference photo, that you have converted to black and white.

Second: to print your black-and-white reference photo, and to print the Skin Tone Value Viewer (the next image). Cut out the tiny holes from the Skin Tone Value Viewer and place it over your reference photo. Compare the tone of the reference photo (which you can see through the tiny hole) to the color of the Skin Tone Value Viewer where the hole is found, and use the pencil displayed there.

| 9B |
| B |
| HB |
| F |
| H |
| 5H |
| 9H |

Third: Use the eyedropper to see which value of the grey tone you have to use.

I have developed the special software, Penpick for this purpose. This software suggests which graphite or colored pencils you should use when you pick the color from your reference photos. This software is a huge help, and many artists, whether beginners or experienced, whether colored pencil or graphite artists, find this software and mobile app version of it very useful. The desktop version even shows the accuracy of the suggestions in percentage, so the closer to 100% the accuracy is, the better the match the suggested pencil is.

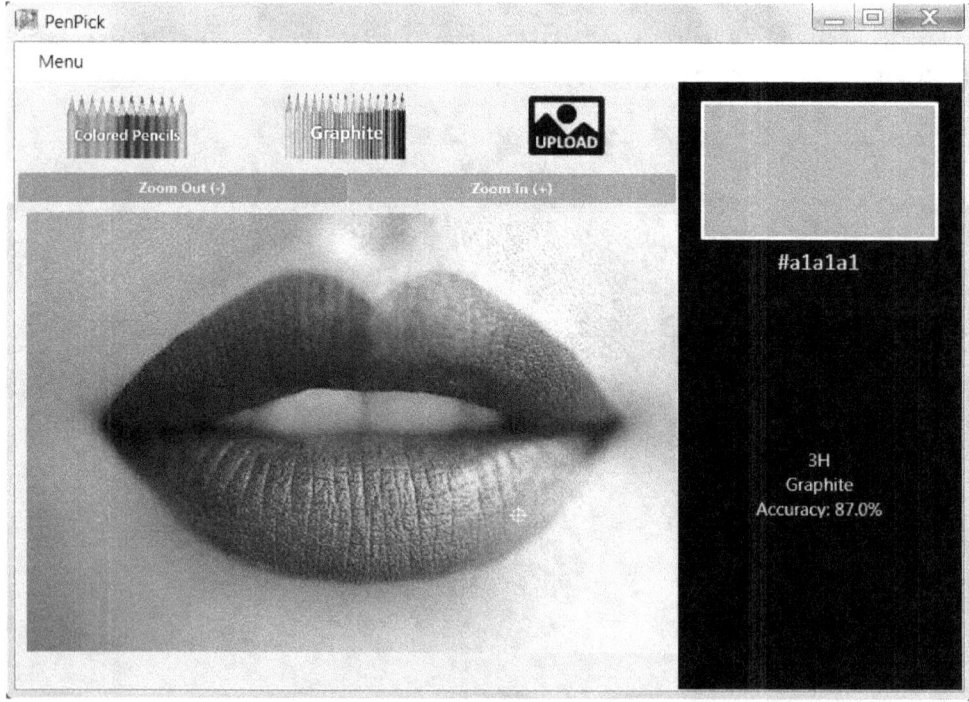

You can get it for yourself at **www.pen-pick.com**

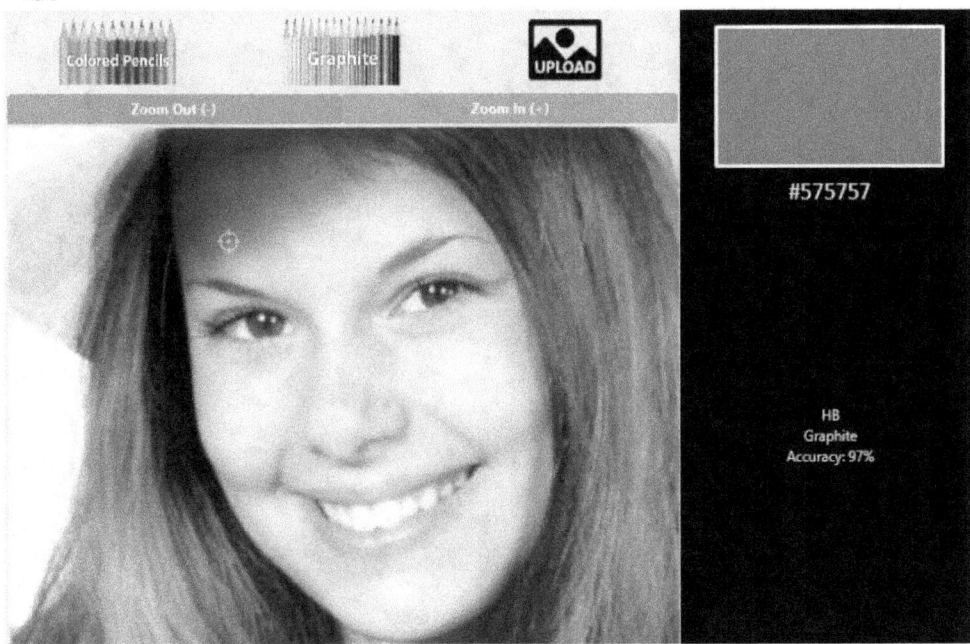

When shading the whole face, we have to give the head a round shape, otherwise it will look flat and cartoonish.

Cut a piece of paper and place it over the surrounding area as shown in the next image. Place it a bit further from the edge to leave the area for reflected light, but you can also erase it later on.

Pick up the graphite powder and apply it using circular motions. Press harder next to the edges of the right and left sides of the face.

Drawing for Beginners

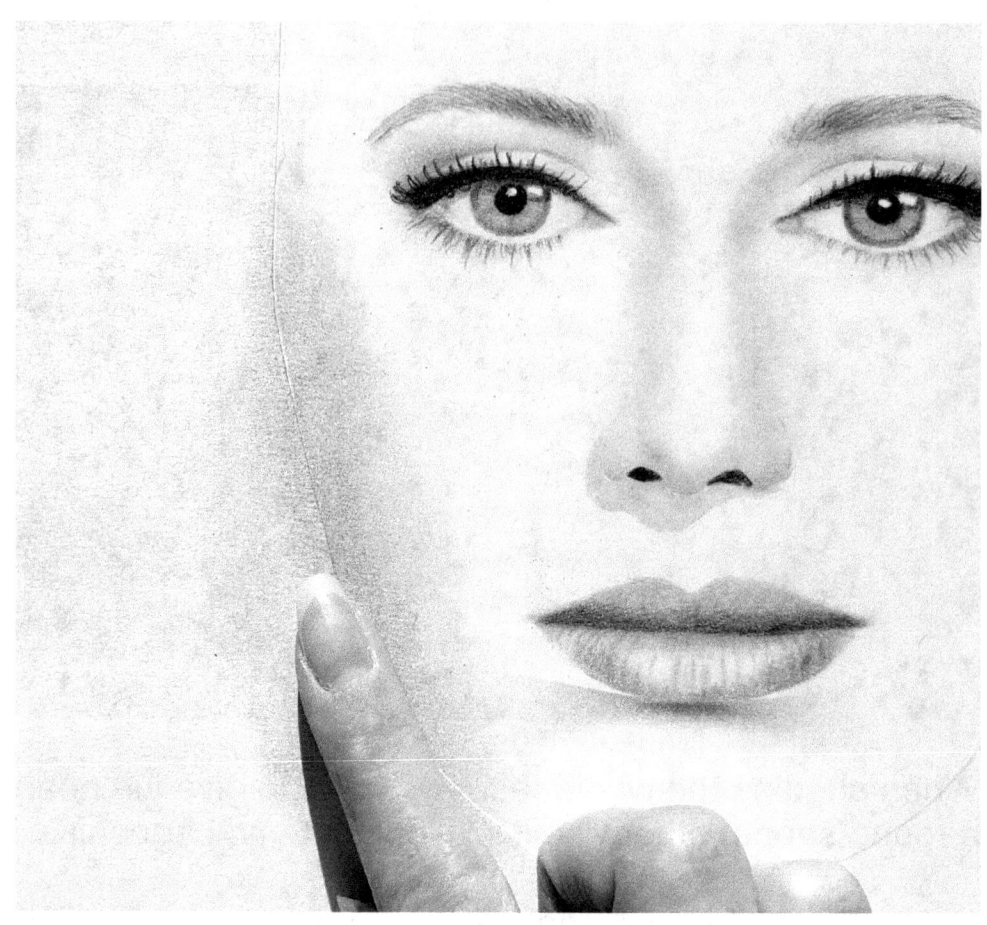

Do the same with both sides of the face.

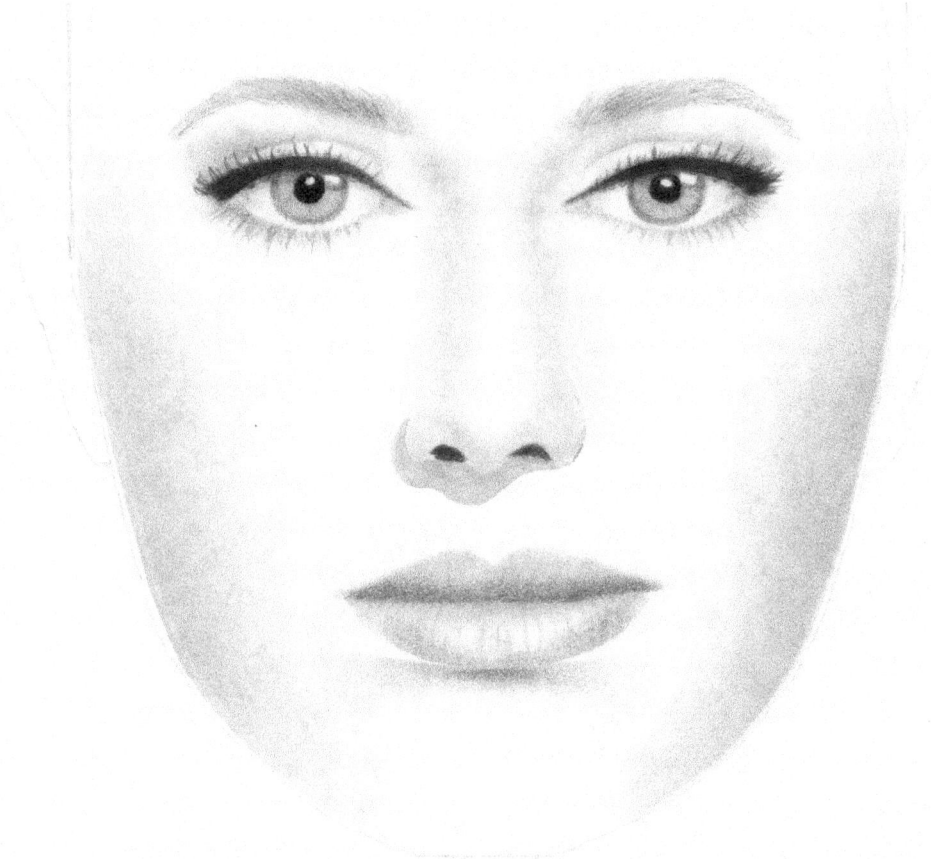

Now you can move onto the chin.

Cut the piece of paper in the shape of the chin and place it over the neck. Leave the tiny area for the reflected light as you can see in the next picture.

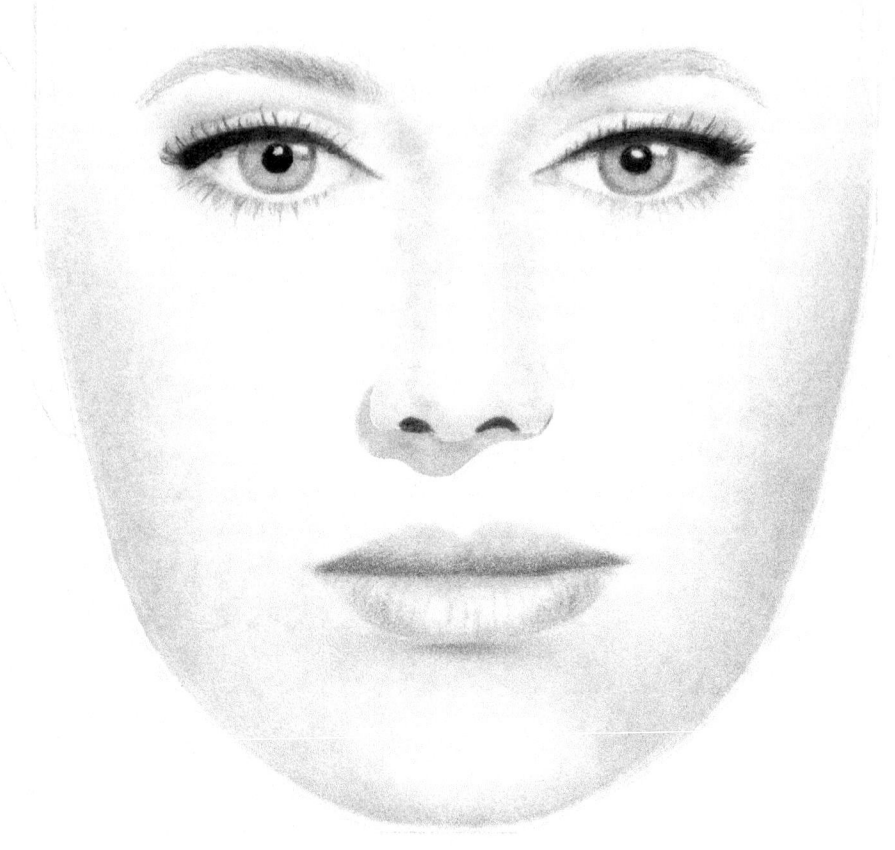

Finally, you can do it around the forehead as well. Here you don't have to place any paper over the hair because it is not a problem if the hair area gets some graphite. It will be shaded and drawn anyway, and the second thing is that there should be a gradient transition between the hair and the skin. The edge between the skin of the forehead and the hair is never sharp, but there are a lot of tiny, hardly visible hairs which makes this area "blurry", otherwise it looks like a person wearing a wig.

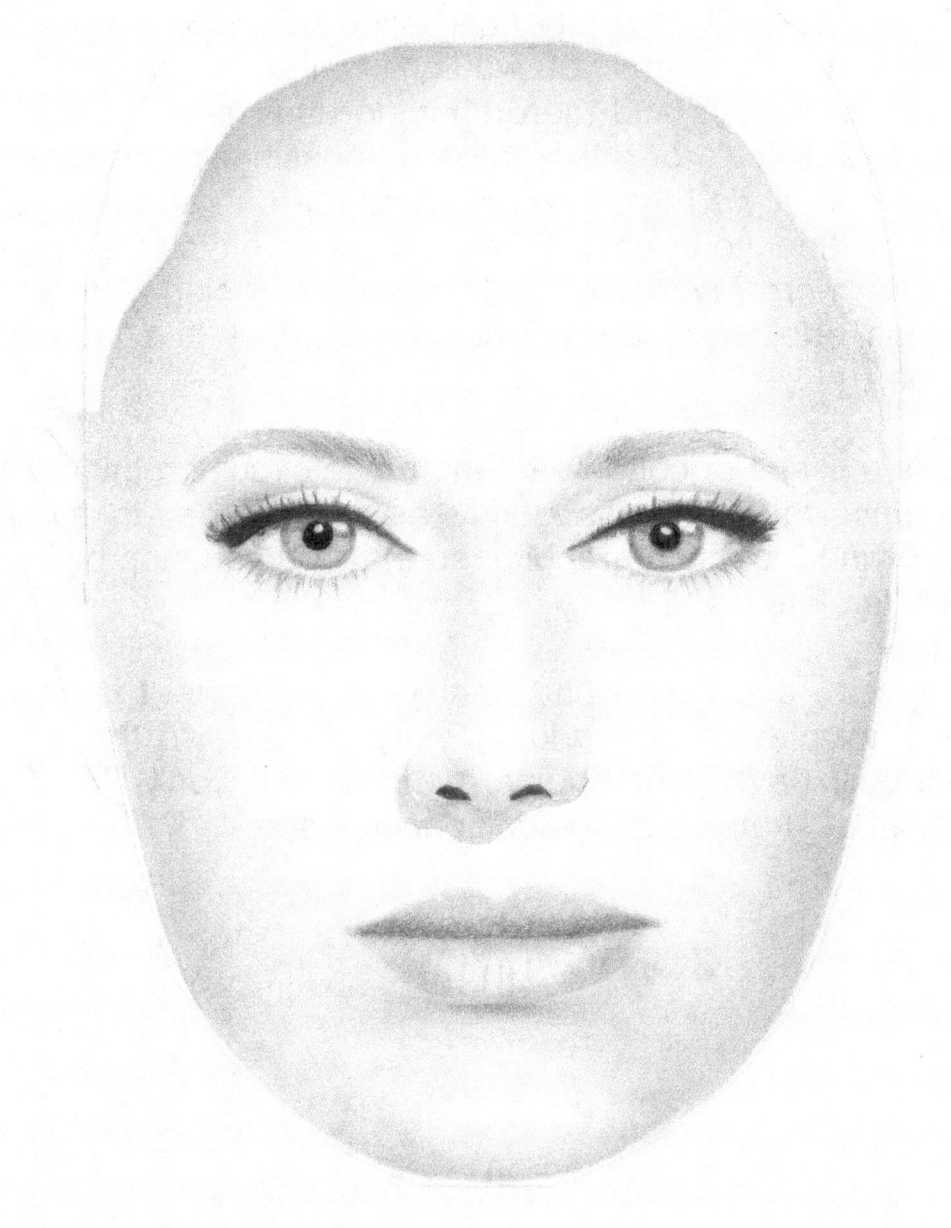

Release the pressure as you shade towards the lower center of the forehead. This is a highly-illuminated area and it has to stay absolutely white.

The final result is pretty pale skin, but I didn't want to shade it a lot so that you wouldn't want to exaggerate it. We can always add more shading and make it darker, but it is difficult, or rather to say impossible, to make the skin pale if we have already created a darker tone. So, if you find your portrait pale so far, you can always make more layers of graphite powder, going over the areas again and again until you achieve the desired tone.

Use a tissue or cotton pad and make circular motions. It is important to press gently as you shade, to avoid applying too much graphite, so that you can stop before it is too late.

You can even scan and print your result as it is now, and try playing with adding more shades, so that you will still have your original work if you won't like the changes that you have additionally made.

SHADING THE SKIN OF THE NECK

In the same manner as we did with the face, or an even better comparison is the kind of shadow that we did with the stem of the wine glass, just this time for the neck both sides have to be much further from each other.

Cut a piece of paper in the shape of the neck, a vertical line with a slight curve at the bottom.

Place it over the background on the right side, to make the vertical line starting just below the curve of the jaw, under the ear, as if it was the continuation of the outline that you can observe in the next image.

The neck is always a bit thinner than the width of the face and the jaw. Apply graphite powder, pressing hard over the cut paper and the edge of the neck, and – as always – release the pressure as you shade towards the highlight, the center of the neck.

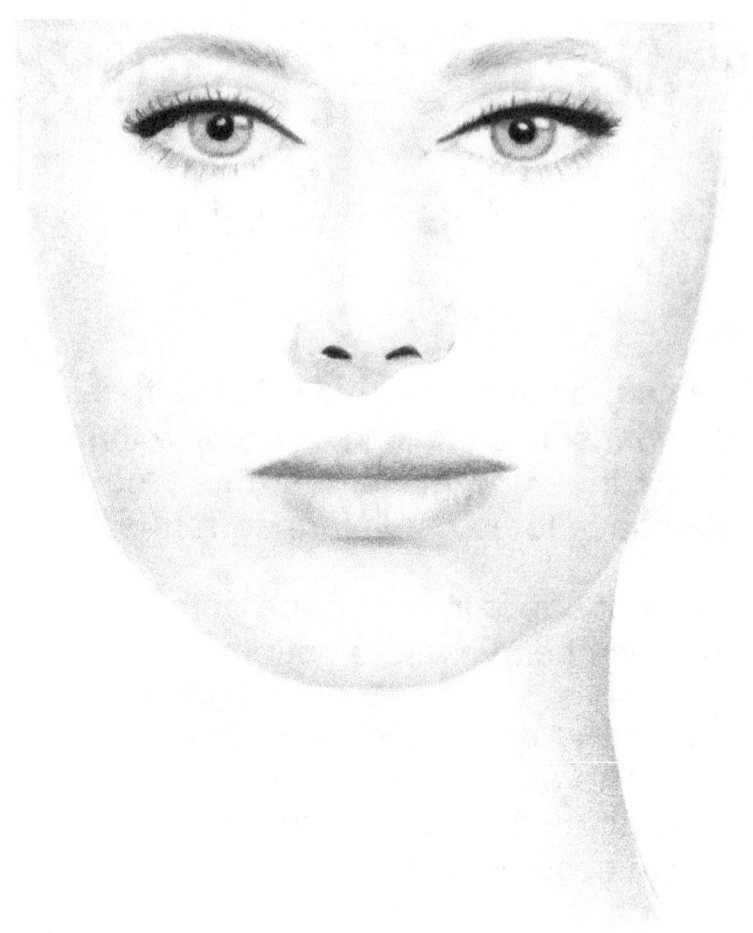

Do the same for the left side of the neck.

The middle of the neck can stay absolutely white, just like the face, because we want it to look highly illuminated.

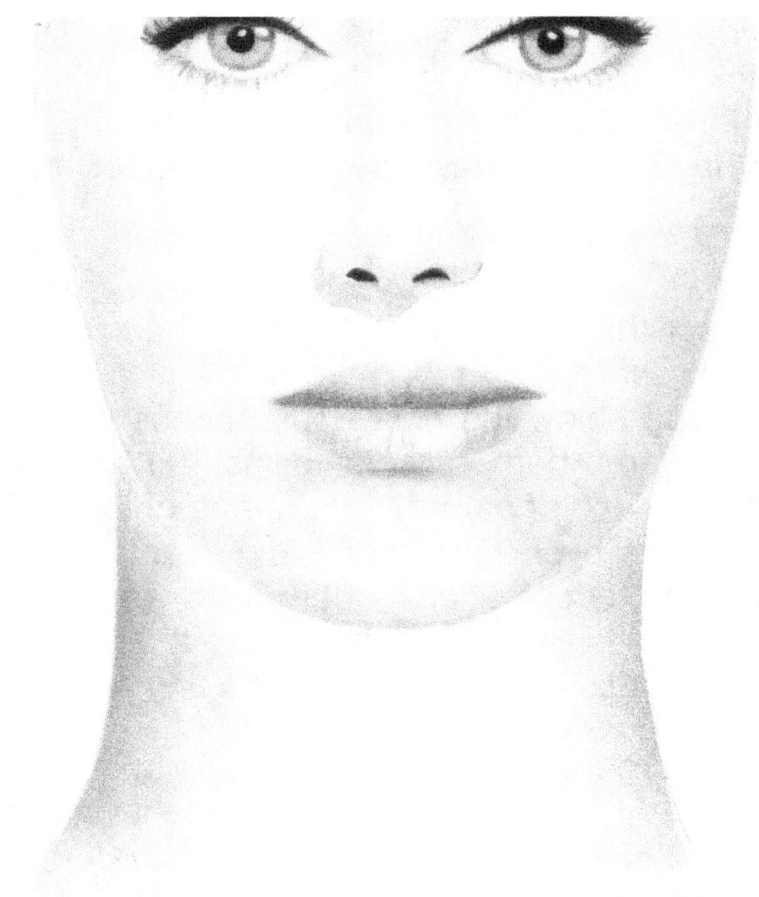

There is only one step left, to create the cast shadow that the jaw casts over the neck.

Here you can see that we have practically only shaded the neck, there is nothing to be drawn in this case here. If you drew a male, you have to add some short or longer hair under the jaw, towards the upper area of the neck.

Remember that we created the cast shadow below the nose with sharp edges and we made it falling towards the left area below the nose. This means that we have to do the same here in order to make it realistic. Here also, cut a piece of paper in the shape of the jaw, which you will place over the jaw to avoid shading it. Leave a tiny line untouched all around the jaw. This line represents the reflected light, analyze the next image to see how it looks after leaving out this tiny area.

Decide where the edge of the cast will be, and place the paper under it, over the neck and shade it with graphite. In the next image you can see how I have outlined the cast shadow making it tiny under the top of the chin, and making it deeper and deeper as I shaded towards the left side of the neck.

Now the reflected light around the jaw becomes more prominent and the neck appears to be further from the viewer's eye. This is achieved with both reflected light and the cast shadow.

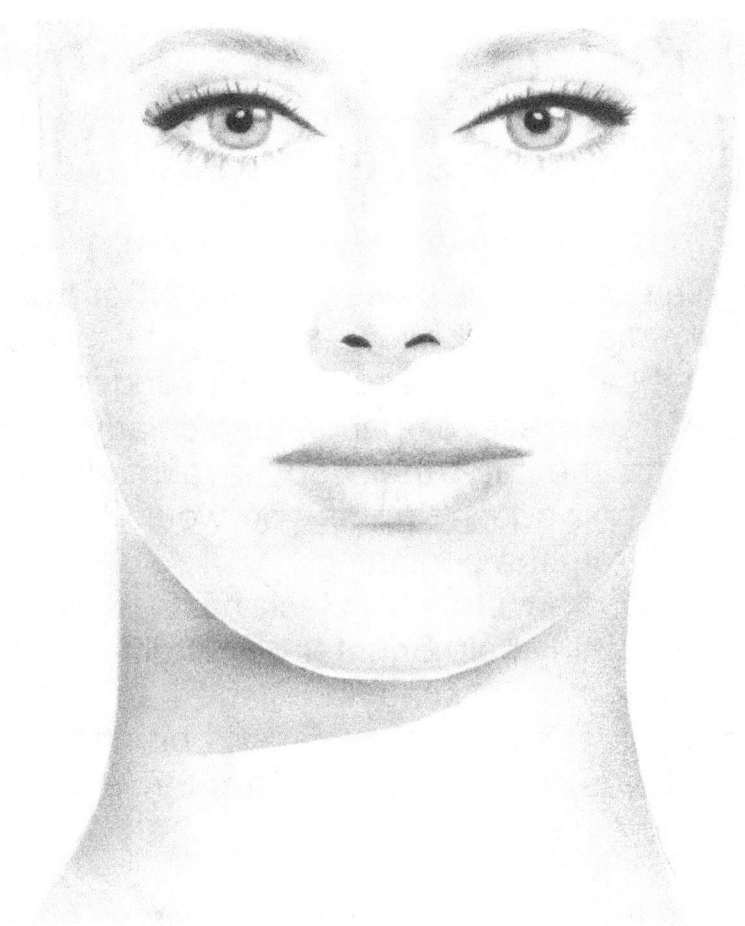

You can see that this is not the kind of the photorealistic drawing that I use to do, but I tried to make it to be doable for the absolute beginner. So, if you have drawn something similar, or even better, you are achieving great progress so keep creating new portraits and working on your drawing skills. Your first drawn portrait doesn't have to be perfect and don't let any result discourage you.

HOW TO DRAW PORTRAIT PART 3
HOW TO DRAW THE HAIR

Drawing the hair is the most difficult part of the portrait for many people. I will show you through the following steps that it can be achieved easily. I suggest trying the hair on a new piece of paper, particularly if you are satisfied with the face that you have made so far. If drawing the hair doesn't go as you would like, you can always start from the beginning.
I want you to draw straight, black hair with me, to see how to make shiny hair. Brighter hair is different to draw. That requires mostly shading. Black hair will show a detailed result of your work, just don't be afraid of using dark pencils. As said, you can always throw the drawing out and start a new one.

The tone of the hair is created by strokes as opposed to the shaded tones of the face. These lines should be drawn fast and firmly and must follow the natural flow of the hair.

I want to draw the hair with the bangs over the forehead. It may appear scary to apply the darker pencils over the white areas of highly-illuminated forehead, but you have to give it a try if you want to learn and experience it yourself. Always practice the strokes on a separate piece of paper.

But let's start with the not so dark HB and filling the area of the hair root. You can grip your pencil with the thumb and forefinger, pressing the pencil with your forefinger in order to shade the larger areas faster. Here you don't have to pay attention to how these strokes look because we will cover them with a darker pencil anyway. This is just the base to cover the hair root and to have some orientation about where the forehead should be found. Kind of warming up before taking the action with dark pencils.

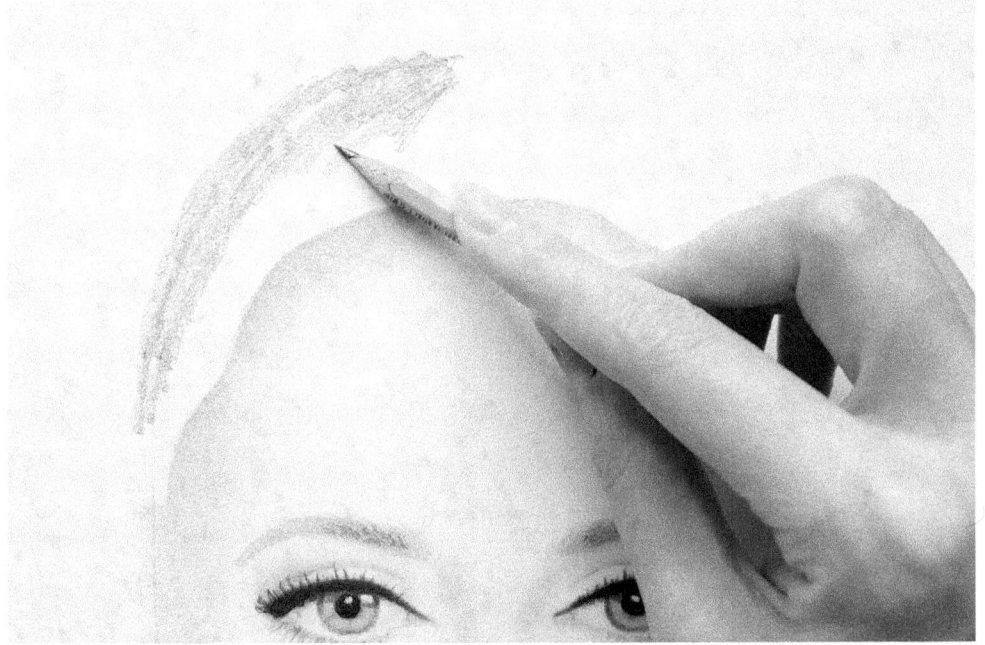

Cover the whole area of the hair root this way, reaching to the top of the ears.

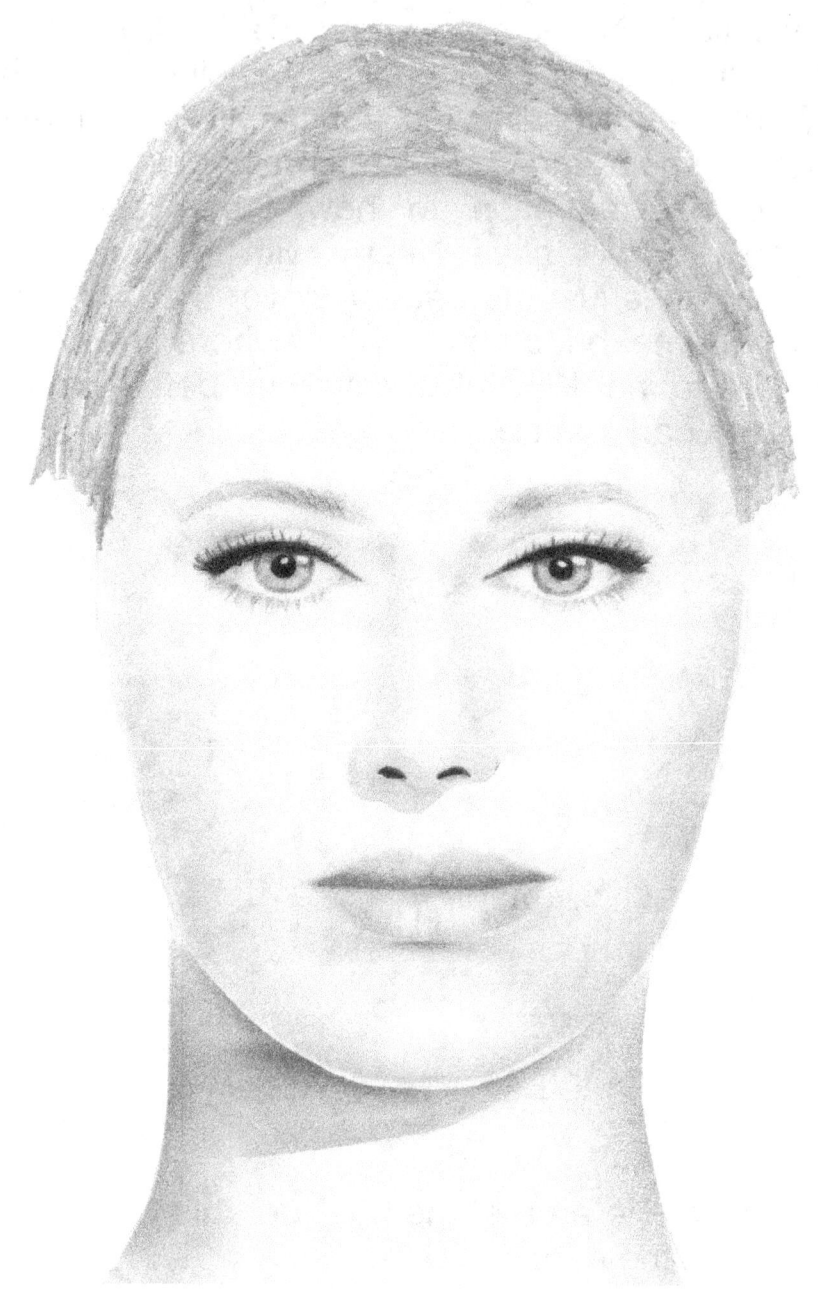

Let's start drawing the bangs using a 6B or darker graphite pencil. The bangs on straight, black hair is always shiny.

To achieve the shiny effect of the hair, there are two steps necessary. It involves drawing the lines from both ends of the hair towards the highlight.

So, let's divide it into two parts for a better understanding. First, using at least a 6B (9B recommended), start drawing the lines from the top of the head towards the forehead and left and right sides of the hairy part of the head above the ears. To help you better understand, I have placed arrows in the next picture, to show you the paths and directions of the pencil strokes that you should apply.

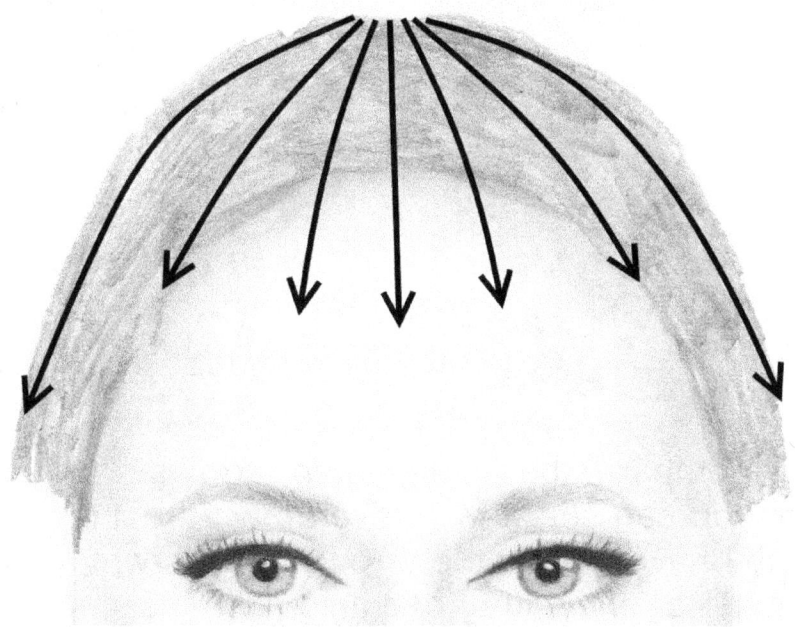

Place the tip of a 9B pencil on the top of the head and draw decisive strokes swiftly, pressing very hard at the top of the head, and releasing the pressure as you reach the end of the line. You should make the lines with different lengths instead of making them all the same length. Some of the lines should go much further than others. Choose randomly which one of them will become longer. This will make it look more natural, and not fake.

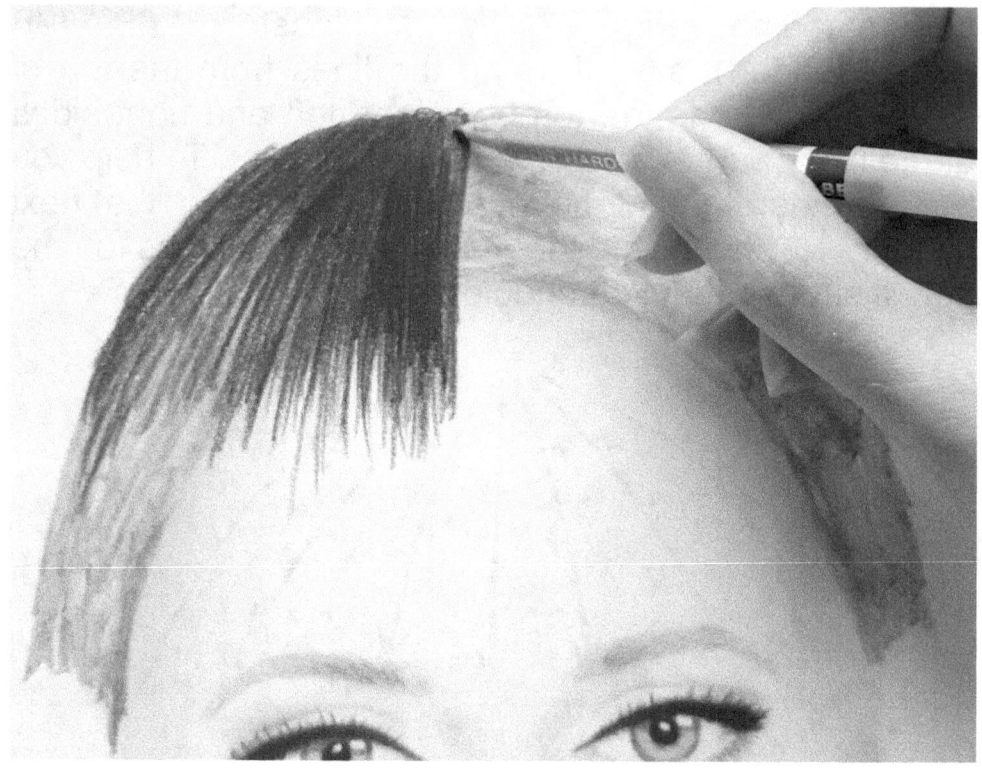

If you compare the image with arrows to the next image, you can see how I have drawn the lines exactly the way I have placed the arrows. This is why I found it important to show the example with the arrows for better understanding. If you observe the black, straight hair, you will notice the directions of the hair's flow and will be able to draw natural hair. Drawing skills are not just about applying the strokes and shades, it is also about observational and memorizing skills and these are important if you want to make lifelike drawings.

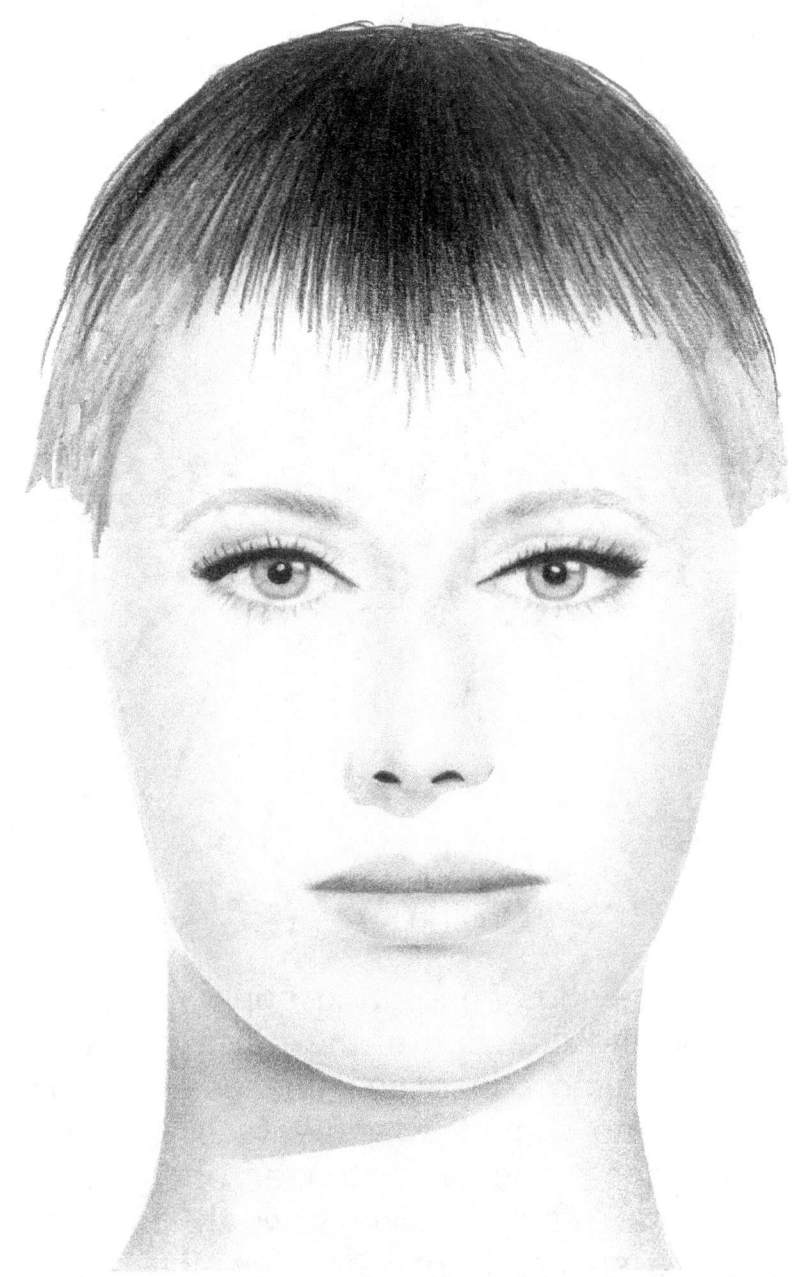

The second part of creating the shiny bangs is to start drawing strokes starting at the other end of the hairs. Here apply the same, pressing hard when starting and releasing the pressure as you reach the area that you want highlighted, in the middle of the forehead. Here you have to decide how long of bangs you want to draw. You can even start right above the eyes, or over the eyebrows, or just like me, a bit further from the eyebrows. Here, it is also important to keep the strokes in the direction of the hair's flow, and here is one more image with arrows to show you where and how you should position these hairs.

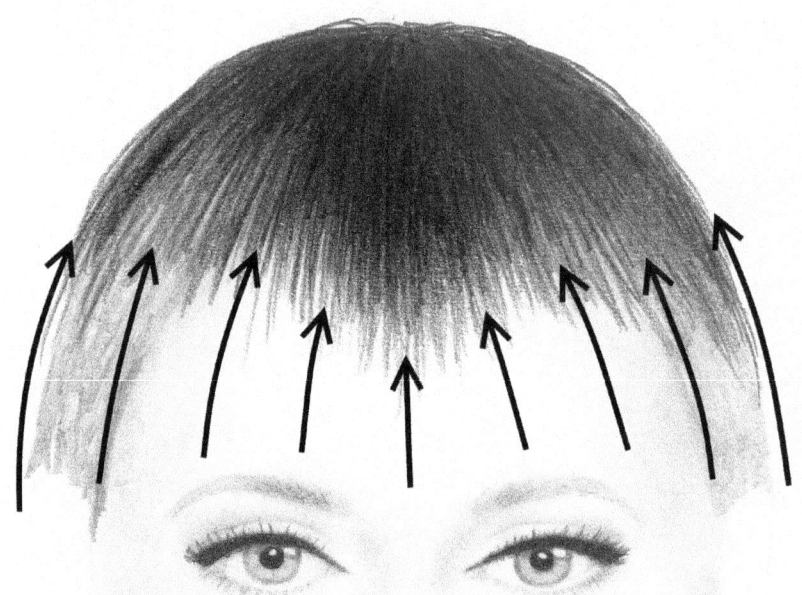

Analyze the previous image and apply strokes one by one following the direction of the hair's growth. It may be boring and time consuming because the hair often takes more time than the whole face, but here you practice patience and persistence, not just drawing skills. The final result is always worth our time. The more time we spend on one drawing, the better it will become. You can start from the middle – just like me - or going from left to right, or from right to left, as you please. Also, on some places, leave some distance, smaller or bigger, between the hair strands because in real life, they are not stuck together. It would look fake.

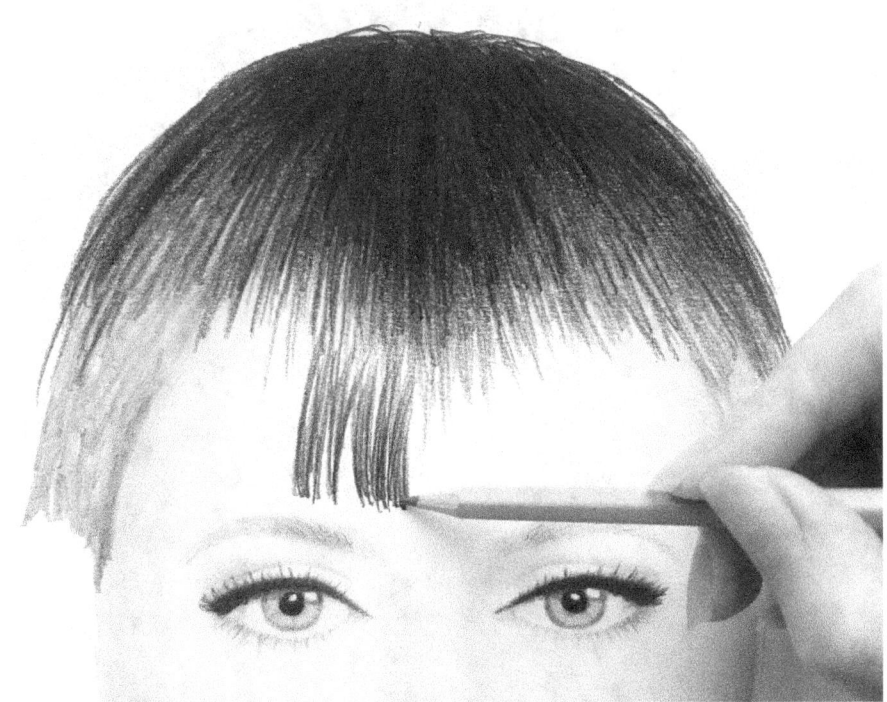

After applying the strokes by the rules in the previous two images and what I have explained, you should have a result similar to mine in the next image. You can see that I have drawn the hair above the temples a bit longer than the hair in the middle of the forehead, but it is also arbitrary. You can make whichever haircut you want. However, I recommend trying more ways and hair styles for practice sake, and to gather experience through trying different approaches. Also, try to make the highlight over the forehead a bit curved, which means that both the left and right sides of it should create a slight arch upwards. This will make the head appear round and the drawing will be much more realistic. So, this shiny highlight should have a curvy shape – as shown in the next image.

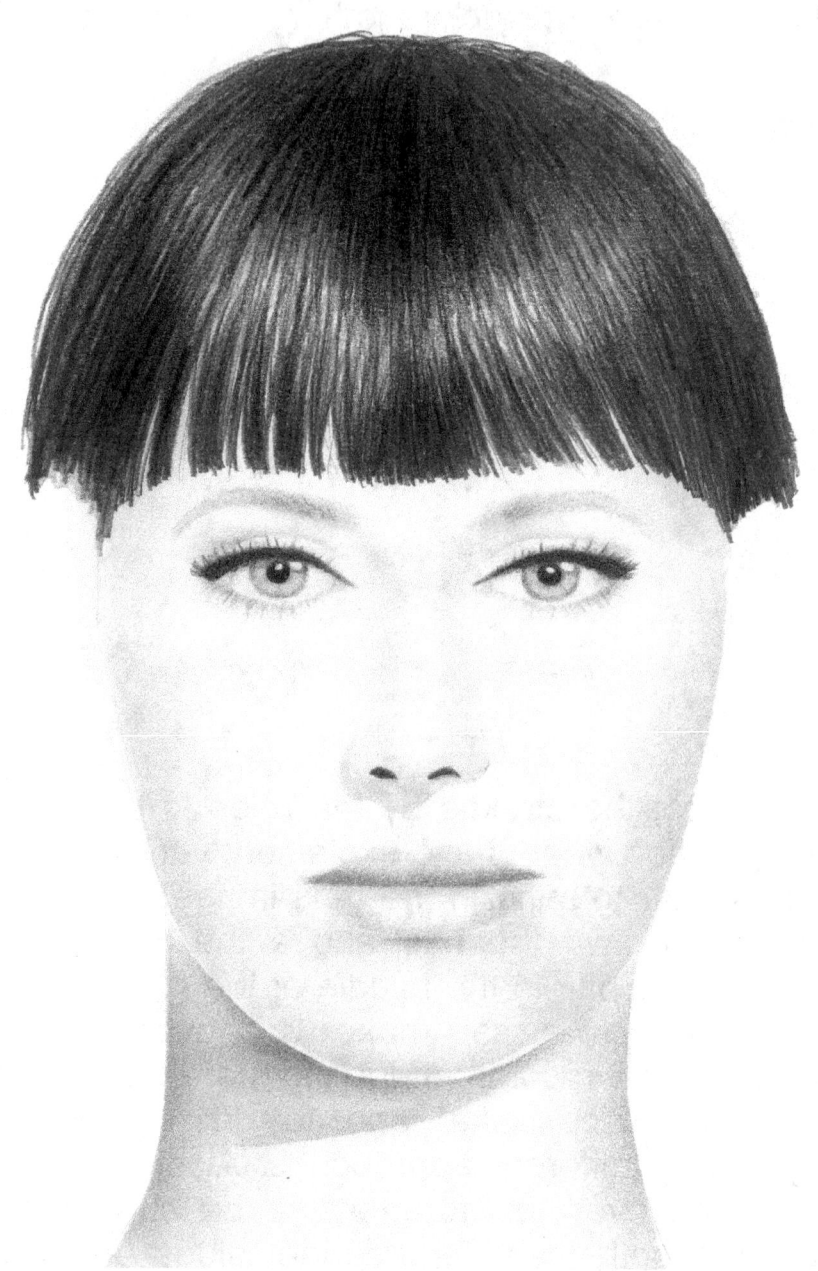

Since the edge between the hair stands and the skin is too sharp now, we should blend them a bit. Also this way we will create tiny cast shadows, that the hair stands cast over the skin. These cast shadows are very small, but we should add them anyway to make it look real. Use a blending stump for this and also use it a bit over the highlighted parts of the bangs.

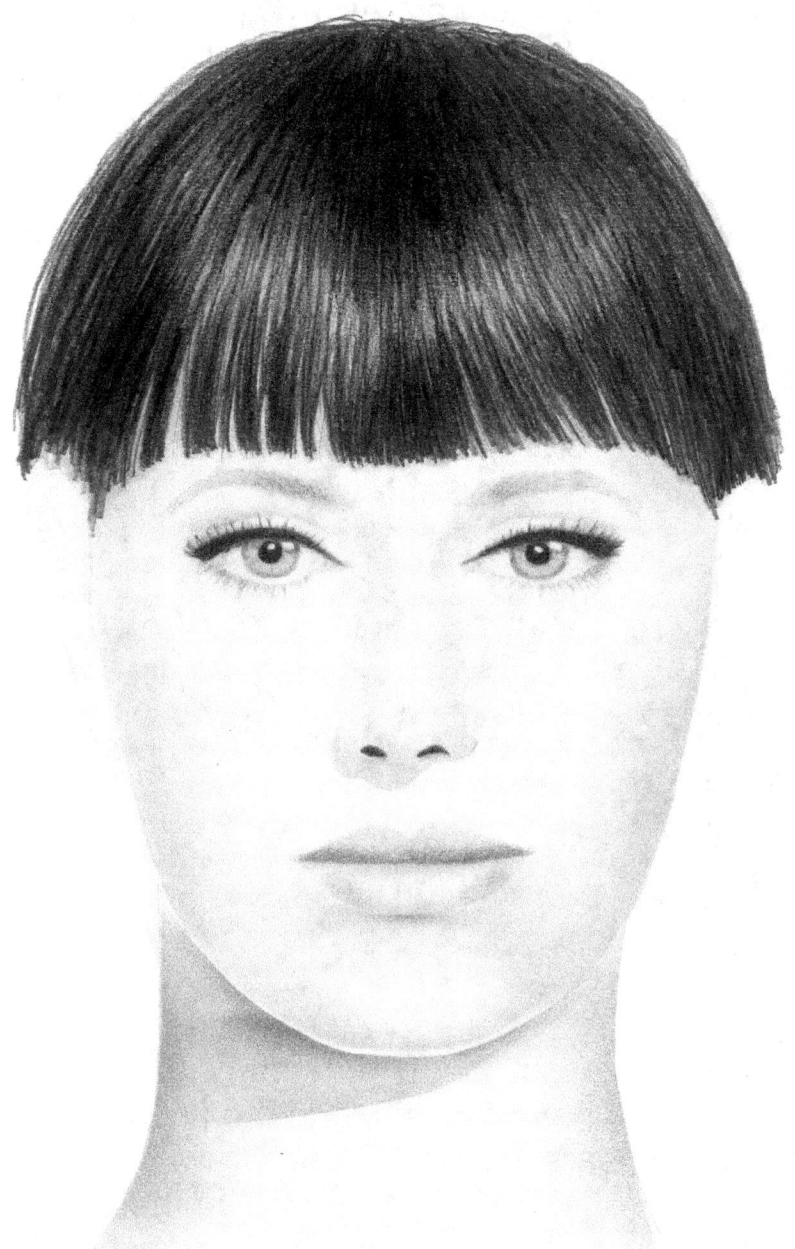

Now you can erase some highlights to create shiny

strands with a well-sharpened eraser. I use a mechanical eraser for this because it allows me to make sharp, tiny hairs over the highlights and to add even more details this way. Always place the tip of the eraser in the middle of the highlights and draw it outwards in the direction of the hair growth. Then place it again over the highlights and draw in the other direction. Maintain this technique from the highlights to the top of the head, and from the highlights towards the eyes and the temples.

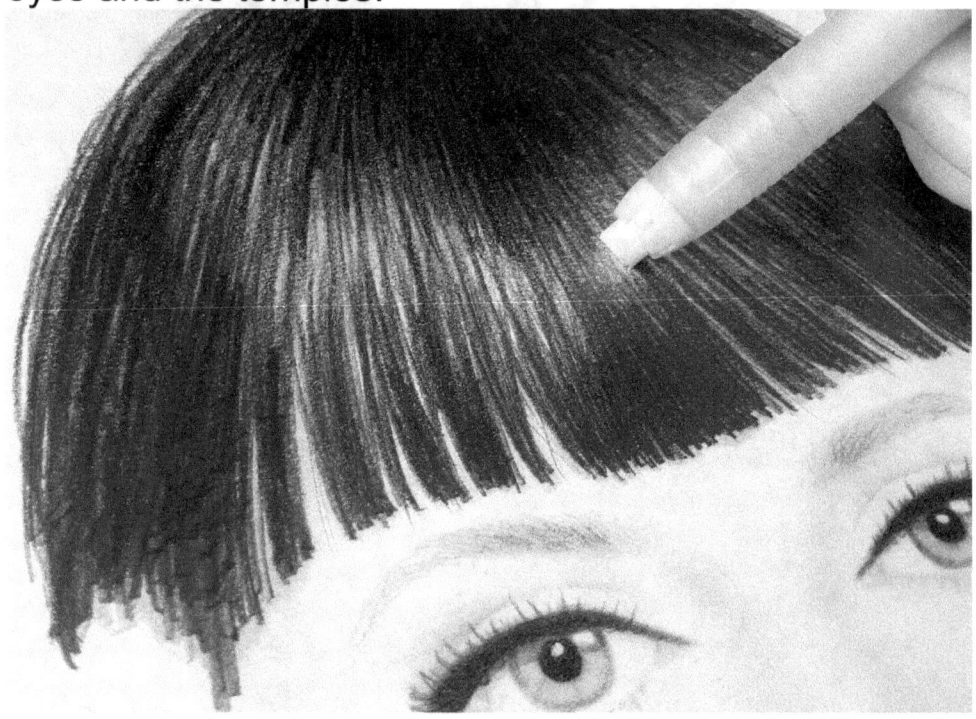

After working a lot with erasers and making the movements as I have described in the previous chapter, the bangs appears much shinier. Draw some random shiny hair over the darkest areas like in the next image. You can even use the knife for creating such hair, but it requires a more experienced hand and be careful with such a knife because you could scratch more than you would like.

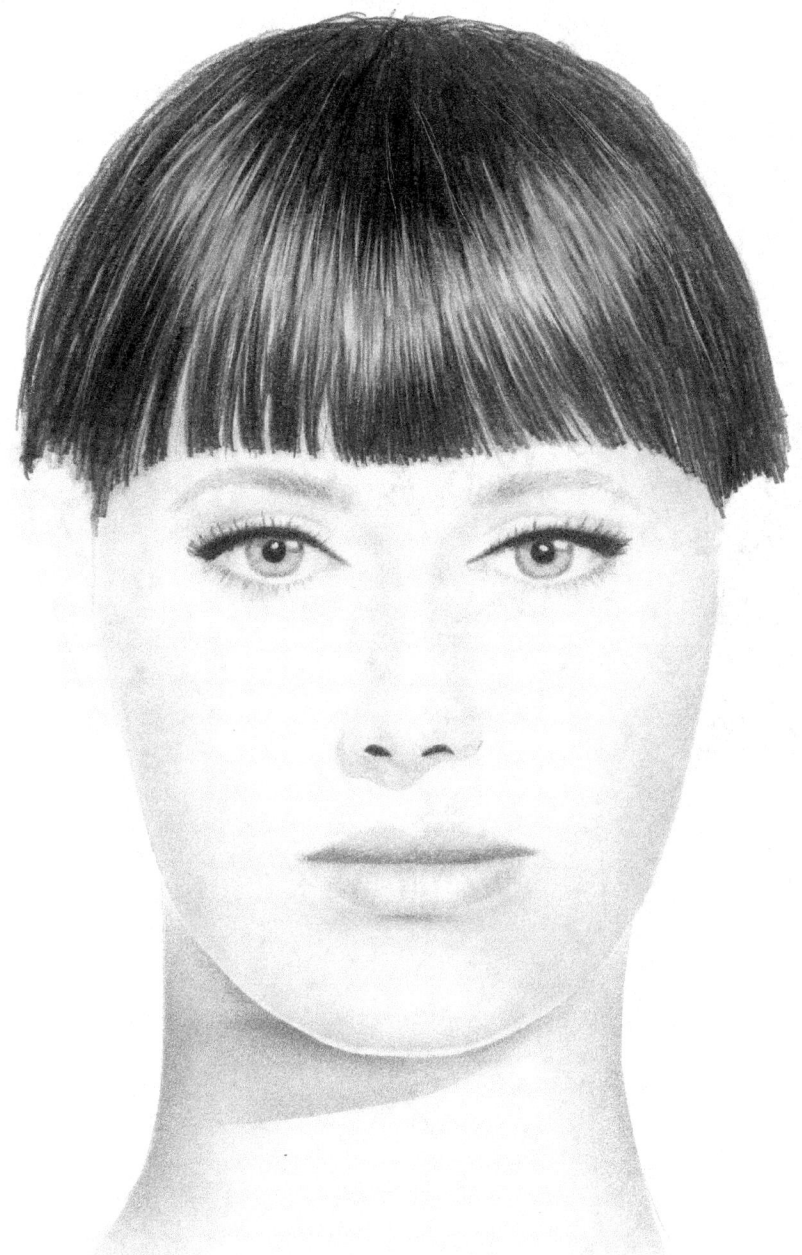

If you are satisfied with the bangs, you can start to draw the falling hair on both the left and right sides. Here I have covered the ear completely and started to draw the lines where I have finished them when I drew the bangs.

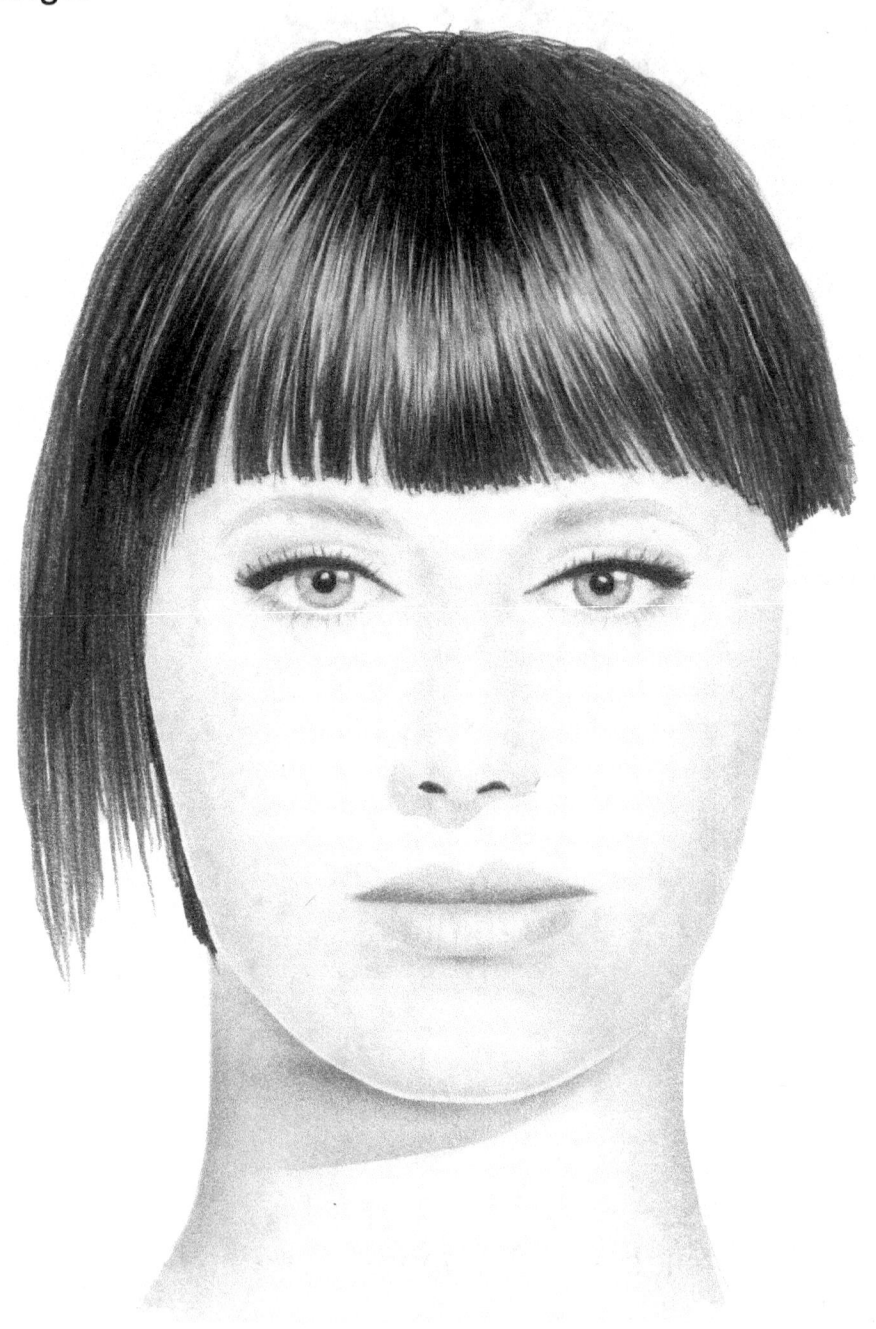

You should continue to draw from those areas, the very left and right sides of the bangs, and to press hard to cover their ends and to make the hair flawless.

Use a 4B or darker for this, while drawing the strokes downwards, release the pressure somewhere in the middle. Here we want to create the same shiny effect that we made with the bangs, so the method is the same. Draw towards the highlights from both sides. Outline the side of the face carefully using the same dark pencil.

Draw the strokes starting at the other end of the hair – where you want it to be – using the same 4B or darker pencil, and also releasing the pressure near and over the highlight in the middle.

You can make more strands. Some of them can bend outwards, some towards the neck, some can be hidden under the rest of the hair or the neck.

Take a look at the next image to see how I have made the strands end differently. You can blend the highlights and make the highlighted hair over it as we did with the bangs. I have left this area like this.

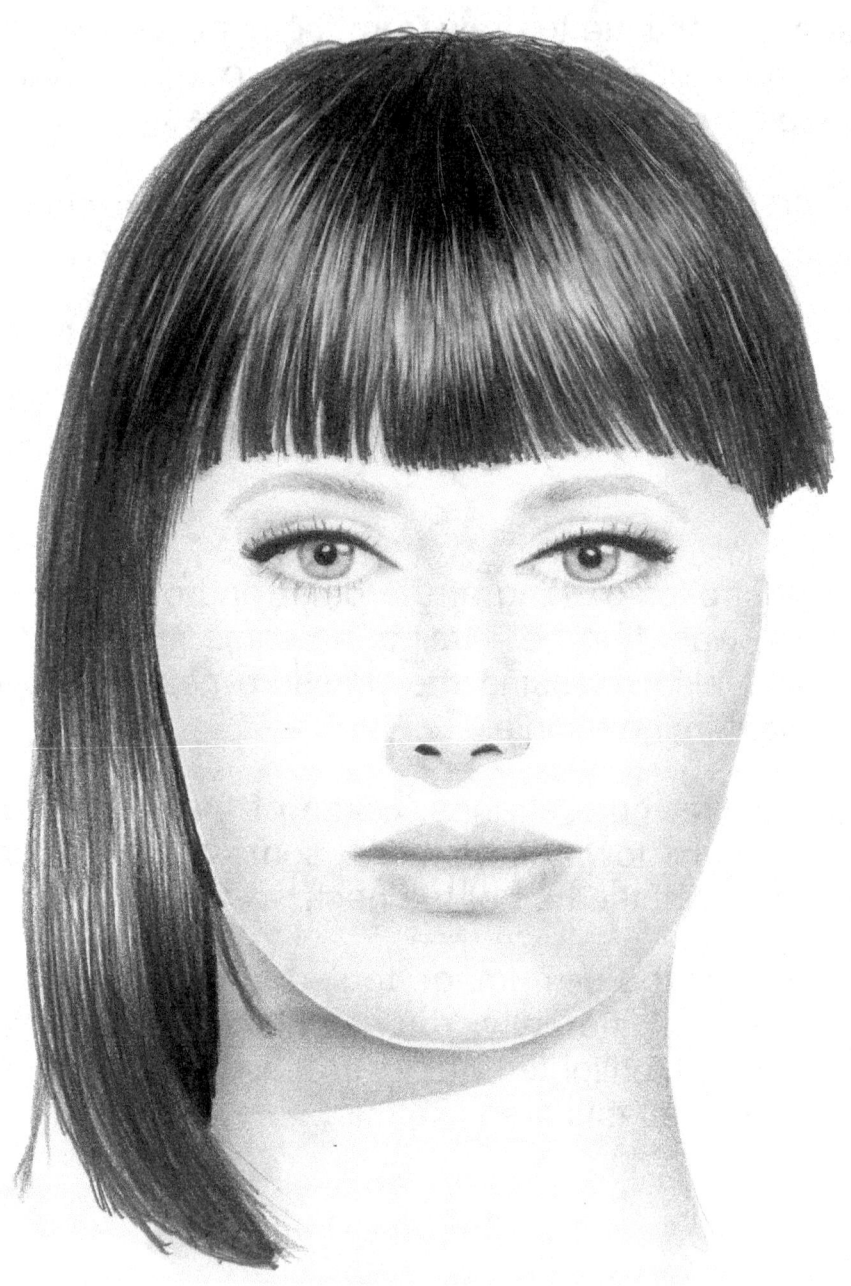

Draw some random hairs with a well-sharpened HB all over the neck and even the face because there are always some hairs that protrude. On the right side of the face I want the hair to flow behind the ear, so that you can learn to shade the ear as well. Here also, cut the piece of paper that you will place all around the ear and use bright graphite powder to shade the edges of the ear. This is enough for the ear. Draw some random, short hairs over the ear to make it more natural.

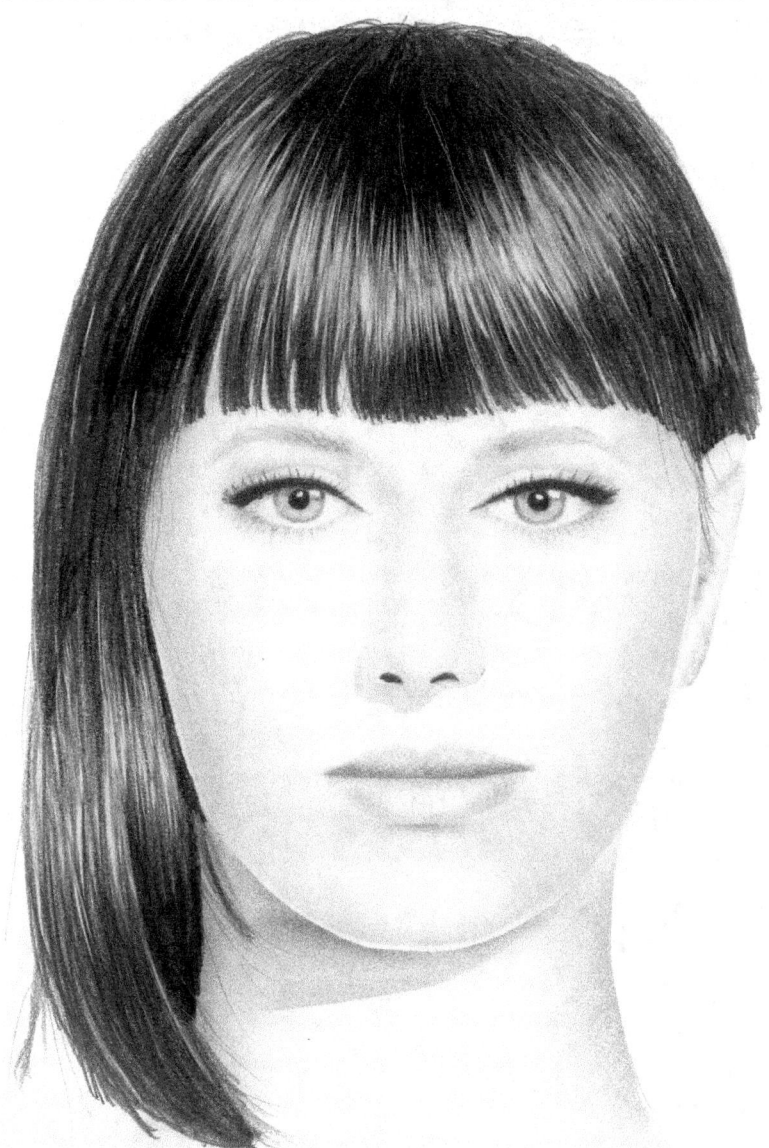

Now you can outline the ear using a 4B or darker and draw the hair that flows behind the ear. As we did on the left side, we have to repeat the same here. Start from the hair we made when drawing the bangs, and draw straight lines towards the middle of the length of the hair. There we have to release the pressure before we lift the pencil off the page. Draw carefully next to the skin of the ear, the face, and the neck because the dark pencil cannot be fully erased.

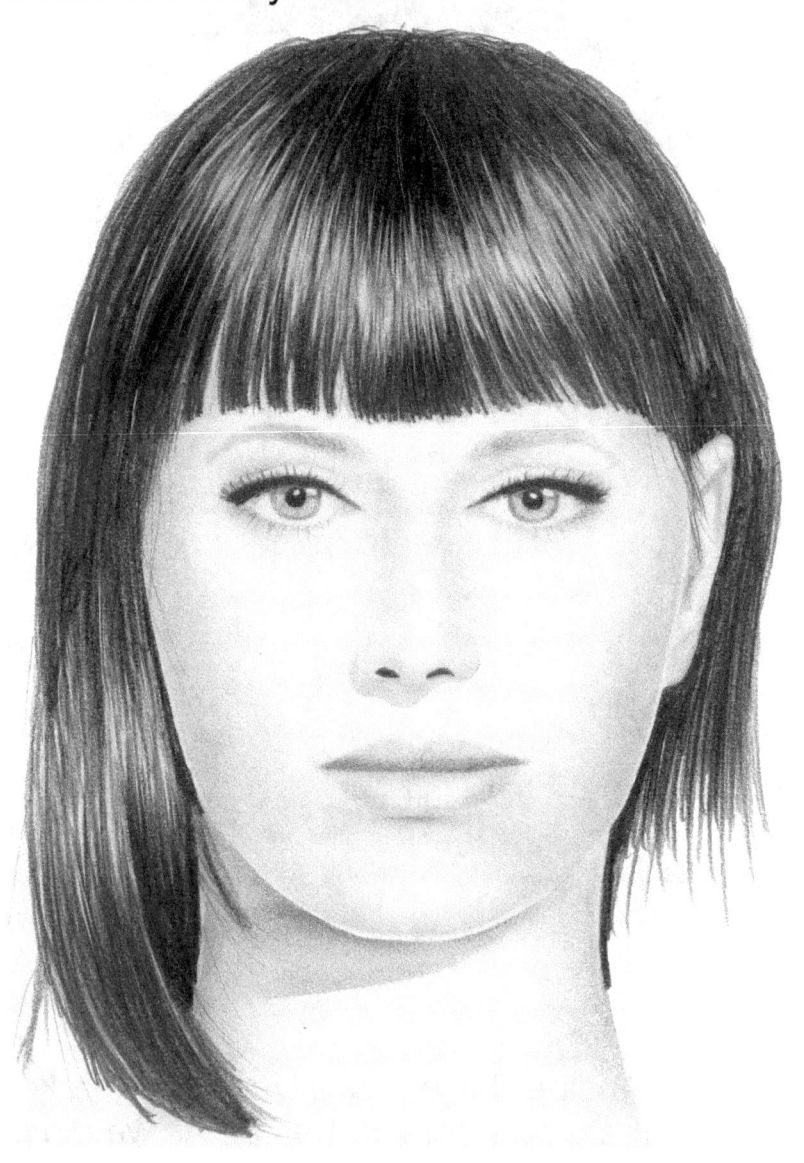

Just like on the left side, do the same here on the right side. Decide where you want your strands to end and how you would like them to bend and start drawing the lines from the bottom to the highlights.

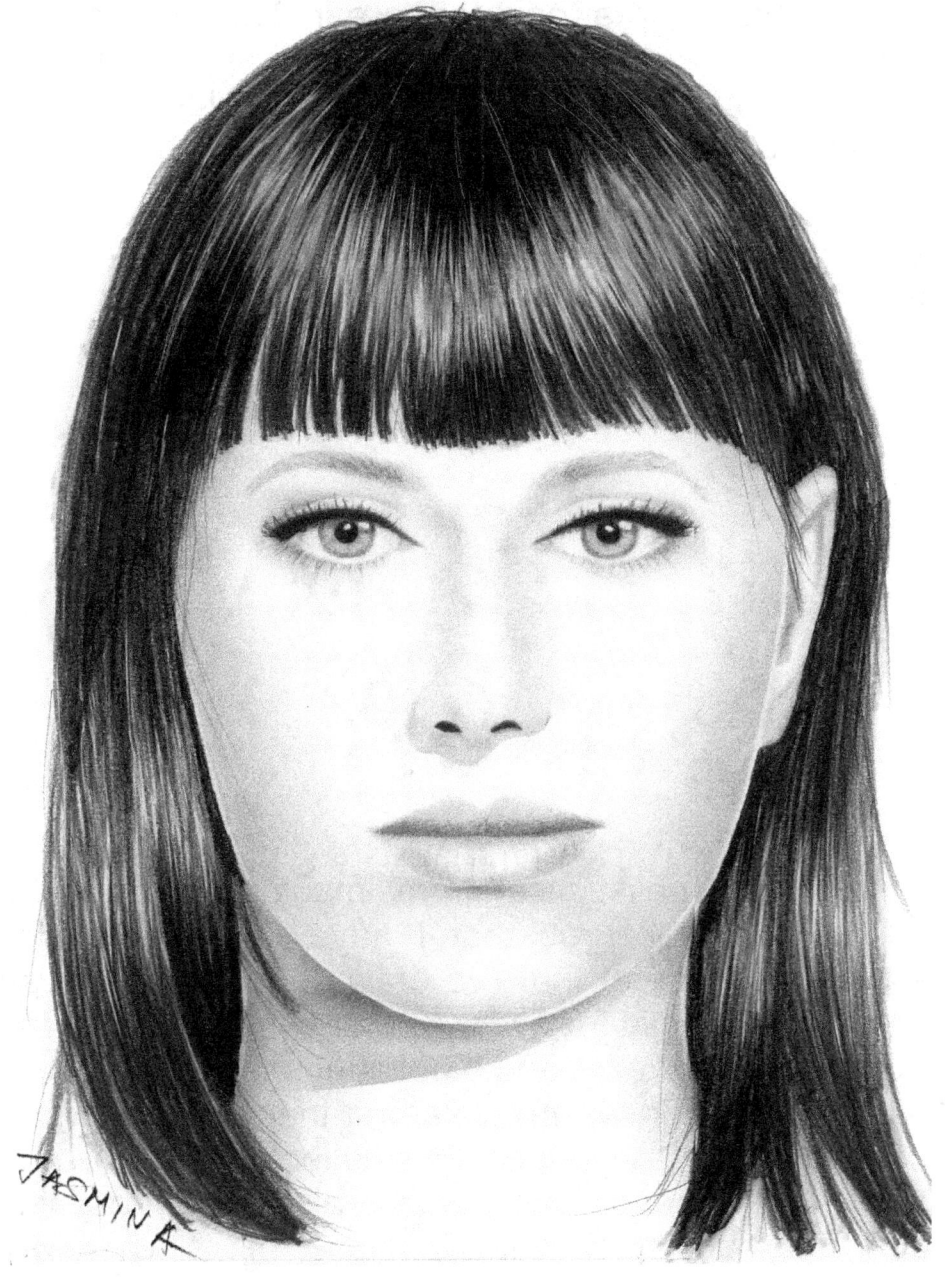

Release the pressure before or over the highlights, every stroke should have a different length. Some should end far before the highlight, some in the middle, and some should extend all over the highlight and end up in the upper area, next to the ear. This way the hair will look shiny and natural. You can blend the highlights with a blending stump and erase some highlighted hairs (like we did with the bangs) if you want.

HOW TO DRAW A CAT

Let's draw a realistic cat from imagination using the method and measures that I have figured out. The measures of the cat that I've drawn for this tutorial are approximately valid for every kind of cat, except the rare breeds with large ears and big, flat noses.

As a first step, draw an equilateral triangle somewhere in the middle of A4 paper, or smaller because we will draw only the head. This equilateral triangle has three equal sides and three equal angles. This is where you decide how big the head of the cat will be. I recommend drawing it approximately 2 inches (5-6 centimeters) per side.

If you cannot make a triangle that has equal sides, draw the horizontal line first. Use a HB graphite pencil and press lightly so the lines can be erased without a trace. If you press hard you will leave embossed "channels" that will remain visible at the end of your drawing. Then take the measure of the length of this line with a dividing tool, keeping the needle in the left and after that in the right end of the line, and mark the mutual point. The ends will meet exactly in the middle under the horizontal line.

In the next image you can see my triangle. This is all we need for the very first step.

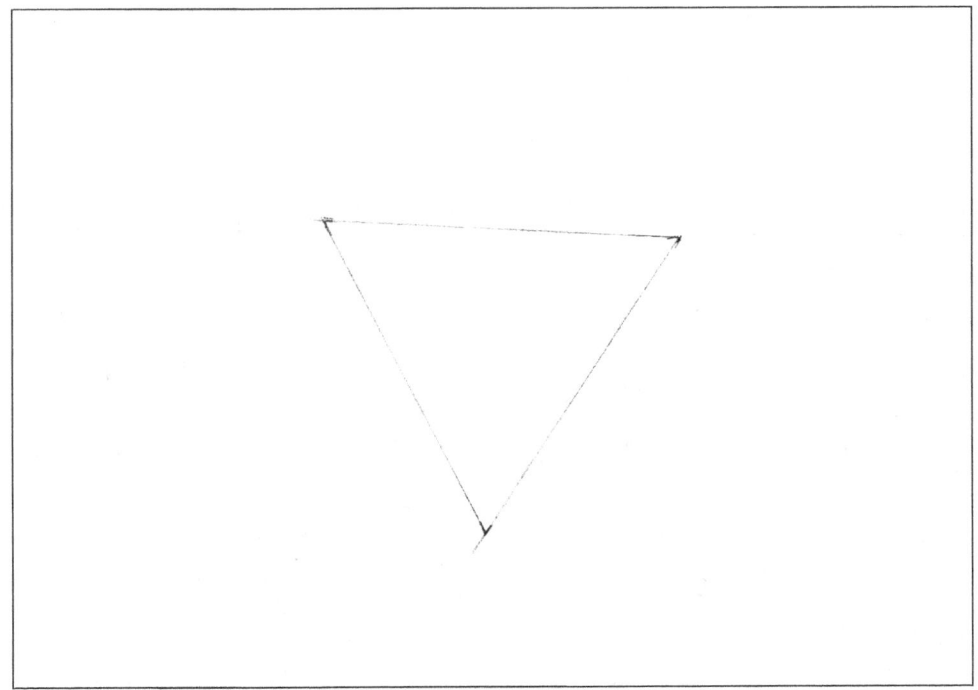

Divide the horizontal line into three equal vertical

sections by drawing two vertical lines as shown in the next image. Don't press hard because you will have to erase these lines.

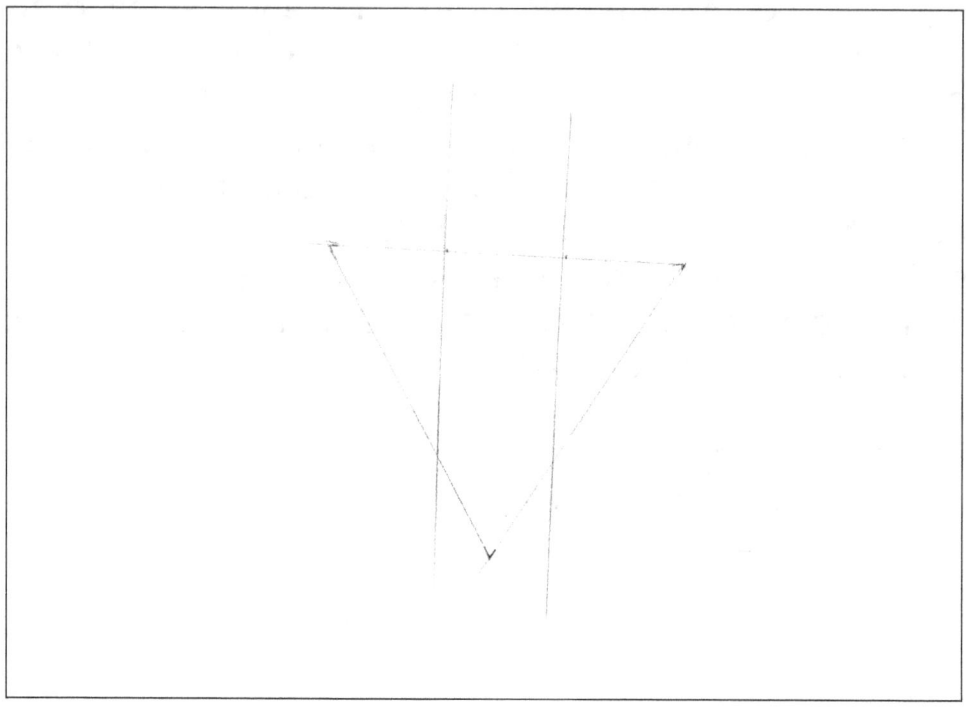

The width of one eye will fit in one section, which means that you can draw two eyes in the angles of the triangle with space for the width of third eye between them. I have drawn a third eye in the next image, but I will erase it before I continue. I just want to show you what I mean so that you will understand the spacing. You could see and make yourself the same with the case of the human portrait in the previous tutorial. Between the two eyes, there is a space for the width of one eye.

You have to decide how wide the pupils of your cat will

be. If a cat is excited or it is nighttime, her pupils will be almost as big as her irises, so the irises will be hardly visible. If a cat is in the direct sunlight, absolutely relaxed, or purring, you can see only a tiny, vertical, line in the middle.

I have chosen the normal width, which you would see when a cat is in her normal environment.

Also, outline the areas for the light reflection and shadows under the upper eyelids. Stay by this step until you have outlined the eyes completely and they look similar to mine.

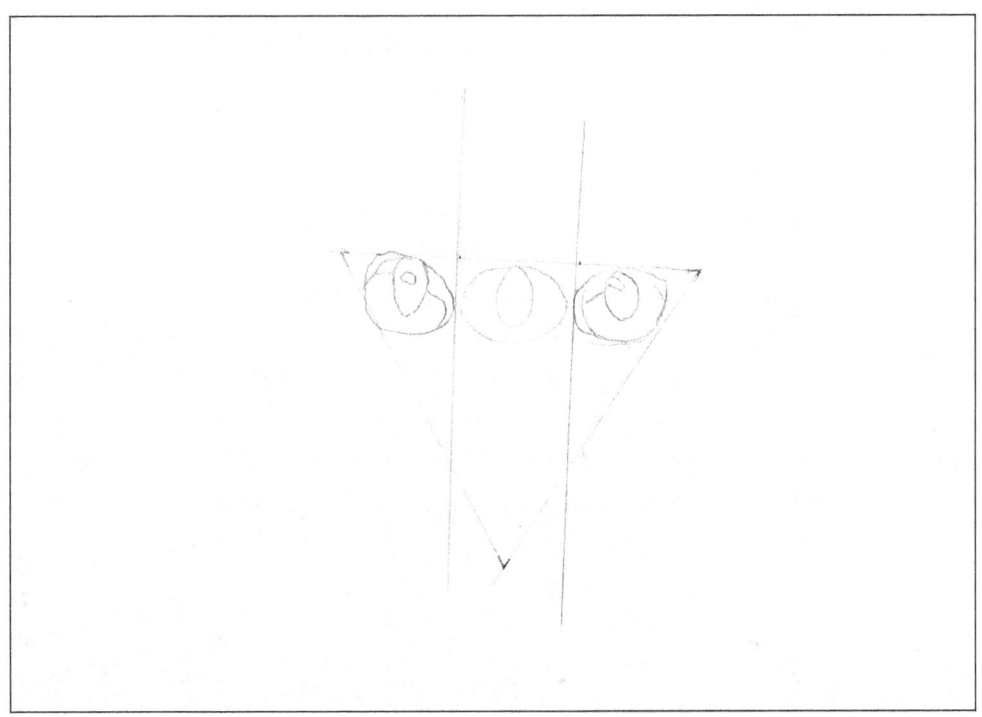

Before you erase the two vertical lines, you need to determine the position of the cat's mouth.

The width of the eye, (marked as D), is the same width

as the width of the mouth. The line of the mouth creates an equilateral triangle in the lower angle of the triangle. You can see what I mean and how it should turn out.

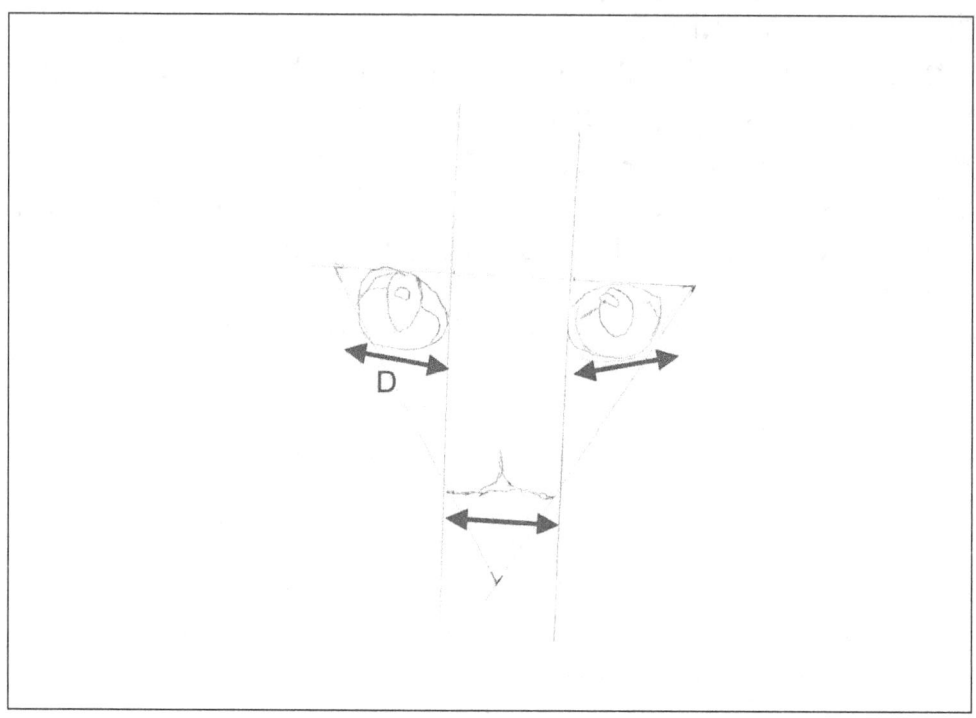

Now you can erase both vertical lines.
Next, mark a dot exactly in the middle of the triangle. Don't make it too dark. In my image the dot is digitally darkened for better visibility, but you should make a bright dot with HB pressing gently. The bottom of the nose should be placed somewhere between the dot and the mouth. I have digitally placed the dashed line so you can see where I mean to draw the bottom of the nose.
The skin of the nose should be drawn near below the red dot. The width of the nose should be about the

same as the height. If you are not exactly sure what a cat's nose looks like, you can check it out on any photo of a cat or copy my outline.

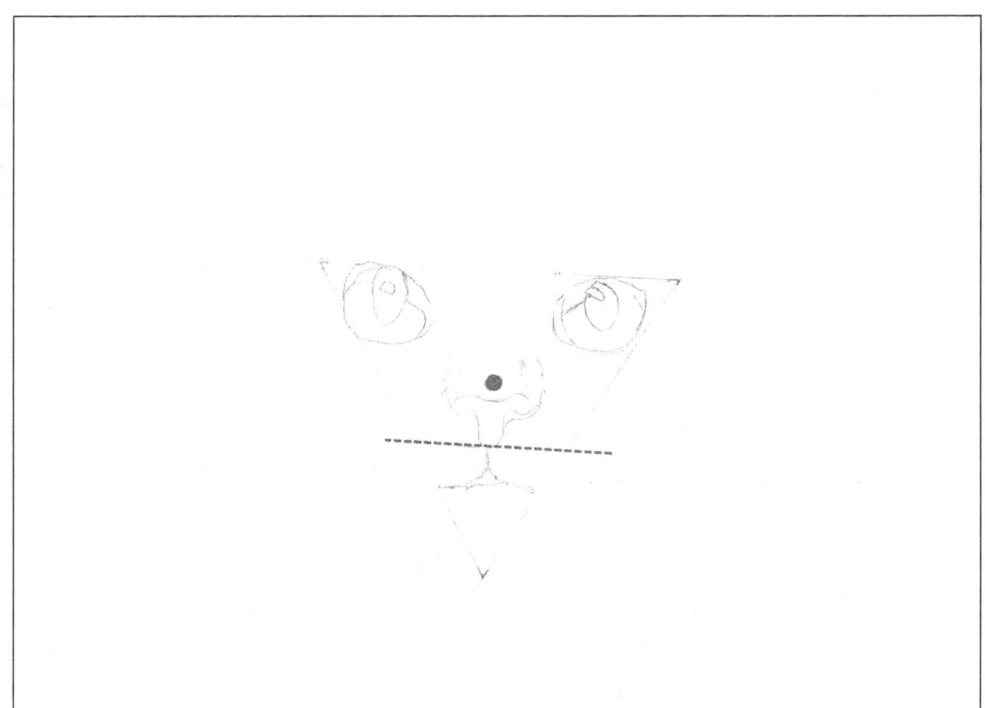

Take a measurement from the dot in the middle of the triangle to any of the angles. In the image I've marked it with an arrowed line (C). Start outlining the top of the cat's head, one C line along further from the top of our triangle. Using the same measurement of the C line again, draw the ears at an angle of the triangle, where I've placed two arrows.

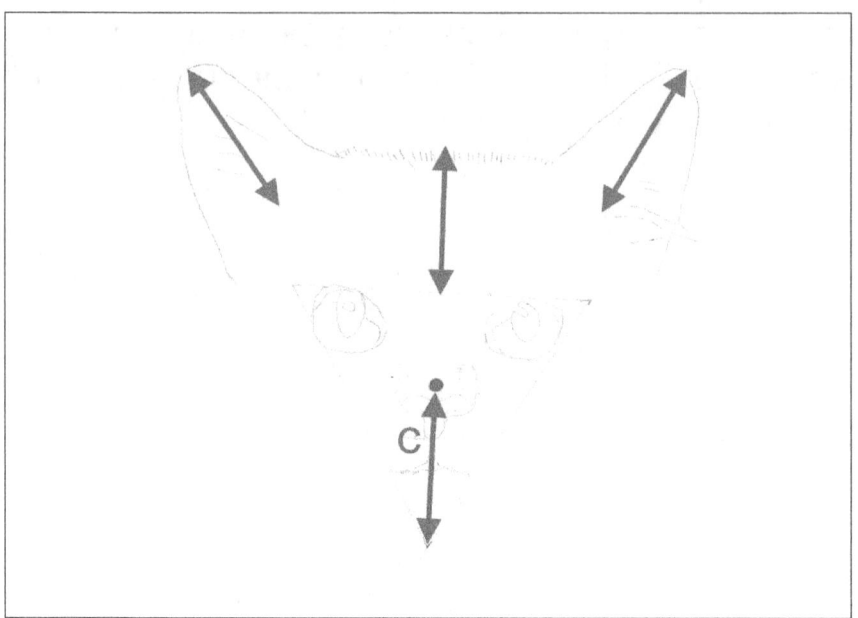

Use the width of the eye, that we marked as an arrowed D line in one of the previous steps, to determine the position of both sides of the muzzle as shown in the next image. Draw tiny dots for the roots of the whiskers in the places where they are naturally found. Look up reference photos if unsure.

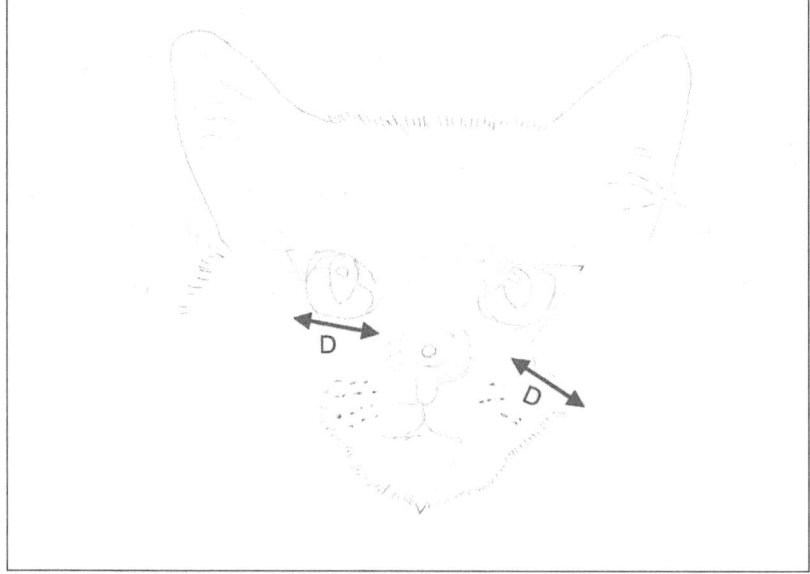

Erase the triangle and add more details such as the placement of shadows or highlights.

Here you have to decide how much of the cat's chest will show. Work all of these preliminary details out now so it's easier to fill it in the other details later.
The next image shows my final sketch.

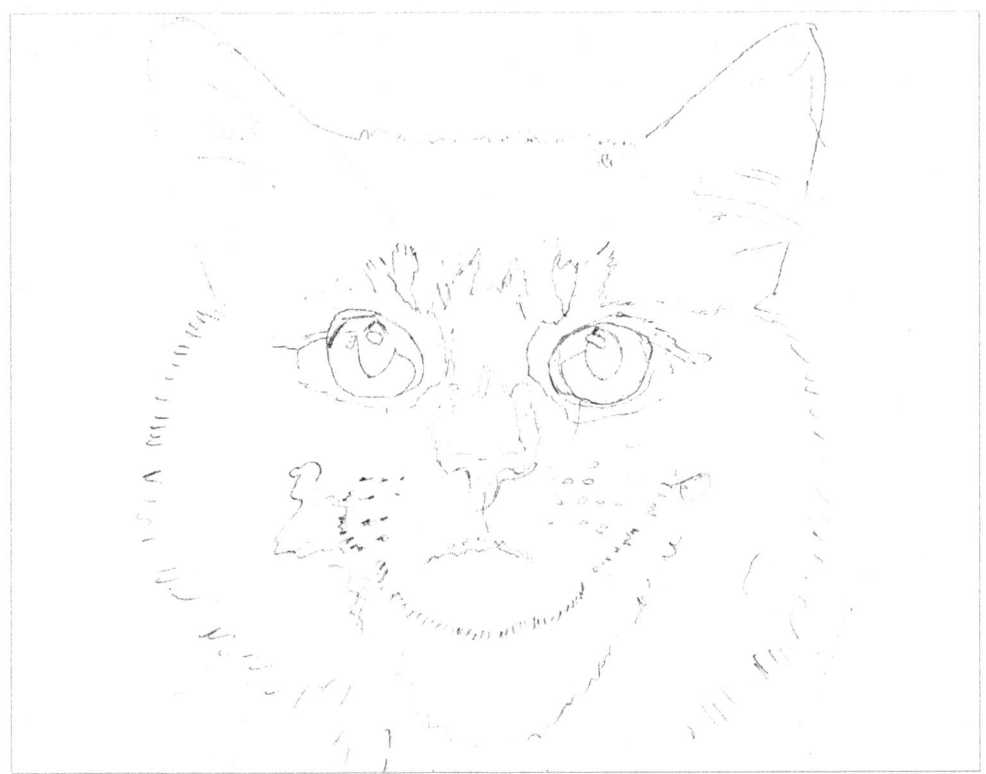

As a first step, fill up the pupils and strengthen the outlines all around the eyes in order to create a thick, black eyelid. Leave the white color of the paper for the reflection of the light. Using the same, darkest pencil, strengthen the nostrils and shadow under her nose. Also, mark the dark fur around her lips. Analyze the next image to see all the areas that I have filled with black.

If the darkest areas look good and are in their proper places, the rest of the drawing will more likely be successful.

So, using 4B or darker, mark the areas for the pupils, nostrils and under the nose, mouth, and the black hair that starts beside the eyes and grows outward. You don't have to use the same patterns as mine, but to draw the values of the fur differently.

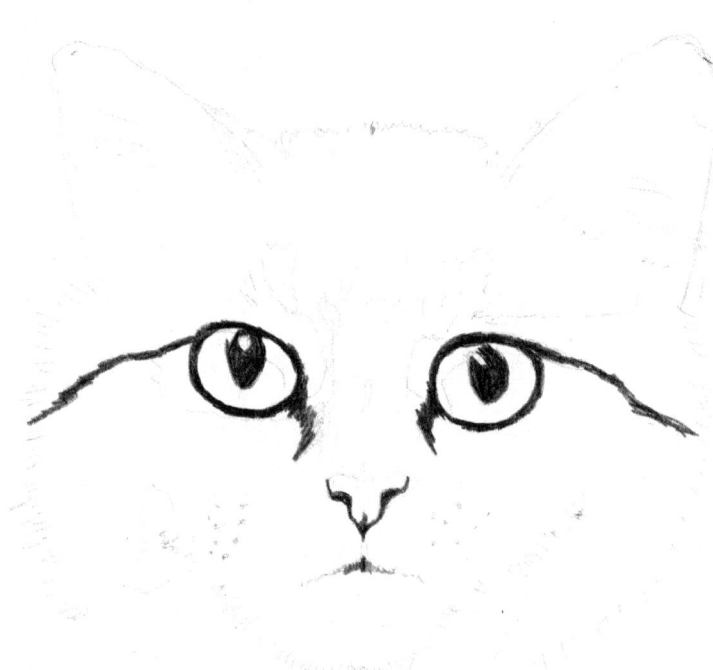

Next, create the cast shadow over the irises. Darken the area under the upper eyelid to give depth to the eyes. Use HB pencil for these areas.

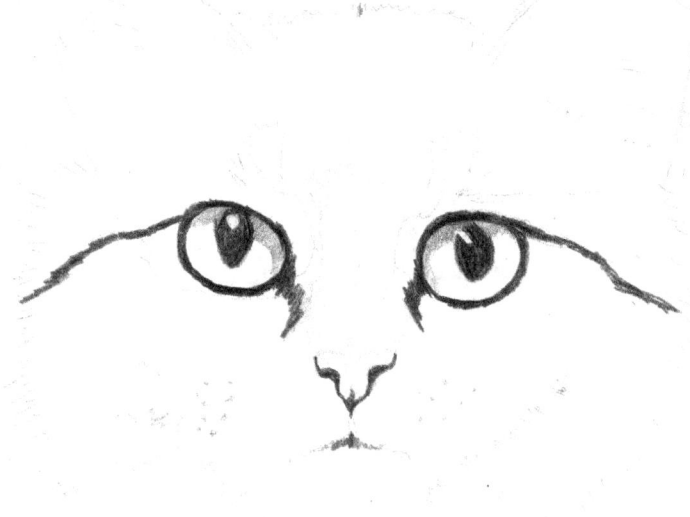

Now you can fill the rest of the irises using a much brighter pencil, such as 2H or brighter, or even the blending stump. Make sure to have the edge between the basic tone of the iris and the shadow cast over its upper area sharp and clearly visible.

At the end, erase the highlights gently where you want. It doesn't matter where you create them, but it's important to keep them symmetrical. You can see in the next image where I have highlighted the iris and do the same if you like it.

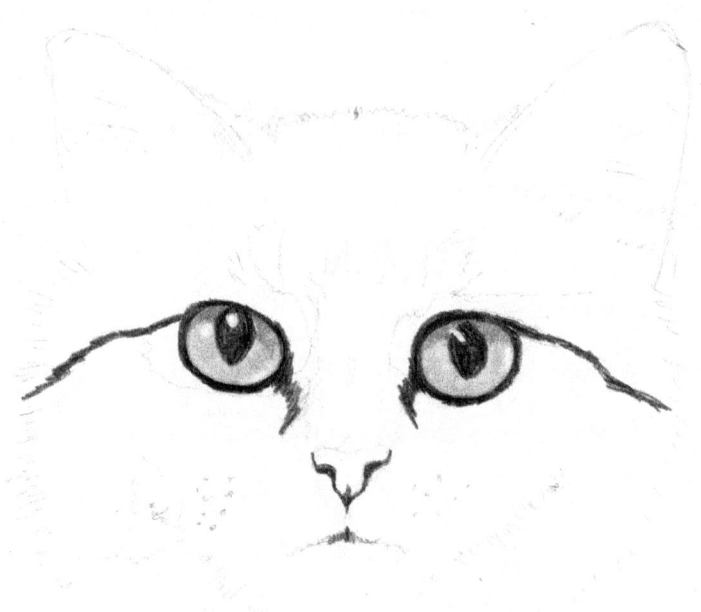

Start to map out the dark stripes over the forehead of the cat. If you are not familiar with cat's fur, examine some photos to learn about the direction of their hair growth. If you have a pet cat or dog, you can learn about that by moving their fur while petting them. I try to draw the usual domestic cat with well-known stripes and patterns.

You can draw a one-toned cat fur, or tuxedo cat, whichever you want, using the same outlining method from this tutorial. The main features of the face can be created with this method, and after that you can do with it what you want.

If you follow my work on social media, or have bought some of my other how-to-draw books, you can see that

when I drew the cat with colored pencils, I sketched it with this "triangle-method" before I started applying color.
I used 2B for these stripes.

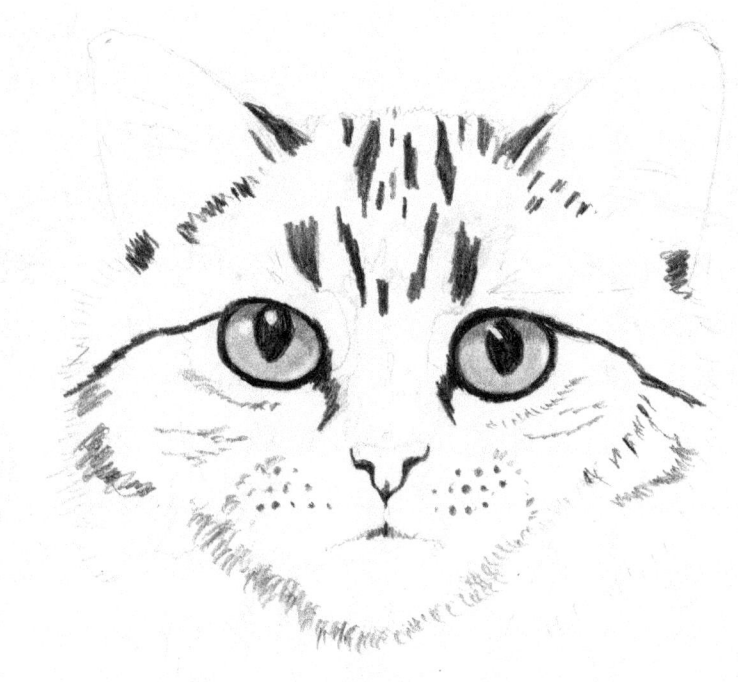

Now you can shade the whole face except her muzzle and around her eyes using cotton pads and graphite powder.

The dot that you have placed in the middle of the face, even if you have it already erased, you probably remember where it was, so use this imaginary dot starting point for drawing all of the hair on her face. All cat's hair grows outwards from this point, and this is how you have to draw it. If you have a cat or dog, you probably have already noticed this when you pet them.

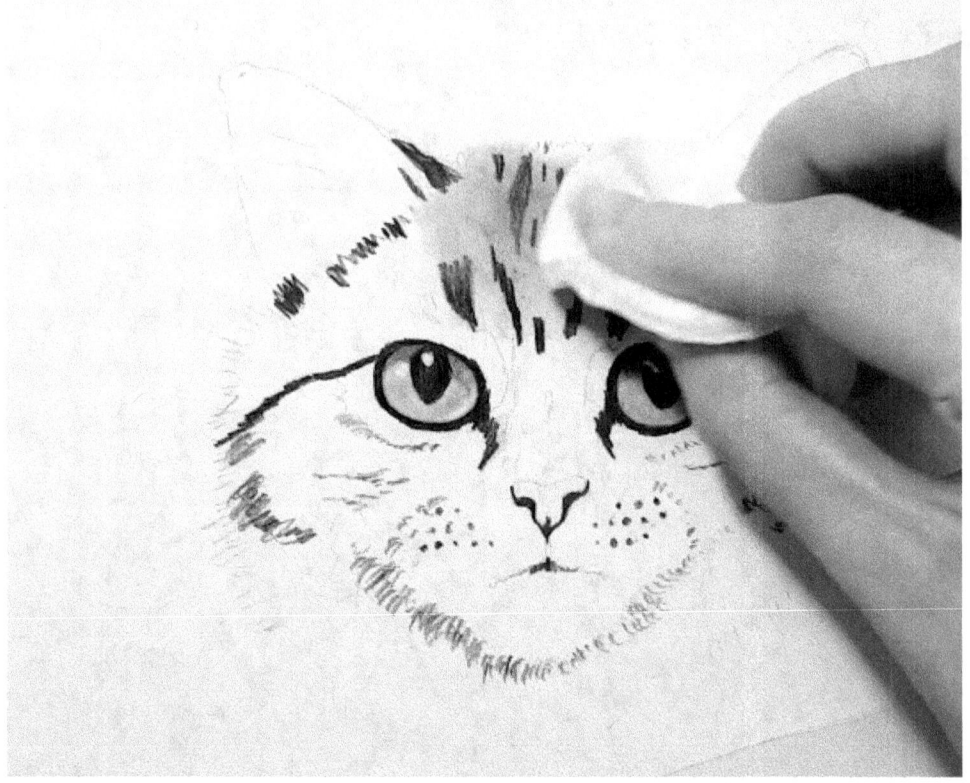

Continue shading the rest of the face with a tissue and graphite powder.

You can use circular motions in order to create an even tone, but here it is not necessarily important because we will be adding hairs and highlights. The area where the whiskers grow should stay white.

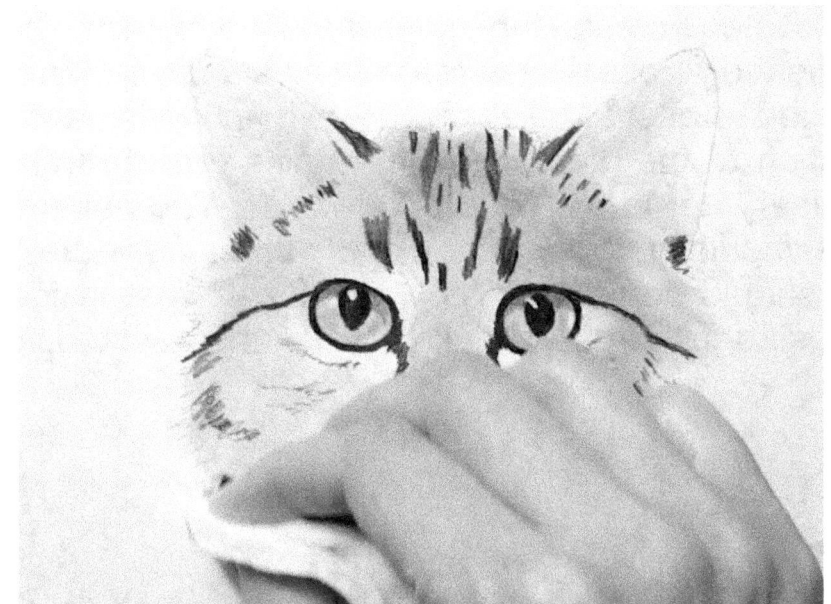

In this next image, you can see how it looks after adding the basic shading. I have removed the blackness from the stripes by blending over them, but they can be darkened again anytime.

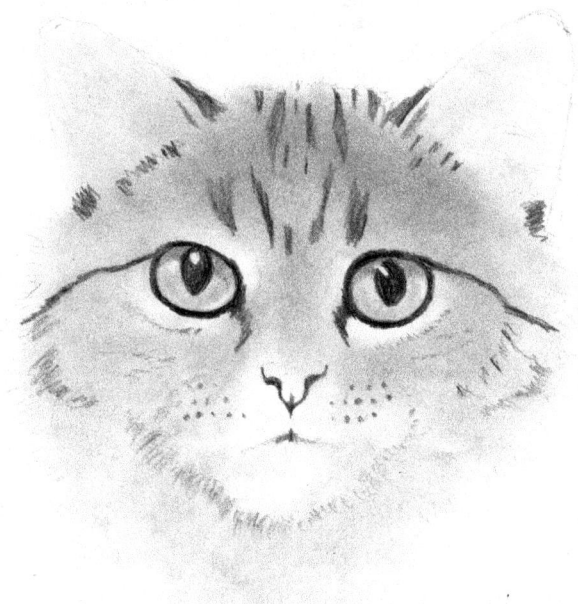

In this step, create the highlighted hairs using a well sharpened eraser, or create the sharp tip on your kneaded eraser. Make short, swift motions, and pay attention to the direction of the hair's growth, from the imaginary dot in the middle, outwards. The hairs of the nose should be very short, and further from the nose they should be longer. They are the longest inside the ears, so don't forget to make them in the ears too.

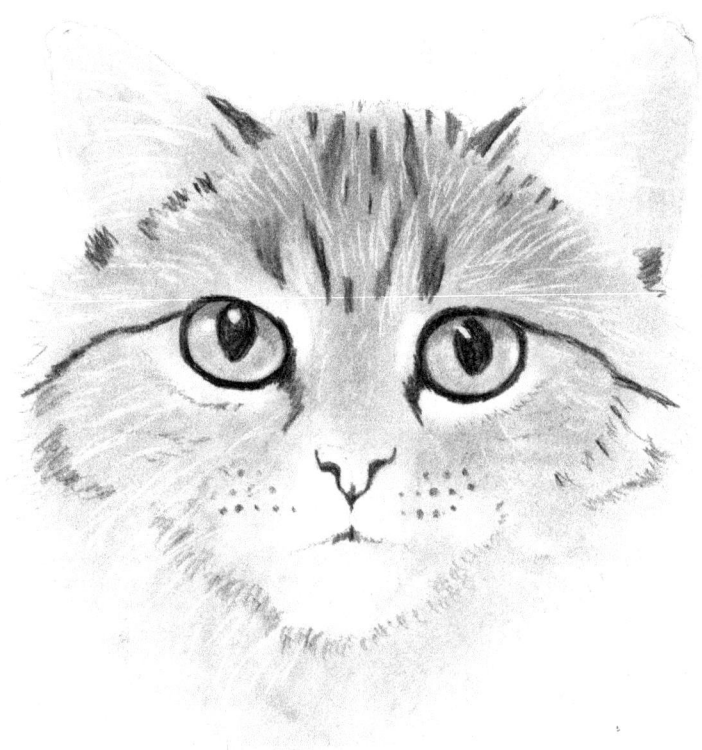

You can shade both sides of the nose up to the forehead using HB, and blend it in with a blending stump. Create a flawless tone gradation as you shade towards the middle of the nose. Compare the previous and the following images to see the difference and what I exactly shaded.

Also, shade around the white fur, which grows around her eyes. Add tiny hairs all around the black eyelid (next to the white hairs) that you marked in the very beginning of this process.

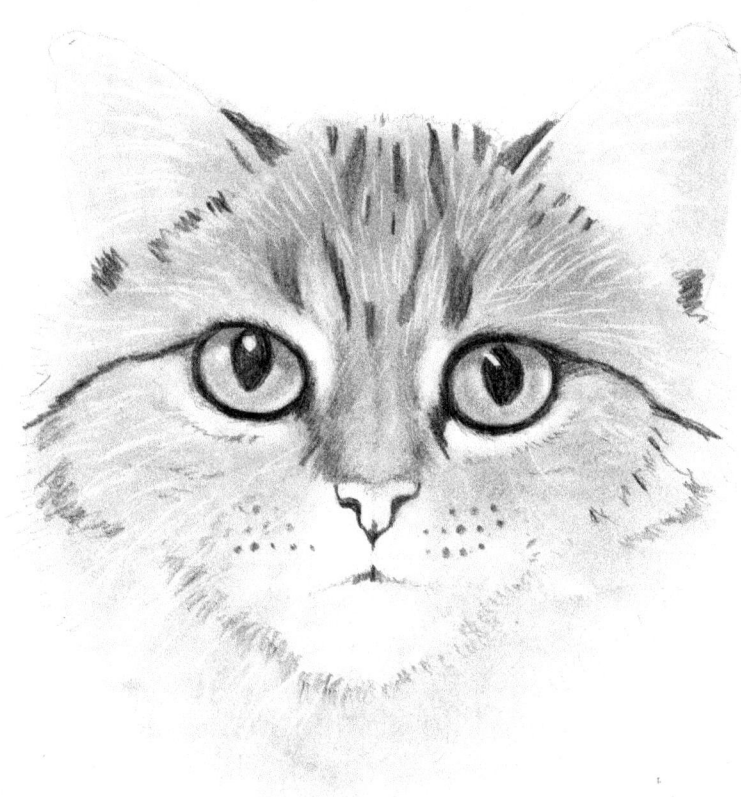

Let's finish the ears by adding the shadows. Use both B and HB and draw in between the previously erased highlights. This step will make the highlighted, long hairs in the ears even more prominent and visible. Use a blending stump to blend these dark areas.

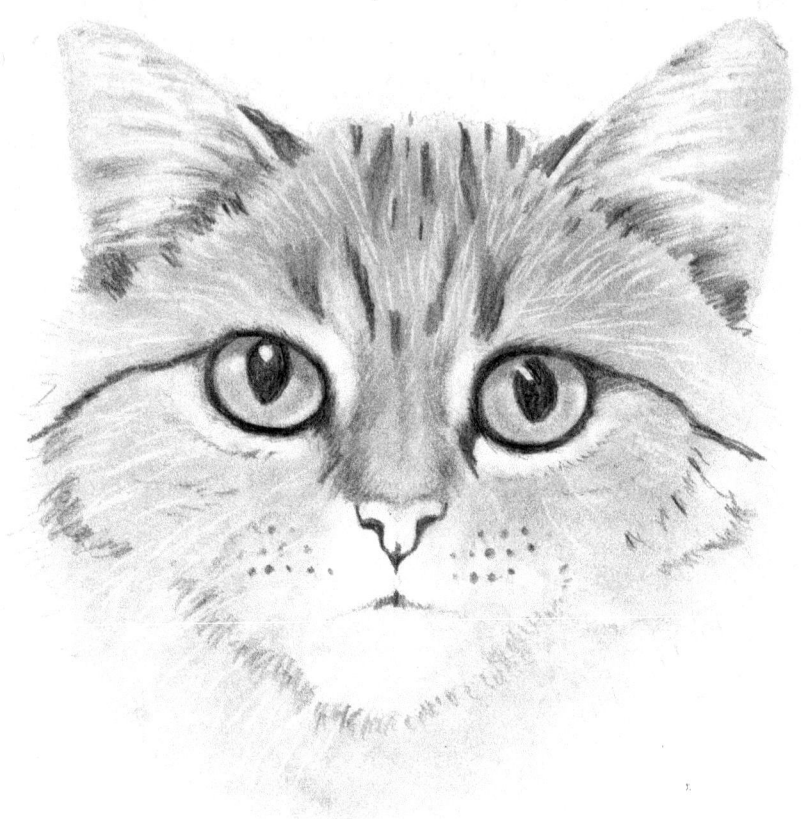

You can finish the face with shading around the muzzle. As mentioned, the middle of the muzzle, and around the mouth should stay white. Draw mid-toned hair on both sides of the face and here also, draw them in between the erased highlighted hairs.

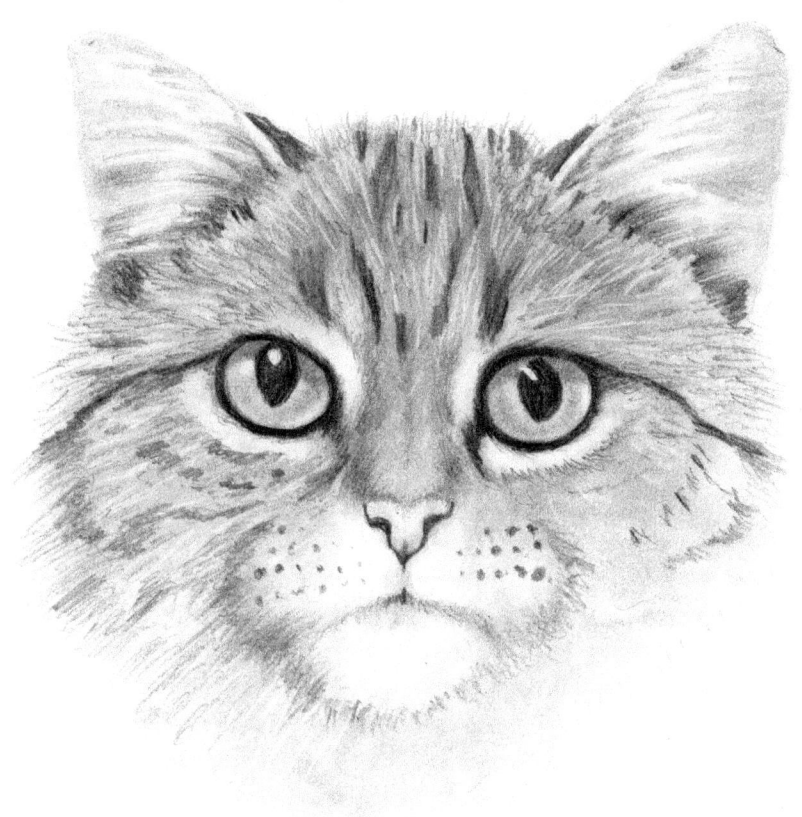

Create the cast shadow under the chin using a HB and a blending stump. You can add as much detail as you want, or leave it like this. You can also improve your result after a few weeks or months of practice. After having gained more experience you can either improve the drawing or create a new one and compare how much you have improved.

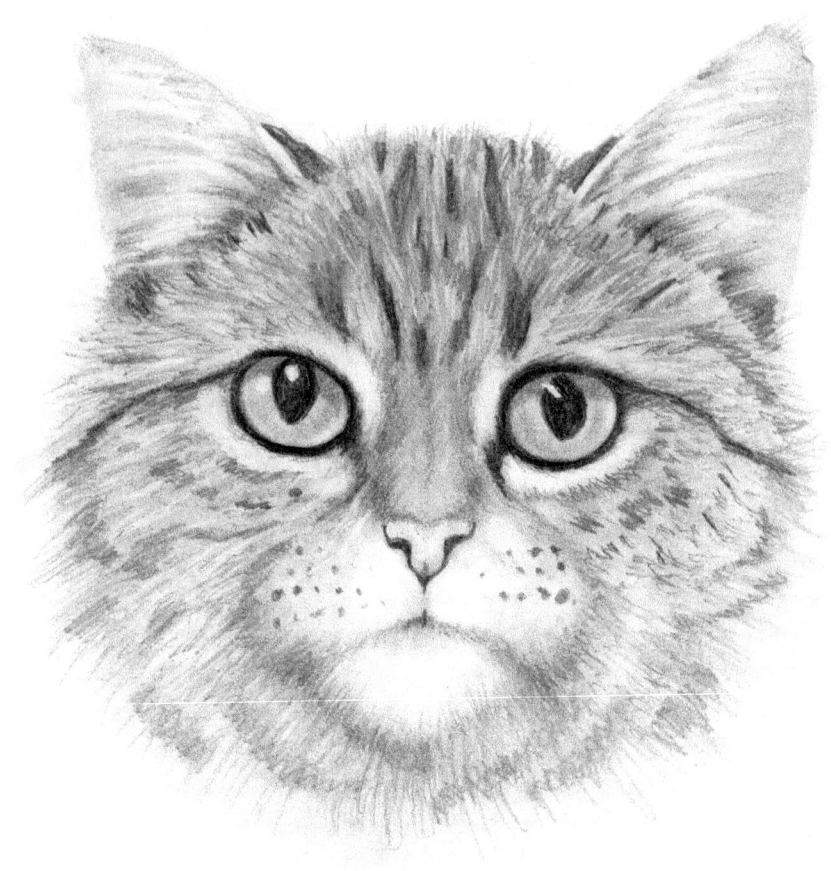

Lastly, draw the whiskers with a 4B pencil.

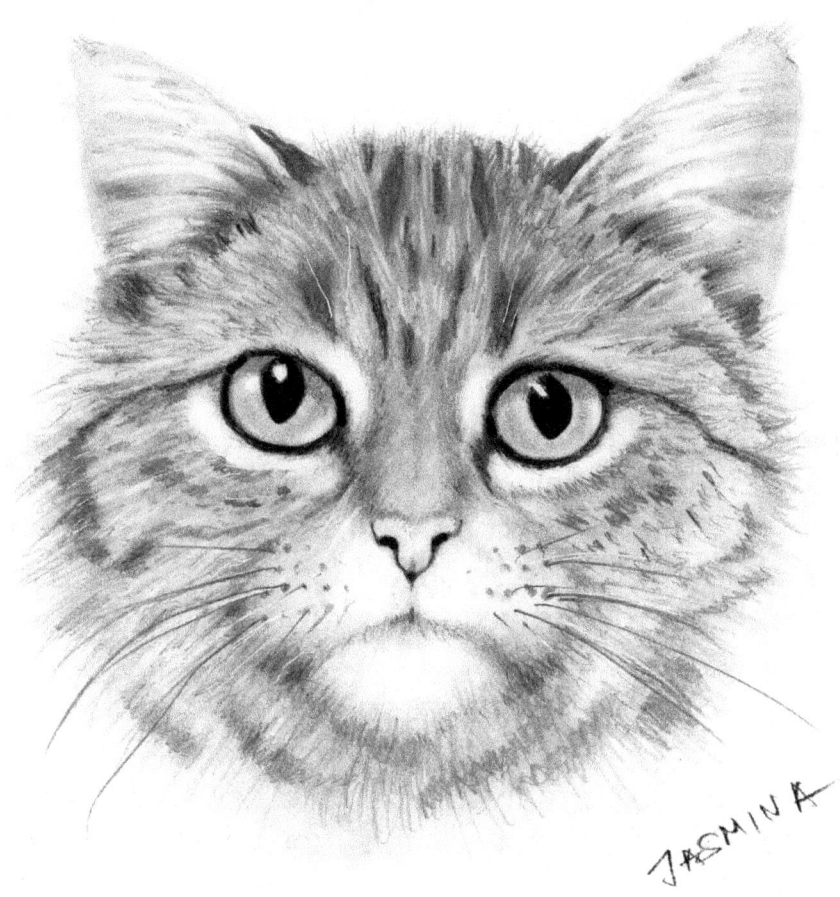

EPILOGUE

I hope that you have followed my instructions, that you enjoyed these tutorials and that you like what you have created so far. I also hope that you fell in love you're your drawings, and that you will continue to practice. If you keep doing it, great results and feelings are yet to come.

Feel free to contact me on social media, through my website www.jasminasusak.com, or via email jasminasusak00@gmail.com, and to ask any questions, to share your thoughts on this book with me, and to show me your drawings. Can't wait to see your results!

INSPIRATION GALLERY

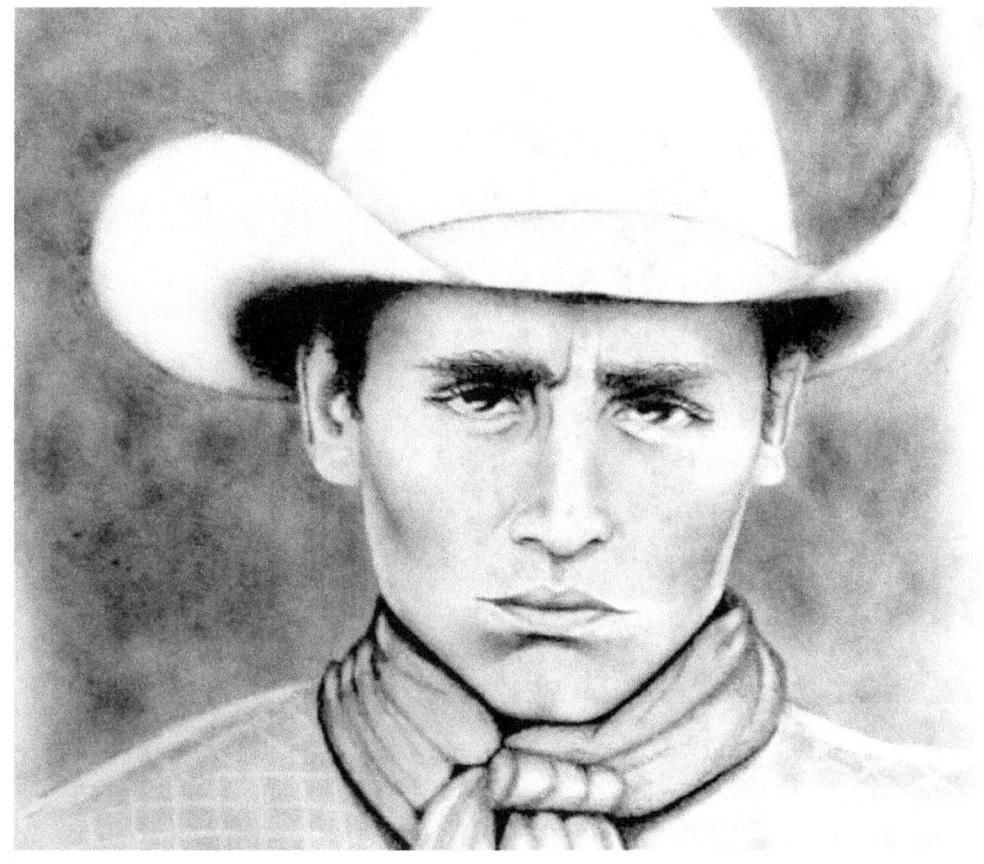

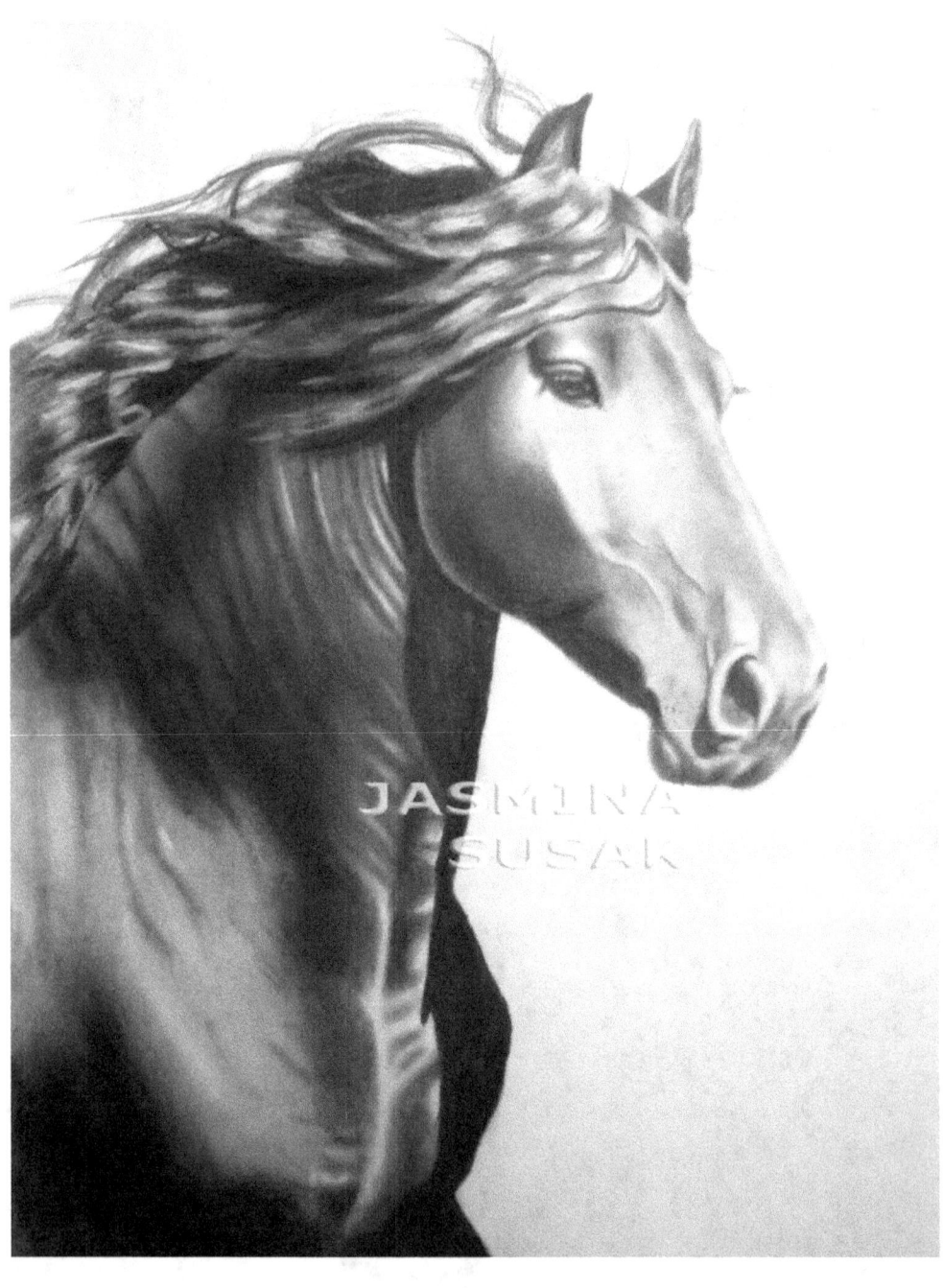

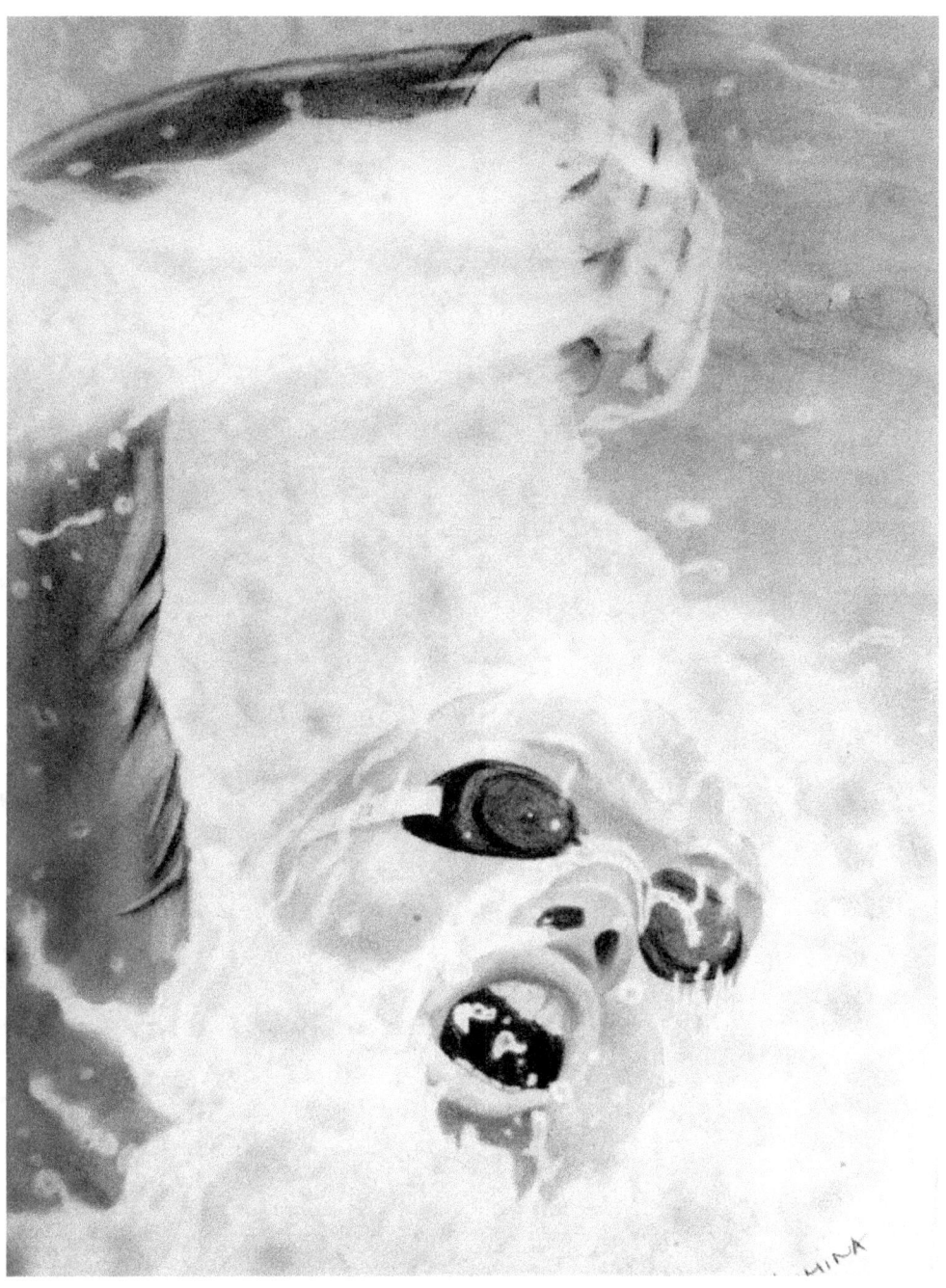

Drawing for Beginners   Page 247

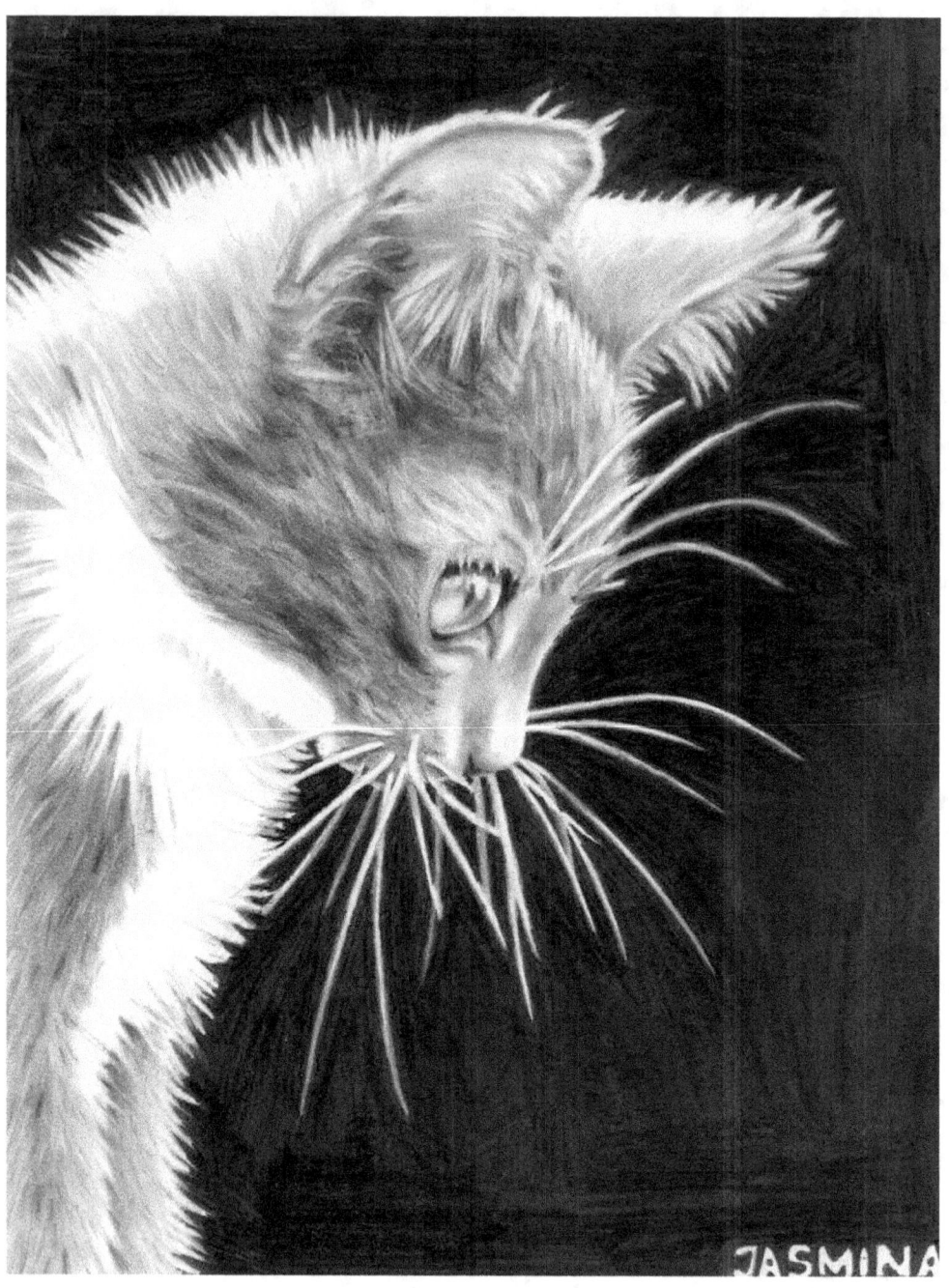

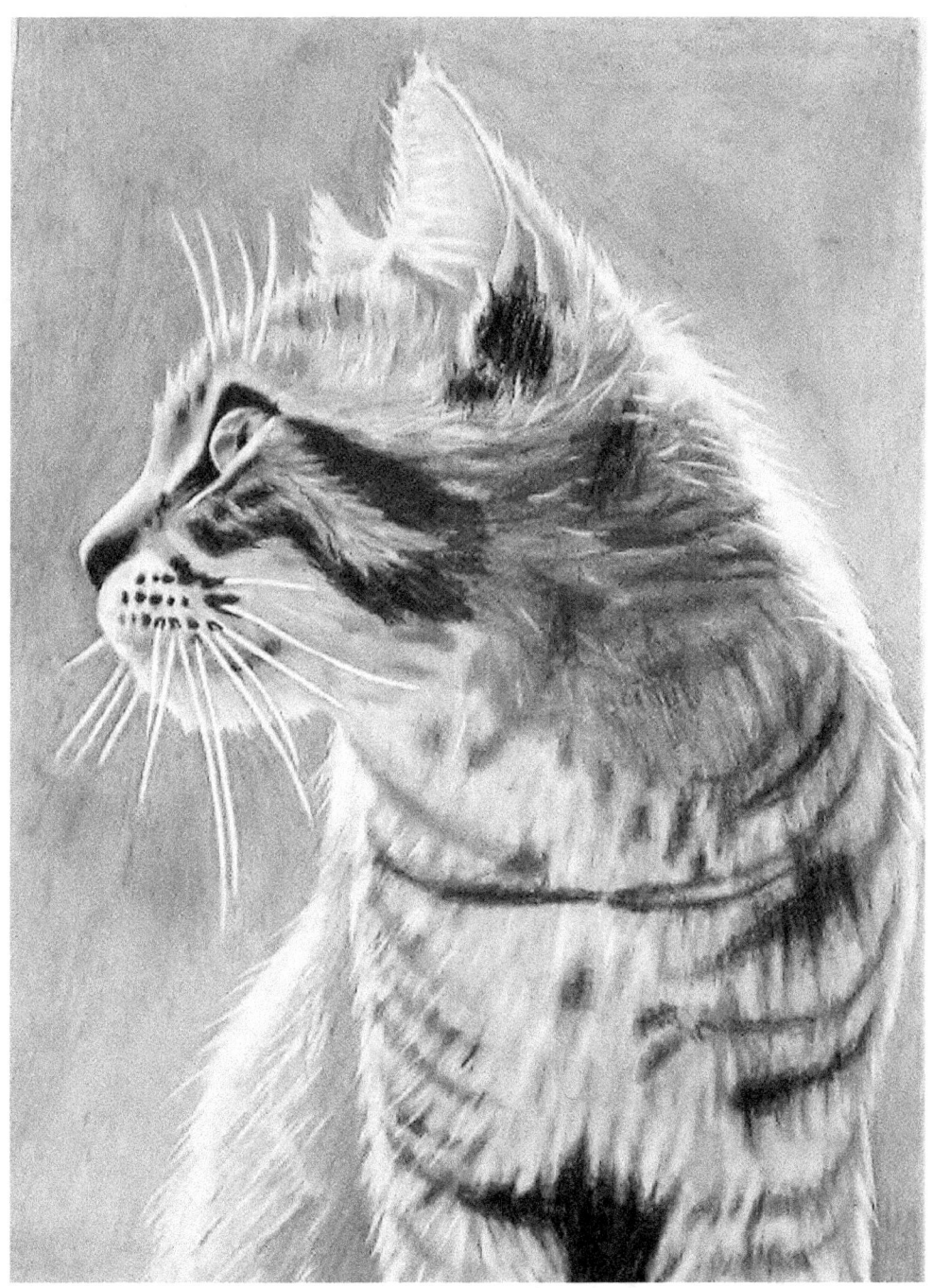

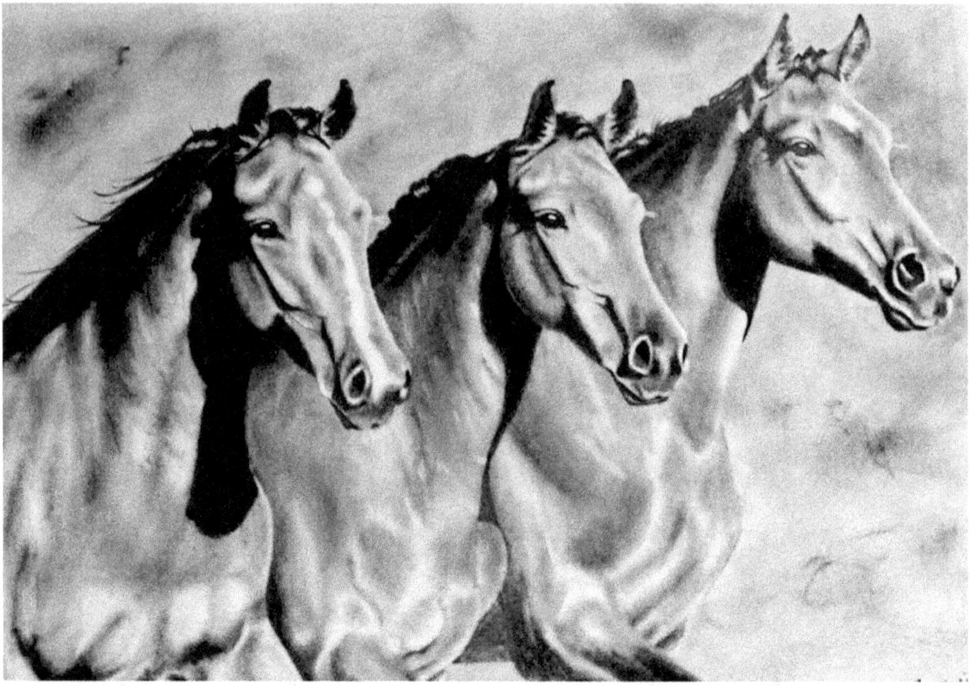

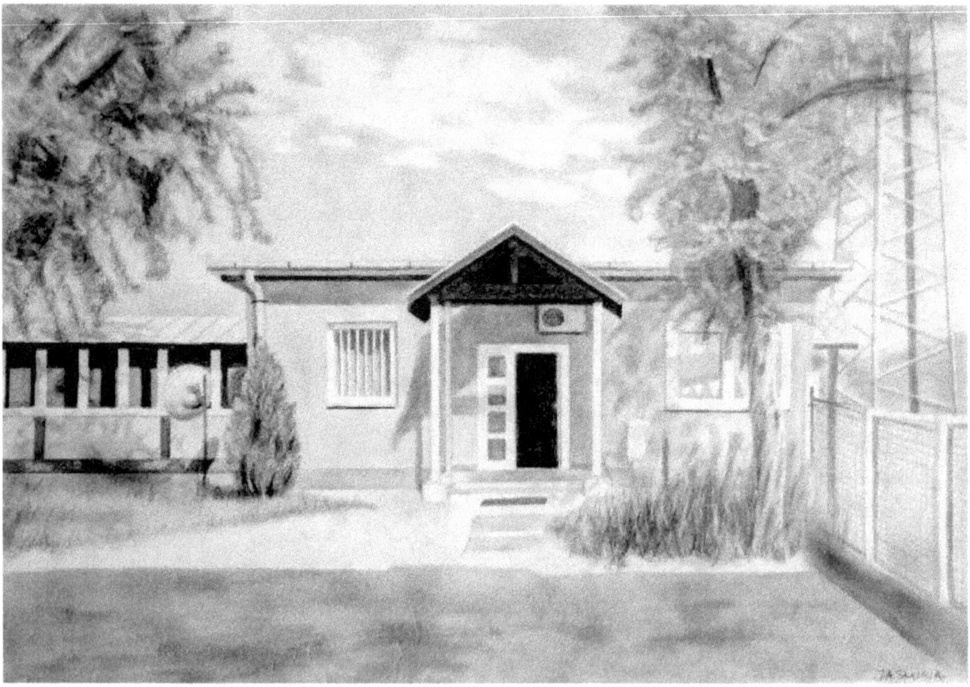

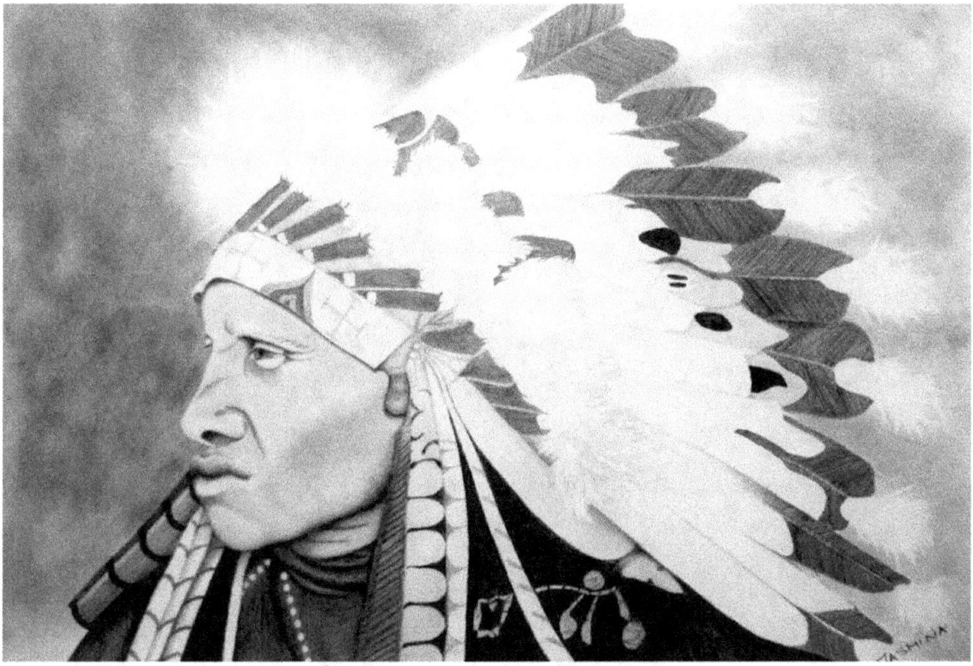

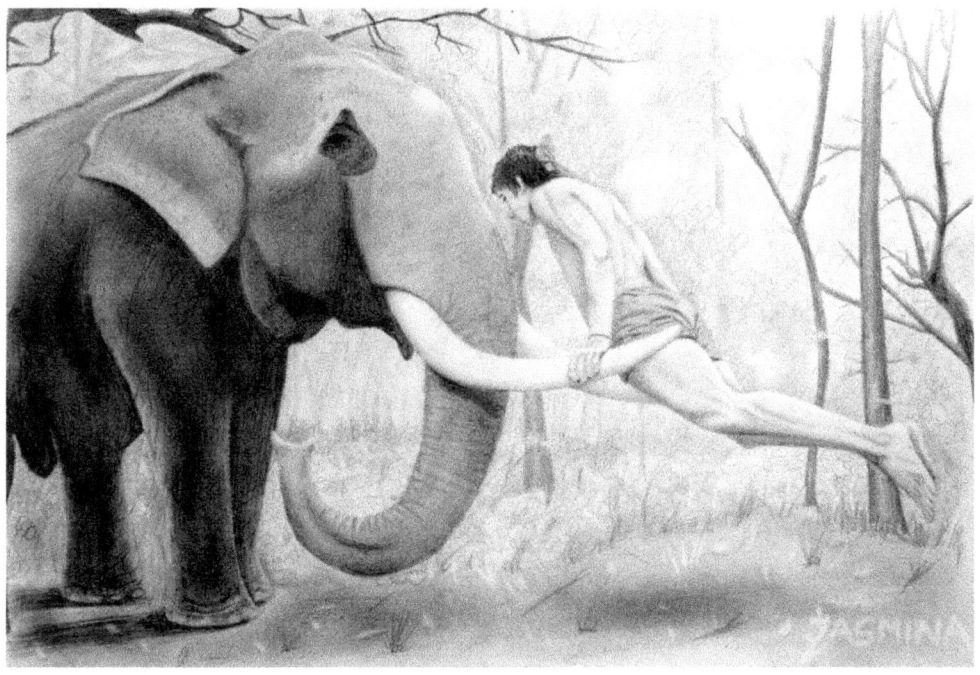

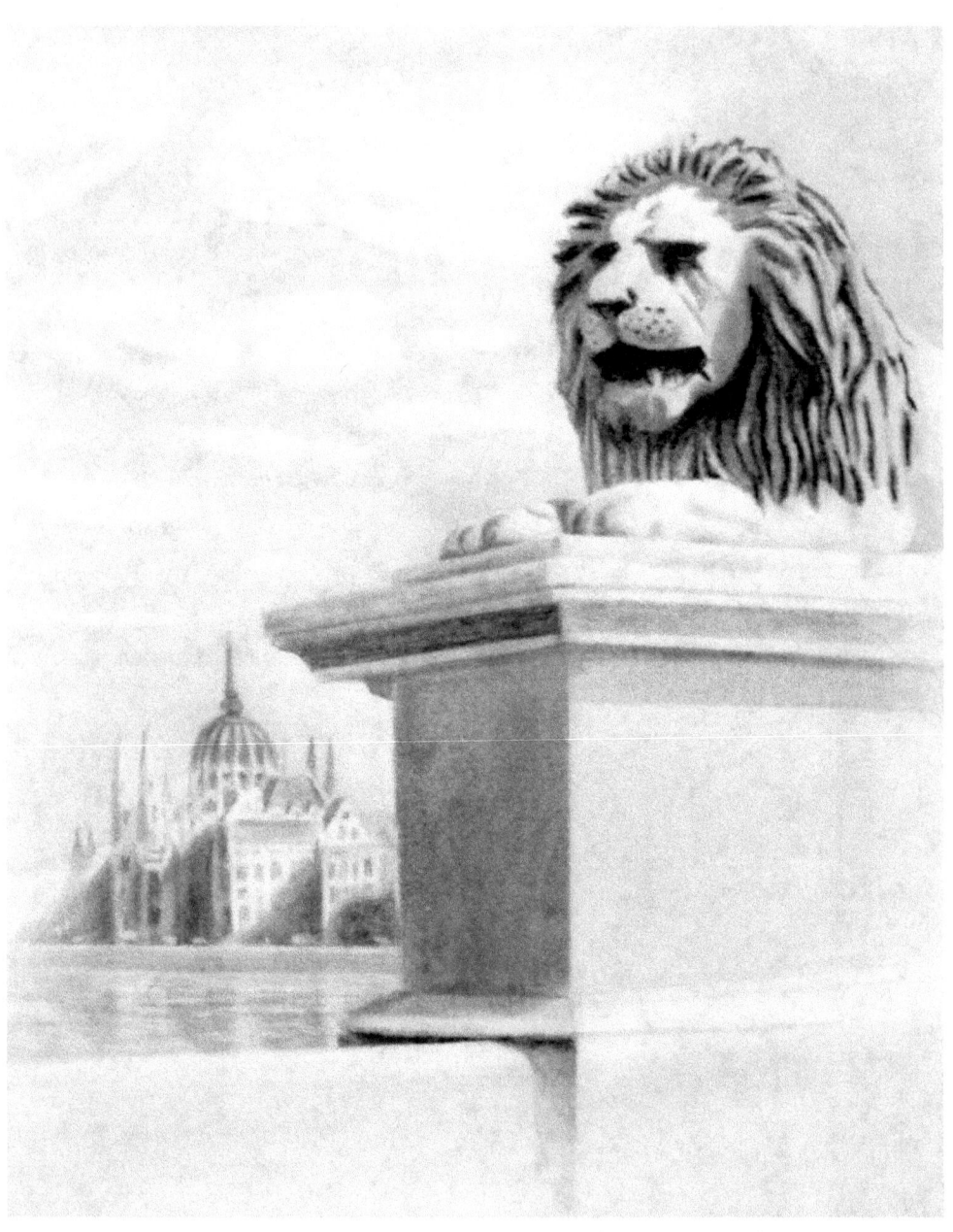

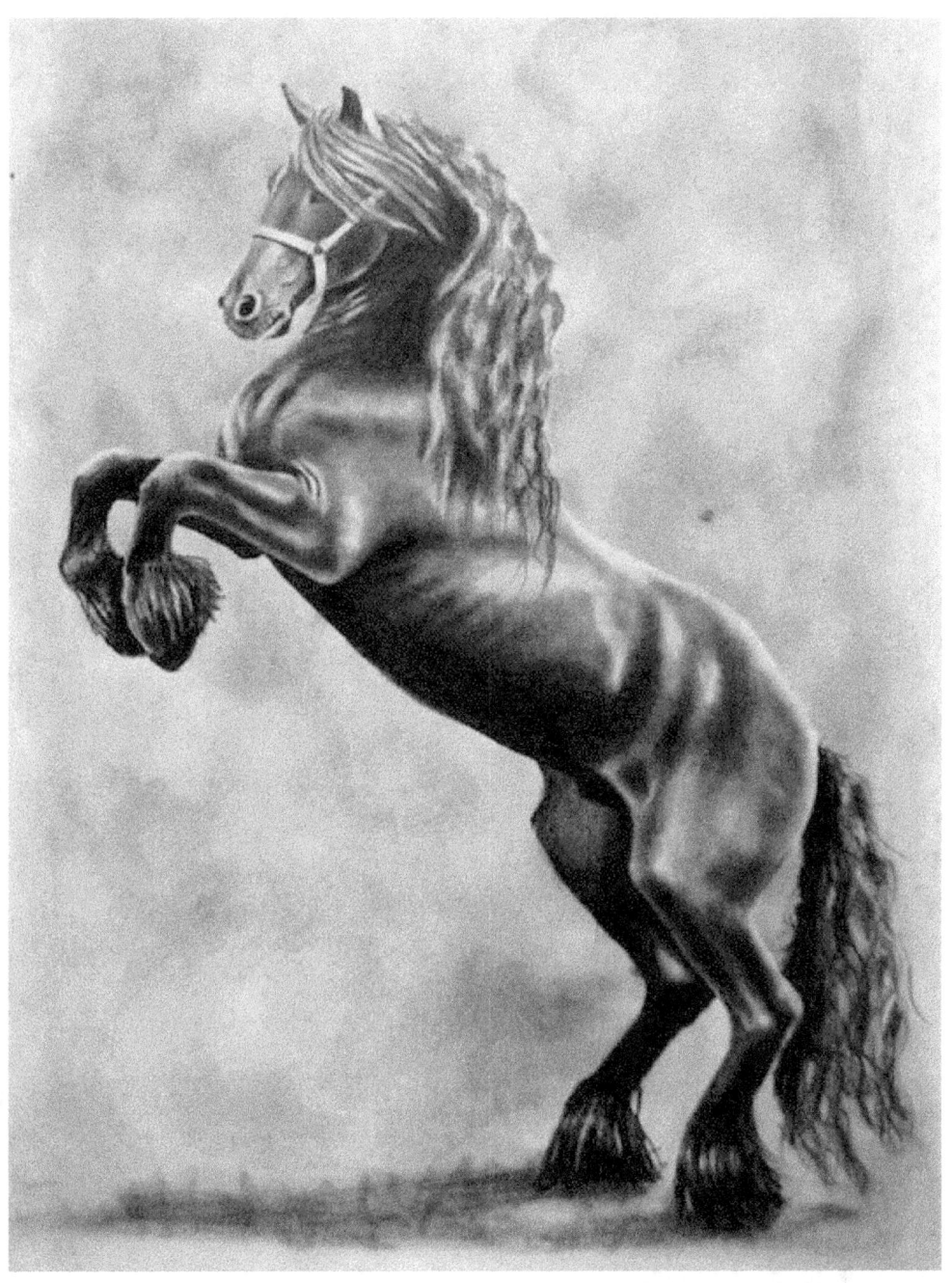

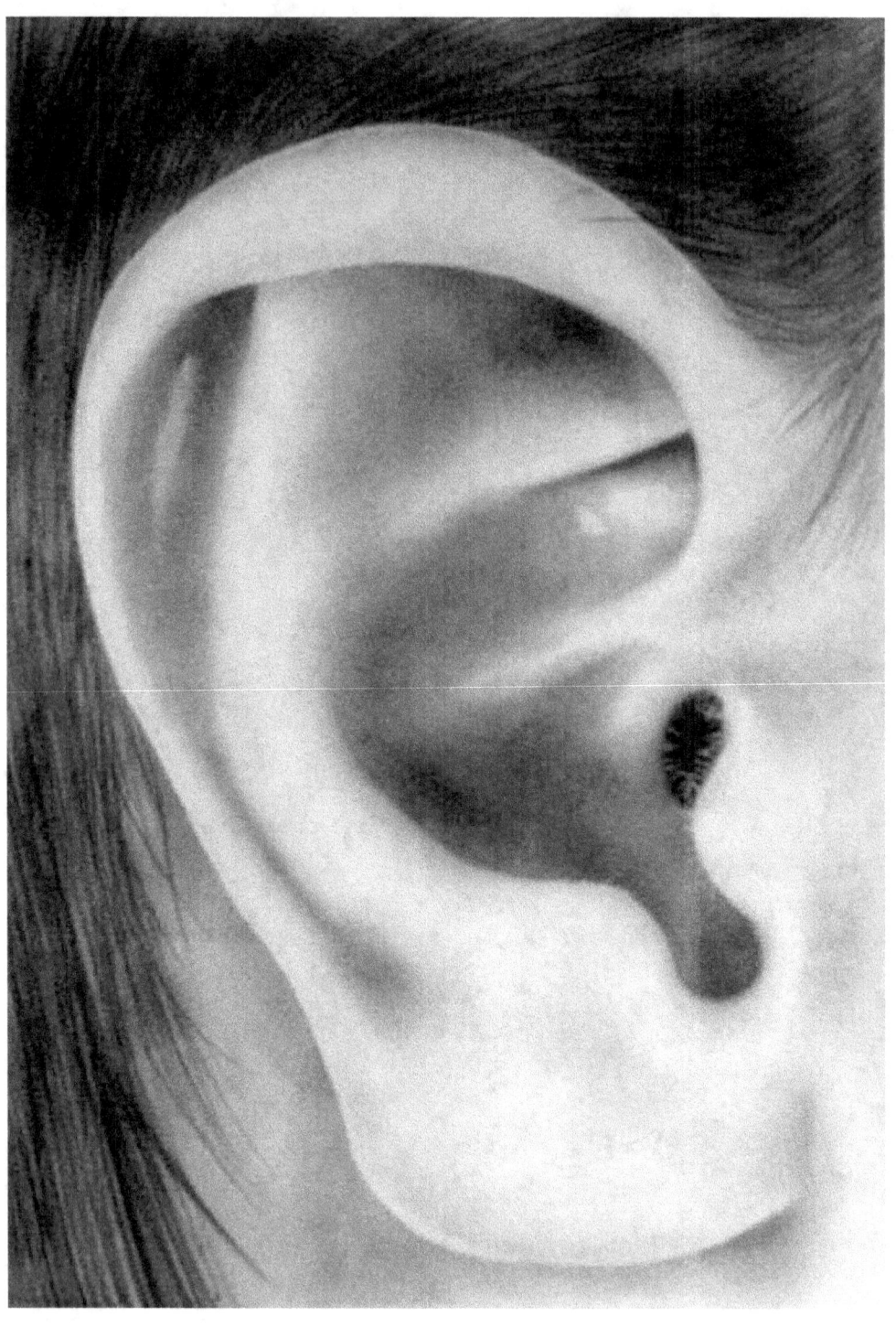

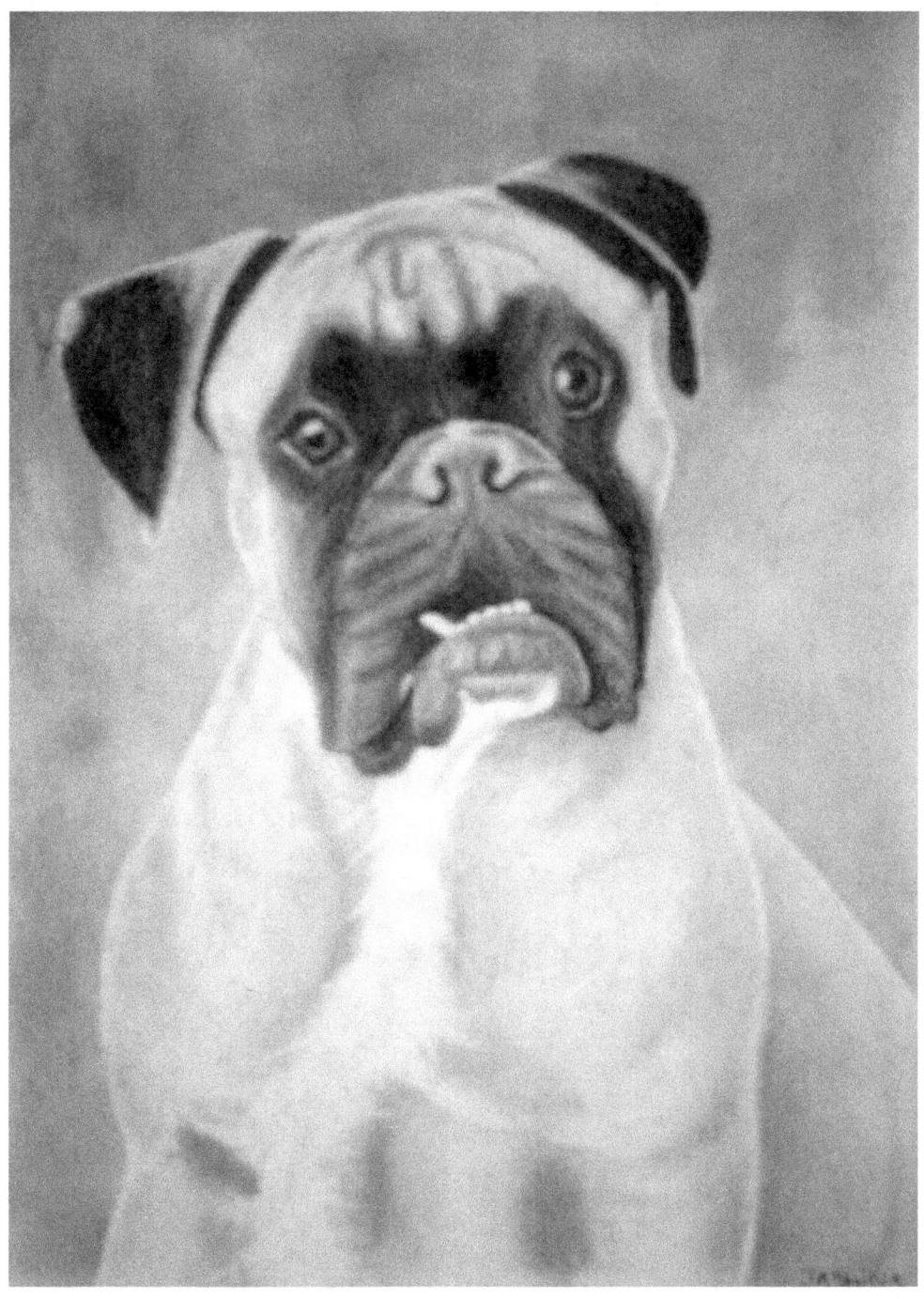

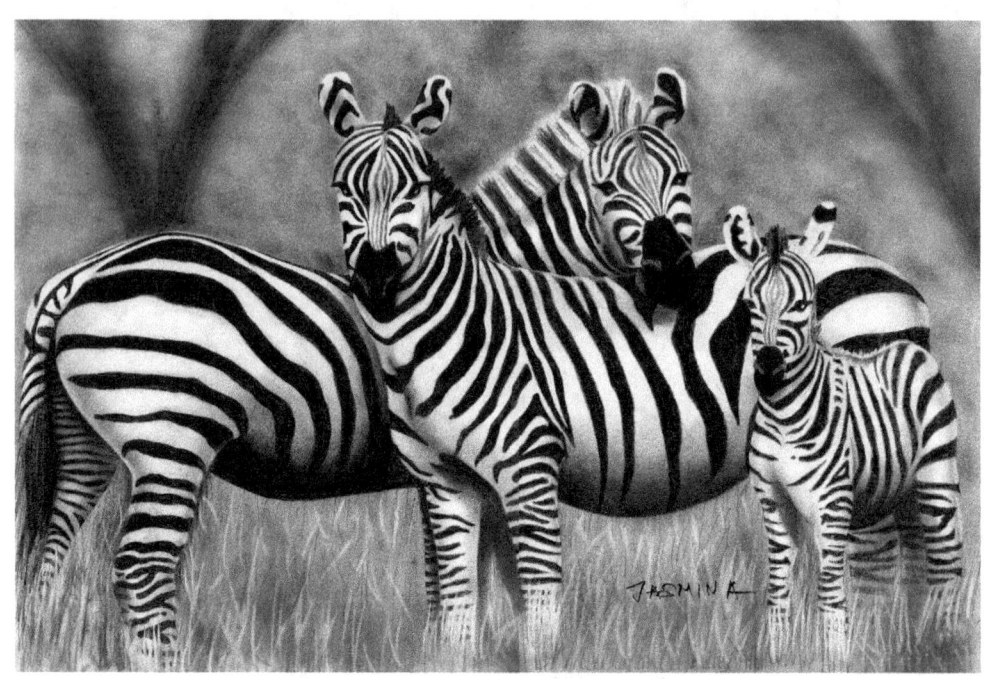
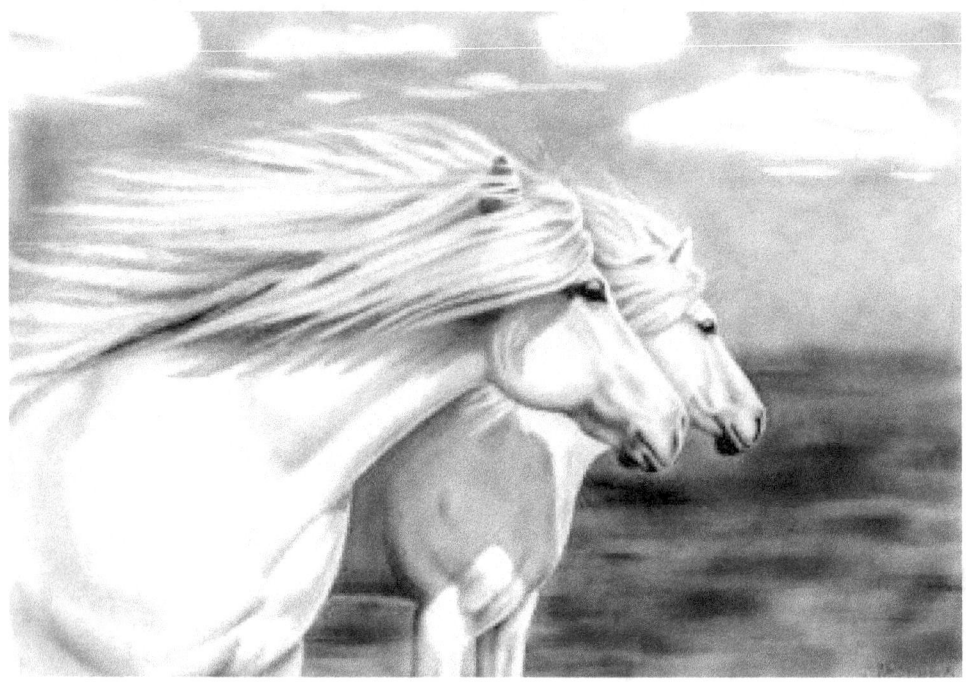

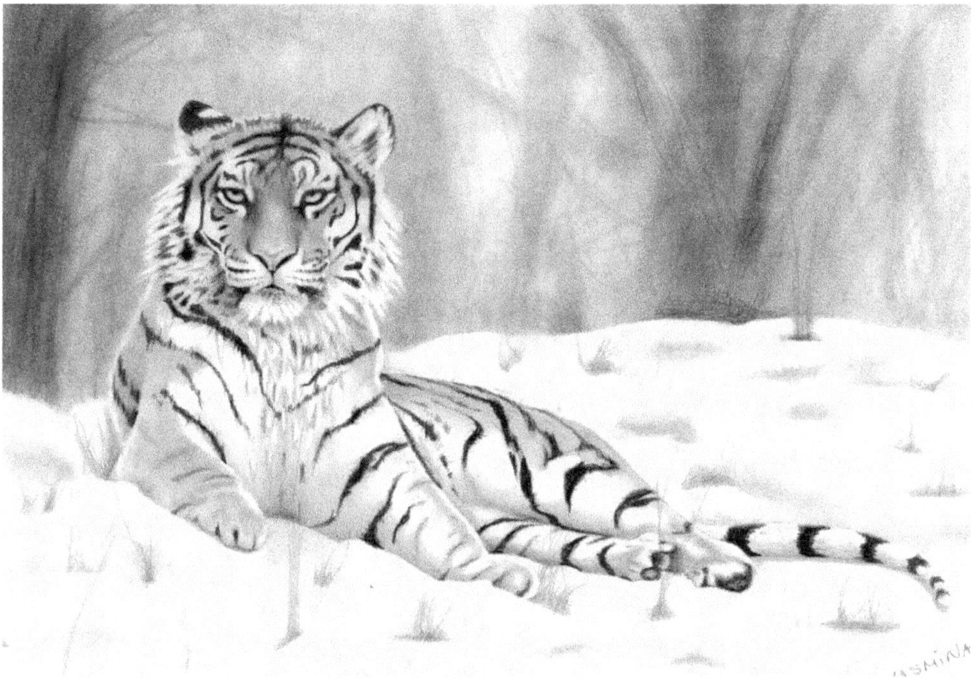

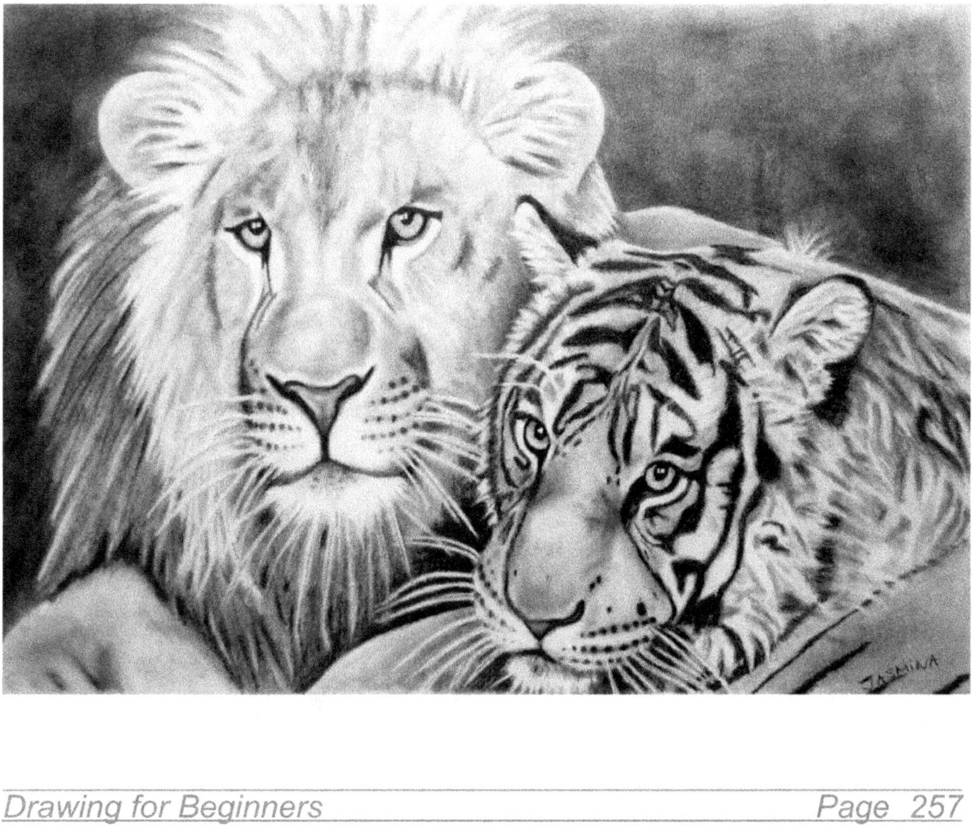

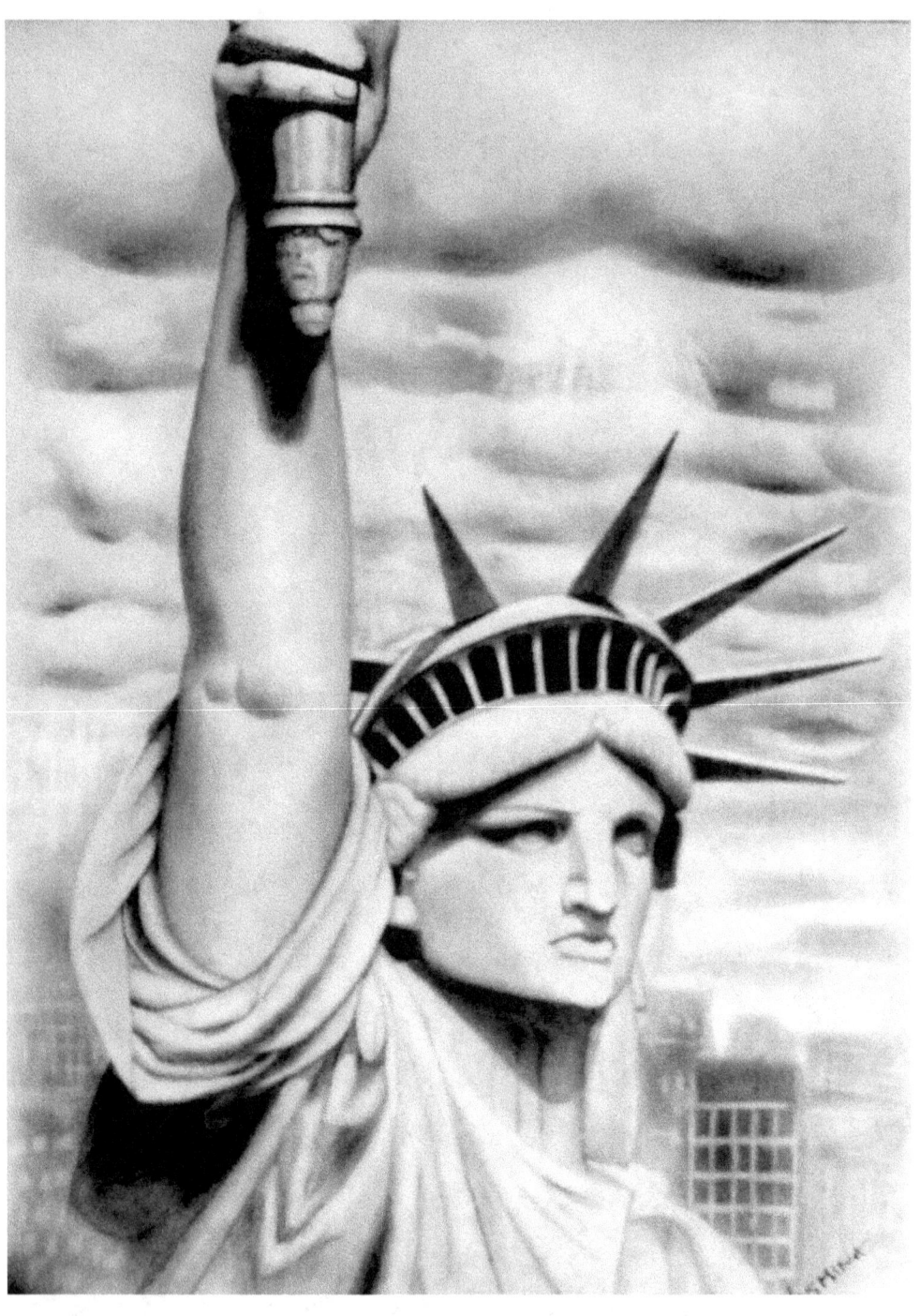

If you want to learn faster and better, I recommend joining my website, **Pencil Drawing Tutor**. As a member, you'll learn through real-time narrated videos, step-by-step written tutorials with pictures, and have 24/7 access to **PenPick Graphite**. You can attach your drawings under any tutorial and chat with other members. The lessons are perfect for beginners, those looking to improve, or anyone who wants inspiration and fun.

Brand new tutorial every WEEK.
Come join us!

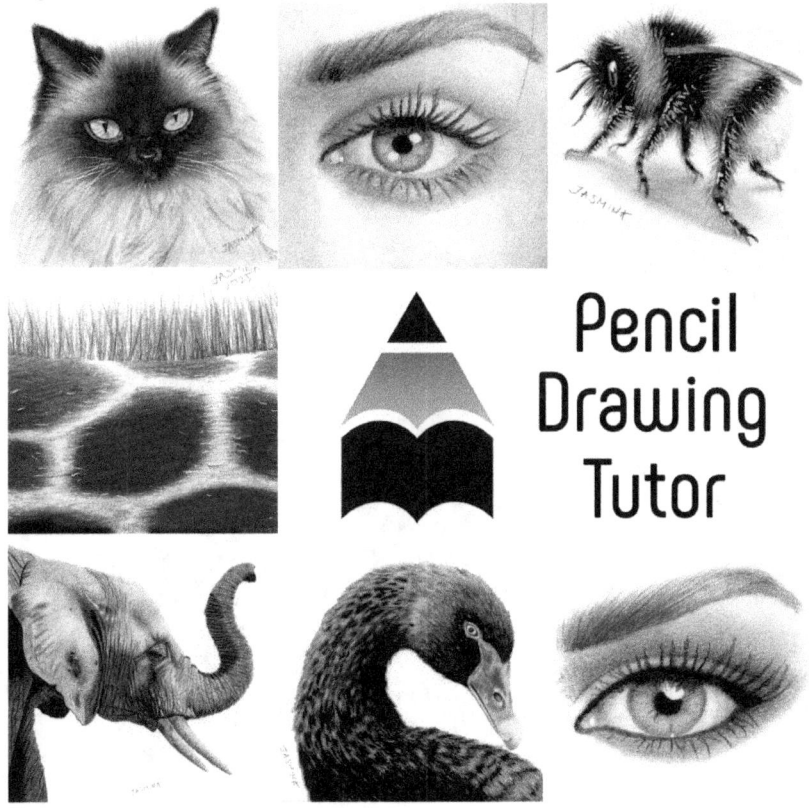

WWW.PENCILDRAWINGTUTOR.COM